HEATH MATHEMATICS
CONNECTIONS

Edward Manfre
James M. Moser
Joanne E. Lobato
Lorna Morrow

HEATH

D.C. Heath and Company
Lexington, Massachusetts / Toronto, Ontario

HEATH MATHEMATICS CONNECTIONS

Edward Manfre

Edward Manfre is a former elementary, intermediate, and secondary schoolteacher who has for over twenty years created classroom materials that encourage thinking. He has also conducted workshops on instructional methods and problem solving.

James M. Moser

James Moser has been a teacher of mathematics at several levels, a teacher educator, a researcher, a curriculum developer, and a state mathematics consultant. He is the author of mathematics textbooks for elementary, secondary, and college students. Currently he is Executive Director of the Wisconsin Mathematics Education Coalition.

Joanne E. Lobato

Joanne Lobato teaches mathematics at Alameda High School in Alameda, California. She has worked as a designer of mathematics software for grades K-8. Joanne conducts research on elementary schoolchildren and frequently presents teacher workshops.

Lorna Morrow

An instructor of mathematics at the University of Toronto, Lorna Morrow has also taught at both the elementary and secondary levels and has written extensively—books, articles, and curriculum materials—on topics in mathematics.

ACKNOWLEDGMENTS
Executive Editor Carol DeBold, **Supervising Editor** Sylvia Clark, **Level Editor** Meg Buckley Springer, **Product Manager** Sara Conkright, **Design Manager** Robert H. Botsford, **Production Coordinator** Donna Lee Porter, **Permissions** Dorothy Burns McLeod **Outside Editorial Assistance:** Sally E. Wilson

The Fraction Bars illustrated and used in this book were created by Professor Albert B. Bennett, Jr., of the University of New Hampshire and Dr. Patricia S. Davidson of the University of Massachusetts, Boston. Decimal Squares were created by Professor Bennett.

ABOUT THE COVER
Cover Design: Linda Fishborne

Cover Photography: Bruno Joachim Studio, (Central Image)
Clark Weinberg / The Image Bank
Theme: Multiplication and division are shown through real-world and symbolic representations of groups, arrays, and sharing—which are the fundamental ideas of multiplication and division.

Published simultaneously in Canada
Printed in the United States of America
International Standard Book Number: 0-669-11901-6
4 5 6 7 8 9 0

CONTENTS

| ● Exploratory | ◐ Discovery | ◐ Linking |
| ◐ Symbolic | ◐ Application | ● Problem Solving |

CHAPTER

4

COLLECTING AND ORGANIZING DATA

● Exploratory	◐ Discovery	◖ Linking
◖ Symbolic	◖ Application	● Problem Solving

CHAPTER

MULTIPLICATION AND DIVISION TO 9

● Exploratory	◐ Discovery	◑ Linking
◐ Symbolic	◑ Application	● Problem Solving

CHAPTER
8   # FRACTIONS

| ● Exploratory | ◑ Discovery | ◐ Linking |
| ◐ Symbolic | ◐ Application | ● Problem Solving |

CHAPTER

11

MULTIPLYING BY 1-DIGIT NUMBERS

| ○ Exploratory | ◐ Discovery | ◐ Linking |
| ◐ Symbolic | ◐ Application | ● Problem Solving |

CHAPTER

12 DIVIDING BY 1-DIGIT NUMBERS

MORE PRACTICE *390*
HANDBOOK *415*

| ◯ **Exploratory** | ◑ **Discovery** | ◐ **Linking** |
| ◑ **Symbolic** | ◐ **Application** | ● **Problem Solving** |

ADDITION AND SUBTRACTION FACTS

Counting Petals
by Aileen Fisher

Somehow flowers
have learned the trick
of practicing arithmetic:

Easter lilies
don't count far—
one, two, three their petals are.

Yellow poppies
count one more.
Roses count to one plus four.

How did dandelions
and such
ever learn to count so much?

...Connections

Science

Counting in Nature Have you ever counted the parts of a flower? The poem tells you the number of petals on some flowers. How many petals do you think are on a dandelion? There may be too many for you to count.

You can make up counting questions for other things found in nature. Look at the snowflake and the spider. How many points are on a snowflake? How many legs does a spider have?

Look at the other pictures on this page. Write a counting question for each one. Can you think of other examples?

USING NUMBERS

This is Main Street in Jeremy's town. You can see Jeremy walking his dog near the Travel Shop.

Jeremy's town is like other towns. It has stores, sidewalks, homes, people, and lots of numbers. These numbers can tell us many things, if we know how to use them.

Work with a partner. Use the picture to solve each problem. Be sure to think about what the numbers mean.

1. What do you think is the name of Jeremy's town?

2. What is the address number of Bob's Bike Shop?

3. It is Saturday in the picture. How many hours is the library open today?

4. Look at the clock on the Town Hall.
   a. What time does it show?
   b. Is it morning or afternoon in the picture? How do you know?
   c. In how many hours will the bike shop close?

5. Jeremy has $5.00 to spend.
   a. Is that enough to buy a dozen muffins at the bakery?
   b. How many is a dozen?

6. Which costs more, the pizza special or the sub special?

7. How many doors do you see in the picture?

8. The side of the bakery is all brick.
   a. Are there more than 50 bricks?
   b. How did you get your answer?

9. The man walking into the bike shop is 6 feet tall.
   a. About how tall is the door to the shop?
   b. About how tall is the bike shop building?
   c. How did you get your answers?

PROJECT • Number Sense

Work with a partner. Find numbers in your classroom or school. Make a chart to show the numbers, where you found them, and what they mean.

Numbers We Found	Where We Found Them	What They Mean
8 fluid ounces	milk carton	how much milk is in the carton
1 to 31	calendar	the days of the month

COUNTING AND ORDERING

The Pine School cafeteria has a new way of serving lunches this year. Every student gets a number. The students are served in order.

Fay has number 81. Ed has 79 and Anna has 82. Of the three students, who will be served first? Who will be served last?

You can find the answer on a number line.

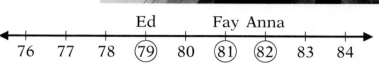

Number 79 comes before 81 and 82. So, Ed will be served first.

Number 82 comes after 79 and 81. So, Anna will be served last.

Number 81 is between 79 and 82. So, Fay will be served after Ed and before Anna.

Think

• The cafeteria has just served number 76. Imagine you are number 85. How many students will be served before you?

Who will be the third person waited on after Fay? Who will be waited on two people before Ed?

You can count on or count back on the number line.

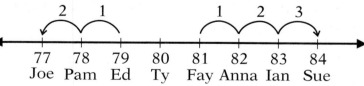

Sue will be the third person after Fay. Joe is two people before Ed.

GUIDED PRACTICE

Write the missing number.

1.

24 25 ■ 27

2.

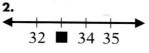

32 ■ 34 35

3.

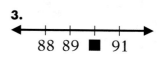

88 89 ■ 91

Write the number the arrow is pointing to.

4.

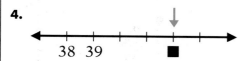

38 39 ■

5.

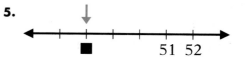

■ 51 52

6. How did you find the answers to exercises 4 and 5?

INDEPENDENT PRACTICE

Write the missing numbers.

7. 81, 82, ■

8. 20, ■, 22

9. ■, 66, 67

10. 44, ■, 46

11. 78, 79, ■, ■, ■

12. ■, ■, 51, 52, 53

Write the number the arrow is pointing to.

13.

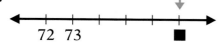

72 73 ■

14.

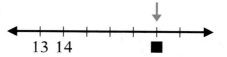

13 14 ■

15.

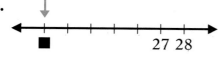

■ 27 28

16.

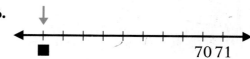

■ 70 71

CHALLENGE • Mental Math

Write the number that is 1 more. Then write the number that is 1 less.

1. 39   **2.** 700   **3.** 568   **4.** 23   **5.** 943

Write the number that is 10 more. Then write the number that is 10 less.

6. 23   **7.** 379   **8.** 568   **9.** 102   **10.** 43

PROBLEM SOLVER'S GUIDE

There are no magic rules to make solving problems easy. But the Problem Solver's Guide can help.

Once we used the Guide to help our family plan a trip to the circus.

ADULTS $5 EACH
CHILDREN $3 EACH

OUR PROBLEM

Mr. and Mrs. Ford and their children, Ed and Ellen, were planning to go to the circus. They wanted to know how much their tickets would cost.

OUR SOLUTION

Understand
What is going on in the problem?
What do we know?
What do we need to find out?

> A family is buying tickets. Tickets are different prices. We need to find the total cost.

Try
We tried to come up with an idea.
We added because we wanted a total.

> $5.00
> + $3.00
> Total ⟶ $8.00

Look Back
We checked if our answer made sense. We saw that we had added without checking the facts carefully.

> $5.00 ⟶ 1 adult ticket
> $3.00 ⟶ 1 child ticket
>
> But there are more than 2 people in the family.

We **tried** again. This time we wrote the cost for each person. The total cost would be $16.

We **looked back** again.
Our answer made sense.

> Mr. Ford ⟶ $5.00
> Mrs. Ford ⟶ $5.00
> Ellen ⟶ $3.00
> Ed ⟶ $3.00

Solve each problem. The Problem Solver's Guide may help. Work with a group.

1. Mr. Ford buys popcorn and ice cream for each of his children. He pays with a $10 bill. How much change should he get back?

2. These 6 clowns make a human triangle 3 rows high. How many more clowns are needed to make a triangle 5 rows high?

3. The dog trainer wants all the dogs to balance on the seesaw. There will be 3 dogs in each basket. Into which basket should each dog go?

POPCORN $1.00
ICE CREAM $2.00

9 Pounds Tucket
8 Pounds Powder
6 Pounds Buster
4 Pounds Buttons
3 Pounds Pebbles
2 Pounds FiFi

PROPERTIES OF ADDITION

Here are three **properties of addition** that may help you add more quickly and easily.

Groups: partners

You will need: counters

▶ Use your counters to add: 8 + 5.

Then complete the number sentence: 8 + 5 = ▧

Then use your counters to add: 5 + 8.

Complete the number sentence: 5 + 8 = ▧

1. What do you notice about the addends and sums in both number sentences?

> An **addend** is a number you add.

The **order property** says that changing the order of addends does not change the sum.

▶ Use your counters to complete the two number sentences:

3 + 0 = ▧

0 + 9 = ▧

2. What do you notice about each sum?

The **zero property** says that if you add zero to a number, the sum equals that number.

▶ Use your counters to complete the number sentences. Add the blue numbers first.

5 + 4 + 2 = ▧

5 + 4 + 2 = ▧

3. What do you notice about the sums?

The **grouping property** says that no matter how you group addends, the sum is always the same.

Write the sum. You may use a calculator.

4. 7 + 5
5 + 7

5. 9 + 0
0 + 9

6. 3 + 2 + 4
4 + 2 + 3

7. 0 + 14
14 + 0

8. 3 + 8
8 + 3

9. 6 + 3 + 4
4 + 6 + 3

10. 72 + 0
0 + 72

11. 41 + 54
54 + 41

12. 9 + 21 + 100
100 + 21 + 9

SUMMING IT UP

13. Does the size of the addends change how the addition properties work? Explain.

14. How can these properties help you add?

PROJECT • Game

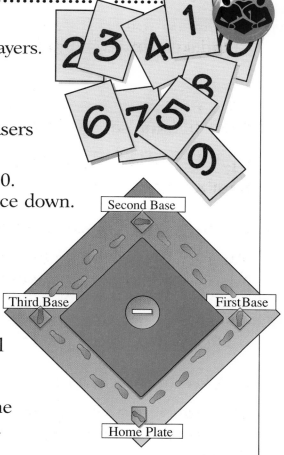

Play Digit Baseball with two or more players.

You will need:

- 22 small cards
- game pieces, such as pennies or erasers
- recording sheet

a. Make 2 decks of cards numbered 0–10. Shuffle them and place the 2 decks face down. Place the game pieces on home plate.

b. Pick 1 card from each pile. Find the sum. Move your game piece that number of footprints on the board.

c. Take turns with the other players until all cards are gone. You score 1 point each time you make a run. Then wait at home plate until your next turn. The player with the most points at the end of the game wins.

USING DOUBLES TO ADD

You can look for doubles when you add.

To find the sum of 6 + 7, you can use the double **6 + 6 = 12** or **7 + 7 = 14.**

Add 1 to the double 6 + 6.

6 + 6 + 1 = 13

Subtract 1 from the double 7 + 7.

7 + 7 − 1 = 13

So, 6 + 7 = 13.

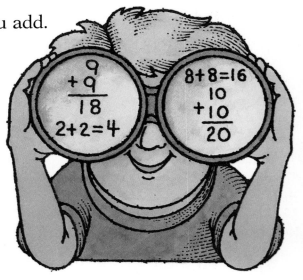

Think

• What double could you use to find the sum of 9 + 8? Would you add or subtract 1?

Other Examples

12 + 12 = 24

12 + 11 = 23

$$\begin{array}{r} 5 \\ + 5 \\ \hline 10 \end{array} \qquad \begin{array}{r} 5 \\ + 6 \\ \hline 11 \end{array}$$

GUIDED PRACTICE

Write the double you could use to find the sum. Then write the sum for each exercise below.

1. 8 + 7   2. 5 + 4   3. 9 + 10   4. 8 + 9

Write the missing sign.

5. 3 + 4 = 3 + 3 ○ 1   6. 6 + 5 = 6 + 6 ○ 1   7. 12 + 13 = 12 + 12 ○ 1

8. In exercises 5–7, how did you know whether to add or subtract 1?

INDEPENDENT PRACTICE

Use the double to write the sum.

9.
$$\begin{array}{r} 5 \\ +\ 5 \\ \hline 10 \end{array} \qquad \begin{array}{r} 4 \\ +\ 5 \\ \hline \end{array}$$

10.
$$\begin{array}{r} 7 \\ +\ 7 \\ \hline 14 \end{array} \qquad \begin{array}{r} 8 \\ +\ 7 \\ \hline \end{array}$$

11.
$$\begin{array}{r} 10 \\ +\ 10 \\ \hline 20 \end{array} \qquad \begin{array}{r} 10 \\ +\ 9 \\ \hline \end{array}$$

12.
$$\begin{array}{r} 15 \\ +\ 15 \\ \hline 30 \end{array} \qquad \begin{array}{r} 15 \\ +\ 16 \\ \hline \end{array}$$

Write the missing sign.

13. $7 + 8 = 8 + 8 \bullet 1$ 14. $9 + 8 = 9 + 9 \bullet 1$ 15. $11 + 10 = 10 + 10 \bullet 1$

Problem Solving

16. There are 8 players on Jackie's soccer team and 1 more than that on Tanya's team. How many players are there?

17. In art class, 10 students are making clay pots and 10 are making potato prints. One student leaves. How many students are there now?

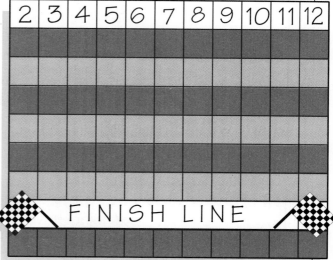

PROJECT • Game

Play this addition game with 2 or more players.

You will need:
  • a game board for each player
  • 2 number cubes

a. Take turns with the other players. Roll the number cubes. Find the sum of the 2 numbers. On your game board, mark an X under the sum.

b. Keep rolling the number cubes and marking an X under the sum. The first player to mark an X below the Finish Line wins.

2	3	4	5	6	7	8	9	10	11	12

FINISH LINE

NOT ENOUGH INFORMATION

Work with a partner to solve each problem. If there is not enough information, tell what you need to know.

1. Harriet has 5 coins. An apple costs 45¢. Does Harriet have enough money to buy one?

2. A postcard costs 15¢. Charlie has some dimes. Is this enough to buy a postcard?

3. Luis has some pencils. If he gives 3 of them away, how many will he have left?

4. Tim had some crayons. He gave 3 to Tiffany. Now he has 5 crayons left. How many crayons did Tim start with?

5. In Miss Butterworth's class, 10 of the students are boys. There are 6 students who have brown hair. How many students are in the class?

6. The movie *Martians* begins at 6:30 at Midtown Theater. José and Roger leave their house at 6:00. Can they get to the movie before it begins?

SECTION REVIEW

for pages 2–12

Write the number the arrow is pointing to.

1.
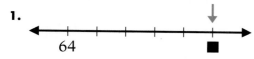

2.

3.
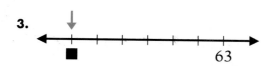

4.
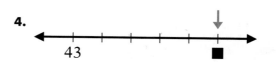

5.
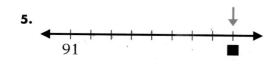

6.
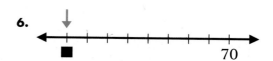

Write the missing numbers.

7. 62, 63, ▓, ▓, ▓, 67

8. 75, 76, ▓, ▓, 79

9. 13, 14, ▓, 16, ▓, ▓, 19

10. 41, 42, ▓, ▓, ▓, 46

11. 88, ▓, ▓, ▓, 92

12. 95, ▓, ▓, 98, ▓, 100

Write the sum.

13. 4
      $+\ 5$

14. 5
      $+\ 4$

15. 5
      $+\ 6$

16. 6
      $+\ 7$

17. 3
      $+\ 7$

18. 5
      $+\ 5$

19. 8
      $+\ 0$

20. 9
      $+\ 8$

21. 9
      $+\ 6$

22. 8
      $+\ 7$

23. 7
      $+\ 7$

24. 5
      $+\ 7$

25. 8
      $+\ 3$

26. 9
      $+\ 9$

27. 6
      $+\ 4$

USING TENS TO ADD

You can look for 10's when you add. To add 7 and 4, break up one addend to make a sum of 10. Then add the rest of the addend to get the sum.

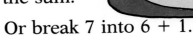

Break 4 into 3 + 1.

$$7 \rightarrow \quad 7$$
$$+4 \rightarrow +3 + 1$$
$$\overline{10 + 1 = 11}$$

So, 7 + 4 = 11.

Or break 7 into 6 + 1.

$$7 \rightarrow \quad 6 + 1$$
$$+4 \rightarrow +4$$
$$\overline{10 + 1 = 11}$$

Think

- How can looking for a 10 help you find the sum of 9 + 6?

Other Examples

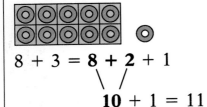

$$8 + 3 = 8 + 2 + 1$$
$$\diagdown \diagup$$
$$10 + 1 = 11$$

$$5 \rightarrow \quad 5$$
$$+7 \rightarrow +5 + 2$$
$$\overline{10 + 2 = 12}$$

GUIDED PRACTICE

Copy and complete the number sentence. You may use counters or make a drawing.

1. 9 + 3 = 10 + ▧
2. 6 + 7 = 10 + ▧
3. 7 + 8 = 10 + ▧

Write the sum. Use mental math when you can.

4. 5 + 9
5. 8 + 6
6. 9 + 7
7. 19 + 7

8. Can you find the sum of 6 + 3 by looking for a 10? Why or why not?

INDEPENDENT PRACTICE

Copy and complete the number sentence.
You may use counters or make a drawing.

9. $3 + 8 = 10 + $ ▓   **10.** $9 + 4 = 10 + $ ▓   **11.** $5 + 7 = 10 + $ ▓

Write the sum.

12. 8
   $+ 4$

13. 8
   $+ 5$

14. 8
   $+ 8$

15. 9
   $+ 6$

16. 9
   $+ 7$

17. $9 + 2$ **18.** $6 + 5$ **19.** $8 + 7$ **20.** $8 + 9$

Problem Solving

21. Mrs. Springer makes 10 apple pies in her bakery. Before lunch, 6 people each buy a pie. Then 5 people come to buy a pie each. How many people could not buy a pie?

22. There are 10 empty seats at the movie theater. There are 14 people looking for seats. How many people can sit down?

PROJECT • Game

Play Tic-tac-toe to Ten by yourself or with friends. Each player will need a number cube.

a. Each player should draw a board like the one at the right.

b. Take turns rolling your number cube. After each roll, write the number in one of the squares on your board. You get 1 point for every row that has a sum of 10.

c. The player with the most points wins. If you play by yourself, try to beat your last score.

Remember that a row can go in three directions.

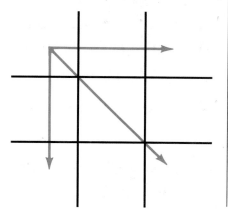

THREE OR MORE ADDENDS

Meg visits a wild animal farm. She sees 8 beavers, 4 pheasants, and 2 red foxes. How many wild animals does she see?

Add 8, 4, and 2 to find the number of wild animals. Remember the grouping and order properties!

● Add: 8 + 4
   Then add 2.

   8 + 4 + 2

   12   + 2 = 14

● Add: 4 + 2
   Then add 8.

   8 + 4 + 2

   8 +   6 = 14

● Add: 8 + 2
   Then add 4.

   8 + 4 + 2

   4 +   10 = 14

Meg sees 14 wild animals.

Think

> • Which of the 3 ways is easiest to add? Why?
> • How are 1 + 3 + 5 = 9 and 5 + 3 + 1 = 9 alike? How are they different?

Finding sums of 10 can help you add 3 addends.

Add: 4 + 6 + 5

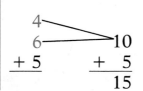

```
 4
 6      10
+ 5    + 5
       15
```

Finding doubles can also help you.

Add: 3 + 8 + 3 + 2

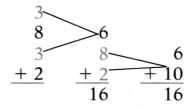

```
 3
 8      6
 3      8      6
+ 2    + 2    + 10
       16     16
```

16

GUIDED PRACTICE

Write the sum. Look for doubles and sums of 10.

1.	2.	3.	4.	5.	6.
3	3	4	5	1	9
7	5	8	5	9	8
+ 3	5	+ 6	+ 5	7	+ 2
	+ 1			+ 3	

7. $7 + 2 + 7$ 8. $5 + 3 + 3 + 1$ 9. $5 + 5 + 9$

10. In exercise 1, which numbers did you
add first? Explain.

....

INDEPENDENT PRACTICE

Write the sum. Look for doubles and sums of 10.

11.	12.	13.	14.	15.	16.	17.
4	6	7	4	4	6	5
6	1	2	4	5	5	6
+ 2	+ 6	3	4	+ 6	+ 4	+ 7
		+ 2	+ 4			

18. $2 + 8 + 8$ 19. $8 + 1 + 2$ 20. $2 + 2 + 5$ 21. $4 + 9 + 1$

Problem Solving

22. Meg sees 7 seals swimming,
2 seals sunning on the rocks,
and 3 seals eating fish. How
many seals does she see?

23. Meg sees 8 bear cubs. There
are 5 cubs running and
3 cubs walking. How many
cubs does she see?

24. In one part of the farm, there
are 4 hawks, 5 turtles,
6 crows, and an empty owl's
nest. How many birds are
there?

25. Meg can take 10 photos with
1 pack of film. She uses
2 full packs. Then she takes
1 more photo. How many
photos has she taken?

 MATH LOG ─────

What other ways do you use to add 3 or more addends?

COUNTING UP OR BACK TO SUBTRACT

The answer in a subtraction problem is called the **difference.** Sometimes you can count up or count back to find a difference.

Subtract: 13 − 9

Count up from 9 until you reach 13. How many numbers did you count?

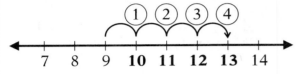

You counted 4 numbers.

So, 13 − 9 = 4.

Subtract: 11 − 3

Count back 3 numbers from 11. What number did you stop at?

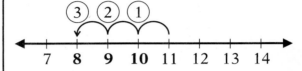

You stopped at 8.

So, 11 − 3 = 8.

Think

- How could you count up or back if you did not have a number line?

GUIDED PRACTICE

Write the difference. You may use the number line to count up or back.

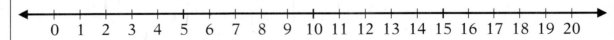

1.	12	2.	16	3.	12	4.	7	5.	15
	− 3		− 8		− 8		− 7		− 0

6.	15	7.	13	8.	17	9.	14	10.	20
	− 8		− 5		− 8		− 6		− 1

11. Explain how you got the answers for exercises 4 and 5.

INDEPENDENT PRACTICE

Write the difference.

12.   9
       − 5

13.   13
       − 6

14.   13
       − 8

15.   15
       − 7

16.   14
       − 4

17. 8 − 5

18. 11 − 5

19. 17 − 9

20. 13 − 0

Problem Solving

21. Ruth gives Anne 10 marbles. Anne gives 2 of them back. How many marbles does Anne have now?

22. Scott is 9 years old. Carmela is 7 years old. How much older is Scott?

....

PROJECT • Game

Play Subtraction Spin with a partner or a small group. You will need a spinner like the one at the right.

a. Pick a number between 1 and 10 and make a subtraction rule. For example, your group's rule could be *Subtract 9*.

b. Take turns spinning the spinner. Subtract the number in your rule from the number you land on. Write the difference on a piece of paper.

c. After everyone has taken a turn, make up a new rule and spin again. Add your differences as you go along.

d. The first player to reach 30 wins.

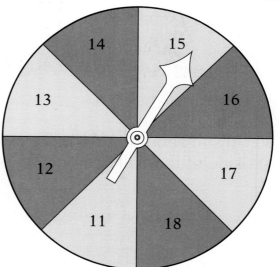

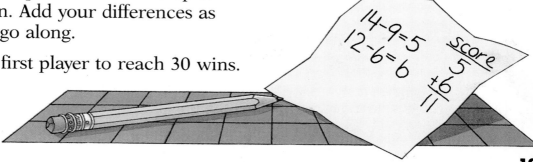

MISSING ADDENDS

In her science class, Alison is using weights and a balance. How many more grams should she put on the left side to make the sides level?

You can use an addition fact to find the answer.

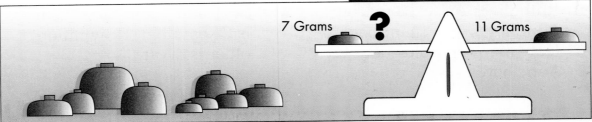

7 Grams **?** 11 Grams

What number added to 7 equals 11?

$$7 + \blacksquare = 11$$

You can add 4 to 7 to equal 11.

$$7 + \mathbf{4} = 11$$

So, Alison should put 4 more grams on the left side of the balance.

Think

• Could you have used a subtraction fact to get your answer? If so, which fact?

You can find the answer using either an addition or a subtraction fact.

So, $7 + \blacksquare = 11$ asks the same question as $11 - 7 = \blacksquare$.

Other Example

$$13 = 8 + \blacksquare \qquad 13 = 8 + \mathbf{5}$$

GUIDED PRACTICE

Copy and complete the number sentence.

1. $5 + \blacksquare = 9$ **2.** $\blacksquare + 8 = 11$ **3.** $8 + \blacksquare = 15$ **4.** $10 = 4 + \blacksquare$

5. $\blacksquare + 3 = 5$ **6.** $13 = 7 + \blacksquare$ **7.** $12 = \blacksquare + 9$ **8.** $\blacksquare + 8 = 17$

9. Tell whether you used addition or subtraction facts to find the missing numbers.

....
INDEPENDENT PRACTICE

Copy and complete the number sentence.

10. $6 + \blacksquare = 11$ **11.** $14 = 9 + \blacksquare$ **12.** $\blacksquare + 9 = 13$ **13.** $10 + \blacksquare = 20$

14. $\blacksquare + 5 = 7$ **15.** $\blacksquare + 7 = 12$ **16.** $8 = \blacksquare + 8$ **17.** $16 = \blacksquare + 9$

Problem Solving

18. Judy is weighing 14 rocks for a project. She has weighed 4 of the rocks. How many more rocks does she need to weigh?

19. By noon, Bill's class made 8 model snakes. At the end of the day, they had 17 snakes. How many model snakes did they make in the afternoon?

20. Nels collected some leaves but 3 of them tore. He has 9 left. How many leaves did he collect?

21. Mark wants to buy a lizard cage that costs $15. He has $7. How much more money does he need?

....
Maintain • Mixed Practice

Write the answer.

1. $\begin{array}{r} 8 \\ + 6 \\ \hline \end{array}$ **2.** $\begin{array}{r} 15 \\ - 8 \\ \hline \end{array}$ **3.** $\begin{array}{r} 7 \\ + 9 \\ \hline \end{array}$ **4.** $\begin{array}{r} 8 \\ + 0 \\ \hline \end{array}$ **5.** $\begin{array}{r} 17 \\ - 9 \\ \hline \end{array}$ **6.** $\begin{array}{r} 20 \\ - 10 \\ \hline \end{array}$

7. $6 + 6$ **8.** $7 + 6$ **9.** $18 - 9$ **10.** $12 - 0$

USING STRATEGIES

If you get stuck, remember....
Tips for Problem Solving
on pages 426–427

The Marvel Magic Show is coming to the Tinton Theater. There is not much time to get tickets. The show will disappear from town in 3 days!

Aisle

A B C D E F G H I J K L M N O

STAGE

Aisle

Solve each problem. Work with a group.

1. Look at Bill and Mindy's tickets. Who will sit closer to the stage?

2. How many seats will be between Bill and the nearest aisle?

3. Red seats cost $3 each. Blue seats cost $2 each. Lynn has $7. She needs to buy tickets for Anne, Shana, and herself. What color seats should she get if they want to sit in the same row?

4. How many red seats are in the theater? How do you know?

5. The show is ready to begin. All the seats are filled except for seat 7 and seat 10 in row G. How many people are in the red seats?

6. There are more blue seats than the picture shows. They go to row Z. Are there more red seats or blue seats in the theater? How do you know?

7. The Amazing Mabel can guess a person's birthday with just a few clues. And so can you! Mabel's friend Mark has a birthday in August. Look at Mabel's questions and Mark's answers. See if you can find on what day in August Mark was born.

8. Try out Mabel's birthday trick on a friend.

Using Subtraction

You can use subtraction to solve different kinds of problems.

► A balloon man has 13 balloons. Then 4 of them blow away. How many balloons does he have now?

$$13 - 4 = 9$$

He has 9 balloons now.

► Juan is making hats for his party. He needs 13 hats. So far, he has made 4 hats. How many more does he need to make?

$$4 + \blacksquare = 13 \text{ or } 13 - 4 = 9$$

Juan needs to make 9 more hats.

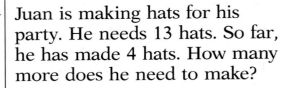

► Coby and Aaron look for starfish on the beach. Coby finds 13 starfish and Aaron finds 4. How many more starfish than Aaron does Coby find?

$$13 - 4 = 9$$

Coby finds 9 more starfish than Aaron.

Think

- There are 17 children at the beach. There are 12 girls. What would you do to find the number of boys?

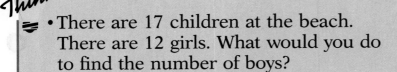

INDEPENDENT PRACTICE

Write the difference.

1. 14
   − 7

2. 14
   − 6

3. 12
   − 6

4. 11
   − 3

5. 17
   − 8

6. 10 − 3

7. 15 − 8

8. 12 − 7

9. 13 − 5

Problem Solving

10. Omar's mother cuts 14 pieces of watermelon for her family. They eat some and leave 8 pieces. How many pieces of watermelon did Omar's family eat?

11. Ruth buys a bag of 8 horns for her party guests. She will give 1 horn to each guest. She has 12 guests. How many more horns does she need?

12. There are 13 friends coming to Eleanor's party. So far, 7 friends are there. How many more friends will come?

13. Eleanor's mother made cupcakes. The children ate 9 of them. There are 6 left. How many cupcakes did Eleanor's mother make?

14. At a picnic, Wendy and 8 friends each eat a hot dog. There are 6 other children who each eat a hamburger. How many more children eat hot dogs than hamburgers?

15. Mrs. Brown used all the money in her wallet. She spent $6 on lunch and $9 on gas. How much money did she have in her wallet?

MATH LOG

Write your own subtraction word problem. Give it to a friend to solve.

ADDING AND SUBTRACTING 9

▶ Ashley wants to add: 6 + 9.

She knows that 10 is 1 more than 9. Here is how she uses that fact to add 9.

6 + 10 = 16

16 − 1 = 15

So, 6 + 9 = 15.

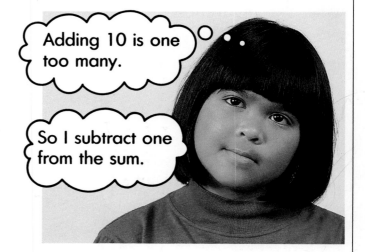

Adding 10 is one too many.

So I subtract one from the sum.

▶ Ashley wants to subtract: 17 − 9.

Here is how she subtracts 9.

17 − 10 = 7

7 + 1 = 8

So, 17 − 9 = 8.

Subtracting 10 is one too many.

So I add one to the difference.

Think

• Why does Ashley add 1 to the difference instead of subtracting 1?

Other Examples

3 + 9

3 + 10 = 13

13 − 1 = 12

So, 3 + 9 = 12.

$$\begin{array}{r} \mathbf{14} \\ -\ \mathbf{9} \\ \hline \end{array} \qquad \begin{array}{r} 14 \\ -\ 10 \\ \hline 4 \end{array} \qquad \begin{array}{r} 4 \\ +\ 1 \\ \hline 5 \end{array} \qquad \text{So,} \begin{array}{r} 14 \\ -\ 9 \\ \hline 5 \end{array}$$

GUIDED PRACTICE

Write the answer. Use mental math when you can.

1.
$$\begin{array}{r} 5 \\ + 9 \\ \hline \end{array}$$

2.
$$\begin{array}{r} 9 \\ + 5 \\ \hline \end{array}$$

3.
$$\begin{array}{r} 13 \\ - 9 \\ \hline \end{array}$$

4.
$$\begin{array}{r} 23 \\ - 9 \\ \hline \end{array}$$

5.
$$\begin{array}{r} 8 \\ + 9 \\ \hline \end{array}$$

6. $9 + 7$

7. $8 + 7$

8. $4 + 9$

9. $15 - 9$

10. How could you use Ashley's ideas about 10 to add and subtract 8?

INDEPENDENT PRACTICE

Write the answer. Use mental math when you can.

11.
$$\begin{array}{r} 9 \\ + 8 \\ \hline \end{array}$$

12.
$$\begin{array}{r} 8 \\ + 7 \\ \hline \end{array}$$

13.
$$\begin{array}{r} 16 \\ - 9 \\ \hline \end{array}$$

14.
$$\begin{array}{r} 9 \\ + 9 \\ \hline \end{array}$$

15.
$$\begin{array}{r} 10 \\ + 10 \\ \hline \end{array}$$

16. $2 + 9$

17. $17 - 9$

18. $6 + 9$

19. $16 + 9$

Copy and complete the number sentence.

20. $5 + \blacksquare = 14$

21. $\blacksquare + 9 = 14$

22. $17 - \blacksquare = 9$

23. $\blacksquare + 0 = 9$

24. $9 + \blacksquare = 12$

25. $13 - \blacksquare = 4$

26. $10 - \blacksquare = 1$

27. $18 - \blacksquare = 9$

Problem Solving

28. Ashley has 16 pictures of whales. Dan has 9. Liz has 14. How many more pictures does Ashley have than Dan?

29. If Ashley gives 7 of her pictures to Dan, how many pictures will they each have?

CHALLENGE • Mental Math

Write the answer.

1. $9 + 53$

2. $37 - 9$

3. $40 - 9$

4. $236 + 9$

FACT FAMILIES

▶ Dave reaches into a jar and pulls out 6 red counters and 5 blue counters. What number sentences can he write?

He writes: $6 + 5 = 11$ and $5 + 6 = 11$.
He has 11 counters.

▶ How many counters would he have if he put the blue ones back? Because $11 - 5 = 6$, he would have 6 counters.

▶ How many counters would he have if he put the red ones back? Because $11 - 6 = 5$, he would have 5 counters.

The 4 number sentences are called a **fact family.**

Here is a fact family for 4, 8, and 12:

$4 + 8 = 12$ $\qquad$ $12 - 8 = 4$

$8 + 4 = 12$ $\qquad$ $12 - 4 = 8$

Think

- How many addition sentences are in each fact family above? How many subtraction sentences?

- How many numbers are in each fact family?

Other Examples

$8 + 8 = 16$ $\qquad$ $9 + 0 = 9$ $\qquad$ $9 - 0 = 9$

$16 - 8 = 8$ $\qquad$ $0 + 9 = 9$ $\qquad$ $9 - 9 = 0$

GUIDED PRACTICE

Write a fact family for the number sentence.

1. $7 + 5 = 12$ **2.** $15 - 8 = 7$ **3.** $9 + 9 = 18$ **4.** $13 - 5 = 8$

5. Why are there only 2 number sentences for exercise 3?

INDEPENDENT PRACTICE

Write the number sentence that is missing from the fact family.

6. $9 + 3 = 12$ **7.** $6 + 9 = 15$ **8.** $20 - 10 = 10$ **9.** $6 + 7 = 13$
     $3 + 9 = 12$ $15 - 9 = 6$ $7 + 6 = 13$
    $12 - 3 = 9$ $15 - 6 = 9$ $13 - 6 = 7$

Write a fact family using the numbers.

10. 3, 11, 8   **11.** 11, 6, 5   **12.** 13, 9, 4   **13.** 7, 7, 14

Write a fact family using the numbers. Then write a word problem using the numbers.

14. 2 parents, 5 boys, 7 people   **15.** 7 spotted cows, 3 black cows, 10 cows

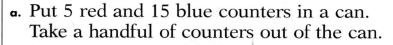

PROJECT • Probability

Work with a partner. You will need a can and counters in two different colors, such as red and blue.

a. Put 5 red and 15 blue counters in a can. Take a handful of counters out of the can.

b. Count the number of blue and red counters. Write a fact family for the counters you picked. Put the counters back.

c. Repeat steps a and b 4 times.

d. What do you notice about the number of red and blue counters you pick?

USING STRATEGIES

The Gators and Tigers are in a close game.
The fourth inning has just ended.

Teams	Innings						Runs
	①	②	③	④	⑤	⑥	
Gators	0	3	0	4			
Tigers	0	2	3	1			

Work with a partner. Solve each problem.

1. What is the score of this game so far?

2. After which inning were the Tigers
   winning?

3. If each team scores 9 runs in the next 2
   innings, who will win the game?

4. Which of these scores below cannot be
   the final score of this game? Why not?

   9 to 7   10 to 2   6 to 4

The game is over, but 2 numbers fell off the
scoreboard.

Teams	Innings						Runs
	①	②	③	④	⑤	⑥	
Gators	0	3	0	4	1		10
Tigers	0	2	3	1	3		9

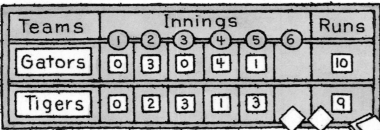

5. How many runs did the Gators score in
   the last inning?

6. How many runs did the Tigers score in
   the last inning?

7. Make up your own problem about this
   game. See if a friend can solve it.

SECTION REVIEW

for pages 14–30

Write the sum.

1. $\begin{array}{r} 5 \\ + 6 \\ \hline \end{array}$	2. $\begin{array}{r} 9 \\ + 3 \\ \hline \end{array}$	3. $\begin{array}{r} 7 \\ + 5 \\ \hline \end{array}$	4. $\begin{array}{r} 9 \\ + 8 \\ \hline \end{array}$	5. $\begin{array}{r} 8 \\ + 3 \\ \hline \end{array}$

6. $\begin{array}{r} 4 \\ 7 \\ + 1 \\ \hline \end{array}$	7. $\begin{array}{r} 2 \\ 4 \\ 4 \\ + 3 \\ \hline \end{array}$	8. $\begin{array}{r} 3 \\ 8 \\ + 5 \\ \hline \end{array}$	9. $\begin{array}{r} 4 \\ 6 \\ + 4 \\ \hline \end{array}$	10. $\begin{array}{r} 2 \\ 5 \\ 5 \\ + 8 \\ \hline \end{array}$

11. $4 + 5 + 6$ 12. $2 + 8 + 9$

Write the difference.

13. $\begin{array}{r} 14 \\ - 7 \\ \hline \end{array}$	14. $\begin{array}{r} 13 \\ - 9 \\ \hline \end{array}$	15. $\begin{array}{r} 13 \\ - 8 \\ \hline \end{array}$	16. $\begin{array}{r} 15 \\ - 6 \\ \hline \end{array}$	17. $\begin{array}{r} 17 \\ - 8 \\ \hline \end{array}$	18. $\begin{array}{r} 12 \\ - 7 \\ \hline \end{array}$

19. $14 - 0$ 20. $13 - 5$ 21. $20 - 10$

Copy and complete the number sentence.

22. $9 + \blacksquare = 16$ 23. $14 = \blacksquare + 5$ 24. $\blacksquare + 9 = 18$

Write a fact family for the number sentence.

25. $7 + 8 = 15$ 26. $9 + 6 = 15$ 27. $14 - 7 = 7$

Problem Solving

28. Rudy wants to play all 11 games at the fair. So far, he has played 5 of them. How many more games does Rudy have to play?

29. Rudy knocked down 10 pins at the bowling booth. Kent knocked down 6 pins. How many more pins did Rudy knock down than Kent?

CHAPTER REVIEW

Language Connection

Each pair of number sentences shows a property of addition. In words, tell what each pair of number sentences means.

Order Property of Addition $2 + 3 = 5$
$3 + 2 = 5$

Zero Property of Addition $3 + 0 = 3$
$5 + 0 = 5$

Grouping Property of Addition $3 + 2 + 1 = 6$
$3 + 2 + 1 = 6$

Test

Write the missing numbers.

1. 46, 47, ▨, ▨, 50

2. 61, ▨, 63, ▨

3. 89, ▨, ▨, 92

4. 54, ▨, 56, ▨, 58

5. ▨, ▨, 40, 41

6. 75, 76, ▨, ▨

Write the sum. Use the double to help you.

7.
$$\begin{array}{r} 6 \\ + 6 \\ \hline 12 \end{array} \qquad \begin{array}{r} 6 \\ + 7 \\ \hline \end{array}$$

8.
$$\begin{array}{r} 8 \\ + 8 \\ \hline 16 \end{array} \qquad \begin{array}{r} 7 \\ + 8 \\ \hline \end{array}$$

9.
$$\begin{array}{r} 9 \\ + 9 \\ \hline 18 \end{array} \qquad \begin{array}{r} 9 \\ + 8 \\ \hline \end{array}$$

10.
$$\begin{array}{r} 10 \\ + 10 \\ \hline 20 \end{array} \qquad \begin{array}{r} 10 \\ + 11 \\ \hline \end{array}$$

Write the answer.

11.
$$\begin{array}{r} 8 \\ 3 \\ + 3 \\ \hline \end{array}$$

12. $15 - 6$

13.
$$\begin{array}{r} 5 \\ 6 \\ + 3 \\ \hline \end{array}$$

14. $18 - 1$

Write the answer.

15. $6 + 4 + 9$

16.
$$\begin{array}{r} 16 \\ - 8 \\ \hline \end{array}$$

17.
$$\begin{array}{r} 15 \\ - 7 \\ \hline \end{array}$$

18. $8 + 2 + 1 + 7$

19.
$$\begin{array}{r} 2 \\ 7 \\ + 1 \\ \hline \end{array}$$

20. $13 - 9$

21.
$$\begin{array}{r} 14 \\ - 7 \\ \hline \end{array}$$

22. $1 + 5 + 3 + 7$

Copy and complete the number sentence.

23. $6 + \blacksquare = 13$

24. $15 = \blacksquare + 9$

25. $\blacksquare + 8 = 15$

26. $18 = \blacksquare + 9$

27. $4 + \blacksquare = 12$

28. $\blacksquare + 6 = 11$

29. $13 = \blacksquare + 8$

30. $20 = 10 + \blacksquare$

Write the number sentence that is missing from the fact family.

31. $9 + 3 = 12$
$3 + 9 = 12$
$12 - 3 = 9$

32. $11 - 7 = 4$
$11 - 4 = 7$
$7 + 4 = 11$

33. $8 + 6 = 14$
$6 + 8 = 14$
$14 - 8 = 6$

34. $9 + 8 = 17$
$8 + 9 = 17$
$17 - 8 = 9$

PROBLEM SOLVING

Solve each problem.

35. There are 8 rooms in Shelley's house and 1 more than that in Josh's house. How many rooms are there in both houses?

36. Carole visits the pet shop. She sees 4 rabbits, 5 turtles, and 3 hamsters. How many animals does she see?

37. This morning, Mr. Carlson had some teddy bears in his toy store. During the day, he sold 10 of them. Now he has 6 teddy bears left. How many bears did he have this morning?

38. Before lunch, Roberto and Carmen made 3 costumes for the school play. At the end of the day, they had made 10 costumes. How many costumes did they make after lunch?

EXCURSION

NUMERATION

LETTER CODES
What has seas without water and cities without people?

You can solve this riddle by using a code. Follow the steps below.

a. First, write the answer for each addition or subtraction exercise.

9	2	12	1
− 3	+ 6	− 6	+ 8
6	8	6	9

Code Key					
A	C	M	P	S	Y
6	7	8	9	12	14

b. Look for each answer in the Code Key. The letter above the number is the code letter.

c. Then write the code letter under each answer.

9	2	12	1
− 3	+ 6	− 6	+ 8
6	8	6	9
A	M	A	P

d. To solve the riddle, you may need to break the letters into two words.

The answer to the riddle is *a map*.

Use the Code Key at the right to
solve the riddles.

Code Key

3	4	5	7	8	9	10	11	12	15	17
C	E	A	F	G	K	L	R	T	U	W

1. What can run but cannot walk?

$$\begin{array}{c} 9 \\ +\ 8 \\ \hline \end{array} \qquad \begin{array}{c} 11 \\ -\ 6 \\ \hline \end{array} \qquad \begin{array}{c} 5 \\ +\ 7 \\ \hline \end{array} \qquad \begin{array}{c} 13 \\ -\ 9 \\ \hline \end{array} \qquad \begin{array}{c} 6 \\ +\ 5 \\ \hline \end{array}$$

2. What is at the end of everything?

$$\begin{array}{c} 7 \\ +\ 3 \\ \hline \end{array} \quad \begin{array}{c} 12 \\ -\ 8 \\ \hline \end{array} \quad \begin{array}{c} 3 \\ +\ 9 \\ \hline \end{array} \quad \begin{array}{c} 6 \\ +\ 6 \\ \hline \end{array} \quad \begin{array}{c} 9 \\ -\ 5 \\ \hline \end{array} \quad \begin{array}{c} 8 \\ +\ 3 \\ \hline \end{array} \quad \begin{array}{c} 17 \\ -\ 9 \\ \hline \end{array}$$

3. What will happen if you throw a blue rock
into the Red Sea?

$$\begin{array}{c} 2 \\ +\ 6 \\ \hline \end{array} \quad \begin{array}{c} 11 \\ -\ 7 \\ \hline \end{array} \quad \begin{array}{c} 8 \\ +\ 4 \\ \hline \end{array} \quad \begin{array}{c} 8 \\ +\ 9 \\ \hline \end{array} \quad \begin{array}{c} 10 \\ -\ 6 \\ \hline \end{array} \quad \begin{array}{c} 7 \\ +\ 5 \\ \hline \end{array}$$

4. What is in front of everyone but cannot be seen?

$$\begin{array}{c} 13 \\ -\ 6 \\ \hline \end{array} \quad \begin{array}{c} 7 \\ +\ 8 \\ \hline \end{array} \quad \begin{array}{c} 4 \\ +\ 8 \\ \hline \end{array} \quad \begin{array}{c} 6 \\ +\ 9 \\ \hline \end{array} \quad \begin{array}{c} 5 \\ +\ 6 \\ \hline \end{array} \quad \begin{array}{c} 13 \\ -\ 9 \\ \hline \end{array}$$

Copy and complete each exercise below.
Use the Code Key to answer the riddle.

Code Key

1	2	3	4	5	6	7	8	9	10
A	M	D	R	T	I	B	H	C	E

5. What should a cat do when it gets
muddy pawprints on a rug?

a. $7 - 4 + 2 + 3 = \blacksquare$

b. $9 + 6 - 7 - 4 + 2 = \blacksquare$

c. $10 - 6 - 2 + 1 = \blacksquare$

d. $5 - 5 + 6 + 3 + 1 = \blacksquare$

Find a riddle you like. Make up a Code Key
and exercises. Exchange papers with a friend.

CHAPTER 2

PLACE VALUE, MONEY, AND TIME

Social Studies

The Abacus One of the oldest tools in math is the abacus. It was invented thousands of years ago. Numbers are shown by sliding beads back and forth. The abacus is still used by people today.

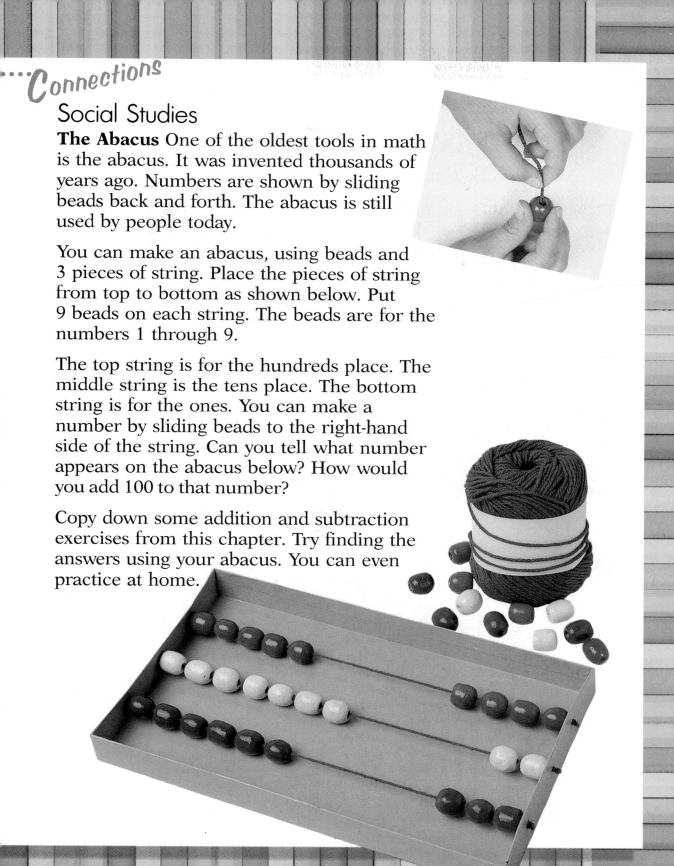

You can make an abacus, using beads and 3 pieces of string. Place the pieces of string from top to bottom as shown below. Put 9 beads on each string. The beads are for the numbers 1 through 9.

The top string is for the hundreds place. The middle string is the tens place. The bottom string is for the ones. You can make a number by sliding beads to the right-hand side of the string. Can you tell what number appears on the abacus below? How would you add 100 to that number?

Copy down some addition and subtraction exercises from this chapter. Try finding the answers using your abacus. You can even practice at home.

TENS AND ONES

The digits 0, 1, 2, 3, 4, 5, 6, 7, 8, and 9 are used to write all numbers.

You can show numbers using counters or place-value blocks. Here are two ways to show 26.

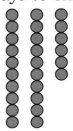

$26 = 20 + 6$ $26 = 2$ tens $+ 6$ ones

Think

- How can you show the number 87 with the fewest blocks?

- How can you show the number 87 with the most blocks?

Other Example

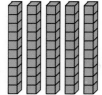

$50 = 5$ tens $+ 0$ ones

GUIDED PRACTICE

Write the number of tens and ones. Then write the number.

1.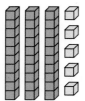

2.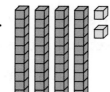

3.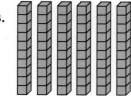

38

Copy and complete the number sentence.

4. 53 = ▢ tens + ▢ ones

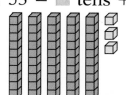

5. 17 = ▢ ten + ▢ ones

6. In exercises 1–5, which number is greatest? How do you know?

· ·

INDEPENDENT PRACTICE

Write the number of tens and ones. Then write the number.

7.

8.

9.

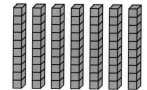

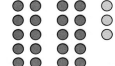

Copy and complete the number sentence.

10. 91 = ▢ tens + ▢ one

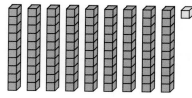

11. 52 = ▢ tens + ▢ ones

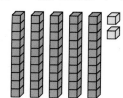

12. 19 = ▢ ten + ▢ ones

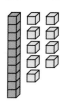

13. 10 = ▢ ten + ▢ ones

CHALLENGE • Number Sense

Find the mystery number. Answer each question.

1. I am the greatest 2-digit number. What number am I?

2. I am the least 2-digit number. What number am I?

39

HUNDREDS, TENS, AND ONES

Our counting system is based on groups of 10.

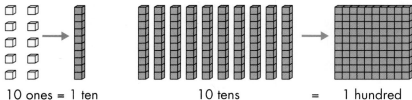

10 ones = 1 ten   10 tens   =   1 hundred

Place-value blocks may help you understand numbers.

Look at the blocks at the right. The blocks show:

2 hundreds + 3 tens + 9 ones, or 239.

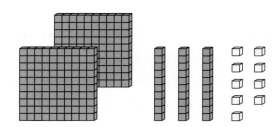

These blocks show:

1 hundred + 0 tens + 2 ones, or 102.

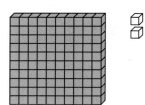

Think

- Why are there no tens blocks used to show 102?

- How would you show the number 120 with place-value blocks?

Other Example

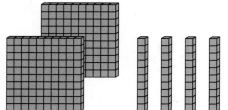

240 = 2 hundreds + 4 tens + 0 ones

GUIDED PRACTICE

Write the number of hundreds, tens, and ones.
Then write the number.

1.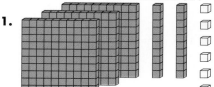

2.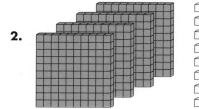

3. Write a 3-digit number with zero tens.
Then write a 3-digit number with zero ones.

INDEPENDENT PRACTICE

Write how many hundreds, tens, and ones.
Then write the number.

4.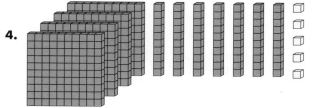

5.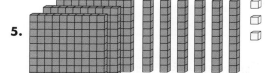

6.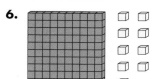

7.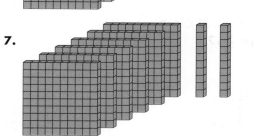

PROJECT • Game

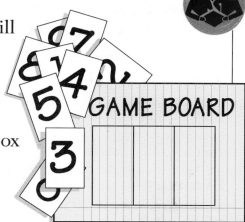

Play Place Value with 2 or 3 players. You will
need 10 cards numbered 0–9. Each player
needs to draw a game board.

a. Shuffle the deck of cards and place them
face down.
b. Each player picks a card and chooses a box
to write the number in. Repeat until the
3 boxes are filled.
c. The player with the greatest number on
the game board wins.

PLACE VALUE

Place-value blocks may help you understand the value of a digit in a number. You can see from the blocks that the **value** of 2 in 324 is 2 tens, or 20.

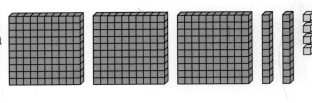

A place-value chart may also help you understand the values of digits.

Hundreds	Tens	Ones
3	2	4
↓	↓	↓
A 3 is in the hundreds place. Its value is 300.	A 2 is in the tens place. Its value is 20.	A 4 is in the ones place. Its value is 4.

You can write the number 324 in different ways.

Expanded form: 300 + 20 + 4

Standard form: 324

You read 324 as "three hundred twenty-four."

Think

- Which digit in 324 has the greatest value? Explain.

Other Examples

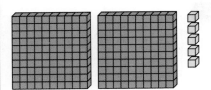

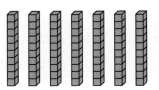

Expanded form: 200 + 5
Standard form: 205
Read: "two hundred five"

Expanded form: 70
Standard form: 70
Read: "seventy"

GUIDED PRACTICE

Write the number in standard form.

1.

2.
Hundreds	Tens	Ones
3	2	0

3.
Hundreds	Tens	Ones
5	0	6

4. seven hundred forty-four

5. 1 ten + 5 ones

6. 600 + 80 + 2

7. Write the numbers in exercises 1–3 in expanded form.

....

INDEPENDENT PRACTICE

Write the number in standard form.

8.

9.
Hundreds	Tens	Ones
	4	9

10.
Hundreds	Tens	Ones
8	6	3

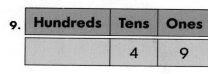

11. three hundred five

12. 9 hundreds + 2 tens

13. 500 + 70 + 2

Write the digit that is in the hundreds place.

14. 524   15. 195   16. 609   17. 326   18. 780

In which place is the digit 6? Write *ones, tens,* or *hundreds.*

19. 629   20. 806   21. 562   22. 65   23. 673

Write the value of the digit 4.

24. 465   25. 342   26. 492   27. 804   28. 45

CHALLENGE • Place Value

Use the digits to write the greatest number.

1. 6, 7, 4   2. 3, 5, 0   3. 7, 8   4. 4, 3, 8

Use the digits to write the least number.

5. 9, 1   6. 7, 5, 8   7. 1, 3, 7   8. 6, 5, 2

PROBLEM SOLVING STRATEGY
USE MODELS

Sometimes you can understand a problem better if you act it out with objects.

We used models to plan a clown show for school.

OUR PROBLEM

We wanted to begin the show with 6 clowns driving onto the stage in a car. First, 5 clowns would get out and juggle. Then 3 of the clowns would get back into the car. We wanted to know how many clowns would be in the car when they drove offstage.

OUR SOLUTION

We began with 6 blocks on the table. These blocks stood for the 6 clowns in the car.

Next, we took away 5 blocks.

Then we put back 3 blocks.

There were 4 blocks on the table. So, there would be 4 clowns in the car when they drove offstage.

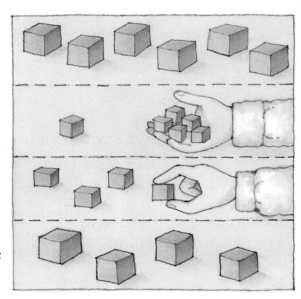

GUIDED PRACTICE

Use models to help you solve the problem.

1. Sarah has 13 peanuts. Tom has 3 peanuts. Sarah wants Tom to have the same number of peanuts as she has. How many of her peanuts should she give to him?

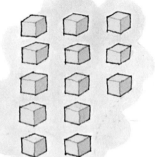
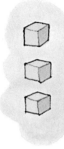

....

APPLICATION

Work in groups to solve each problem. Use models to help you.

2. Alvaro and Carol look for shells at the beach. They find 9 shells. Then they find 6 more. Next, Mrs. Rizzo gives them 3 more. Now they want to share the shells. How many shells should each child get?

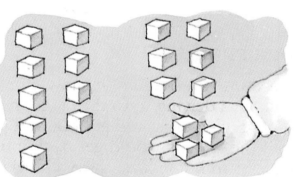

3. Sue folds a sheet of paper in half 4 times. When she opens it up, how many sections will there be?

4. Mr. Davis places 6 statues in a gallery so that they form a triangle. Now he wants the triangle to face the other way. How can he do this by moving only 2 statues?

THOUSANDS

The world's largest ships are the supertankers. They carry oil from one country to another. One French supertanker is 1359 feet long. If the ship stood on end, it would be almost as tall as the Empire State Building.

You can show the number 1359 with your place-value blocks or a place-value chart.

Thousands	Hundreds	Tens	Ones
1	3	5	9

A 1 is in the thousands place. Its value is 1000.

A 3 is in the hundreds place. Its value is 300.

A 5 is in the tens place. Its value is 50.

A 9 is in the ones place. Its value is 9.

Expanded form: 1000 + 300 + 50 + 9

Standard form: 1359

You read 1359 as "one thousand three hundred fifty-nine."

1 thousand = 10 hundreds, or 100 tens, or 1000 ones

Think

- How can you show 2000 with the fewest blocks?

- How can you show 2000 with the most blocks?

GUIDED PRACTICE

Write the number in standard form.

1.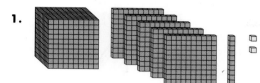

2.
Thousands	Hundreds	Tens	Ones
6	3	7	0

3. 2000 + 900 + 6

4. four thousand fifteen

5. In exercise 2, what is the value of the digit in the thousands place?

....

INDEPENDENT PRACTICE

Write the number in standard form.

6.

7.
Thousands	Hundreds	Tens	Ones
4	6	3	2

8. 3000 + 100

9. six thousand six hundred fourteen

Copy and complete the number sentence.

10. 2450 = ▢ thousands + ▢ hundreds + ▢ tens + ▢ ones

11. 5008 = ▢ thousands + ▢ hundreds + ▢ tens + ▢ ones

Write the value of the digit 7 in the number.

12. 3742　　　　13. 6027　　　　14. 7152　　　　15. 4976

....

PROJECT • Calculator

Play Wipe Out! Use a calculator.

What number can you subtract from the Start number to get the Finish number on your calculator? An example is done for you.

Start	Finish	Wipe Out
327	307	20
9684	684	
1726	1720	
598	98	

LOGICAL REASONING

Joey is thinking of a number between 15 and 25. It does not have a 2 in the tens place. It is not even and it is not 17. What is the number?

Here is a way to find Joey's number.

List the numbers from 16 to 24.

16 17 18 19 20 21 22 23 24

Cross out the numbers that have a 2 in the tens place.

16 17 18 19 ~~20 21 22 23 24~~

Cross out the even numbers and cross out 17.

~~16 17 18~~ 19 ~~20 21 22 23 24~~

The number must be 19. It is the only choice that is not crossed out.

Problem Solving Work with a partner.

1. What is Amy's number? It is between 42 and 54. It does not have a 4 in the tens place. It is not next to 51. The sum of its digits is not 6.

2. In which room did Carl hide a toy? The room is not next to the bedroom. It has no sink. People do not sleep here.

3. What capital letter is Bill thinking of? It comes before *M* in the alphabet. It is not in the word that means this shape. ▭ It is not next to *I* or *J*. It is not made with any curved lines.

4. Make up your own puzzle. Trade with a friend.

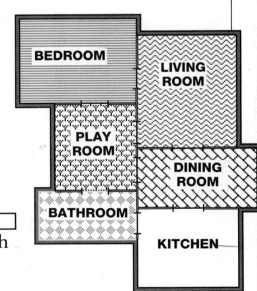

SECTION REVIEW
for pages 38–48

Choose the number the blocks show. Write the letter.

 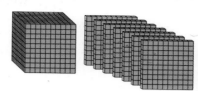

1. a. 145   **b.** 451
   c. 415   **d.** 541

2. a. 1782   **b.** 8721
   c. 2178   **d.** 1728

Copy and complete.

3.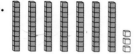

   ▇ tens + ▇ ones

4.

   ▇ hundreds + ▇ tens + ▇ ones

5.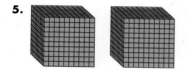

   ▇ thousands + ▇ hundreds + ▇ tens + ▇ ones

Write the number in standard form.

6.

Hundreds	Tens	Ones
9	6	5

7.

Thousands	Hundreds	Tens	Ones
4	3	2	0

8. 2 hundreds + 3 tens + 4 ones   **9.** 7 hundreds + 3 tens + 7 ones

10. 3000 + 600 + 9   **11.** 9000 + 900 + 90 + 9

12. three hundred fifty-seven   **13.** seven thousand two hundred

Write the value of the digit 5.

14. 53   **15.** 175   **16.** 526   **17.** 350

18. 5128   **19.** 1564   **20.** 1005   **21.** 5040

ADDITION AND SUBTRACTION

Place-value blocks and basic facts can help you to understand how to add and subtract tens, hundreds, and thousands.

Add: 200 + 300

Just add the number of hundreds.

2 hundreds	+	3 hundreds	=	5 hundreds
200	+	300	=	500

 Think

• What basic fact helps you to add 300 to 200?

Basic facts can also help you subtract tens, hundreds, and thousands.

You can use the basic fact 8 − 3 = 5 to subtract 3000 from 8000.

$$
\begin{array}{rcl}
8000 & \rightarrow & 8 \text{ thousands} \\
- \ 3000 & \rightarrow & \underline{- \ 3 \text{ thousands}} \\
\hline
5000 & & 5 \text{ thousands}
\end{array}
$$

Other Examples

20 + 50 + 10 = 80   1500 − 800 = 700   6000 + 3000 = 9000

GUIDED PRACTICE

Write the answer.

1.
$$\begin{array}{r} 3 \\ +\ 5 \\ \hline \end{array} \quad \begin{array}{r} 30 \\ +\ 50 \\ \hline \end{array} \quad \begin{array}{r} 300 \\ +\ 500 \\ \hline \end{array} \quad \begin{array}{r} 3000 \\ +\ 5000 \\ \hline \end{array}$$

2.
$$\begin{array}{r} 7 \\ -\ 2 \\ \hline \end{array} \quad \begin{array}{r} 70 \\ -\ 20 \\ \hline \end{array} \quad \begin{array}{r} 700 \\ -\ 200 \\ \hline \end{array} \quad \begin{array}{r} 7000 \\ -\ 2000 \\ \hline \end{array}$$

3. $4000 + 5000$

4. $300 + 400 + 200$

5. $120 - 60$

6. Which basic fact helped you find the answer to exercise 5?

INDEPENDENT PRACTICE

Write the answer.

7.
$$\begin{array}{r} 40 \\ +\ 30 \\ \hline \end{array}$$

8.
$$\begin{array}{r} 500 \\ +\ 200 \\ \hline \end{array}$$

9.
$$\begin{array}{r} 6000 \\ +\ 4000 \\ \hline \end{array}$$

10.
$$\begin{array}{r} 80 \\ +\ 50 \\ \hline \end{array}$$

11.
$$\begin{array}{r} 700 \\ +\ 400 \\ \hline \end{array}$$

12.
$$\begin{array}{r} 90 \\ -\ 30 \\ \hline \end{array}$$

13.
$$\begin{array}{r} 800 \\ -\ 200 \\ \hline \end{array}$$

14.
$$\begin{array}{r} 1000 \\ -\ 700 \\ \hline \end{array}$$

15.
$$\begin{array}{r} 110 \\ -\ 90 \\ \hline \end{array}$$

16.
$$\begin{array}{r} 14,000 \\ -\ 7,000 \\ \hline \end{array}$$

17. $5000 + 1000$

18. $50 + 70$

19. $900 - 500$

20. $30 + 30 + 10$

21. $200 + 100 + 500$

22. $6000 + 2000 + 1000$

Problem Solving

23. How many more blue balloons than red balloons are in the store?

24. Festa City orders a total of 16,000 yellow and blue balloons for a parade. How can the store fill that order?

25. Which do you think would take up more room—all the purple balloons filled or all the gold balloons empty?

BALLOONS AT THE BRIGHT BALLOON STORE	
Color	Number of Balloons
red	5000
yellow	9000
blue	8000
silver	900
purple	200
gold	300

ROUNDING

Work with a partner.

Look at the folded number line. Each peak shows a number that is halfway between 2 tens.

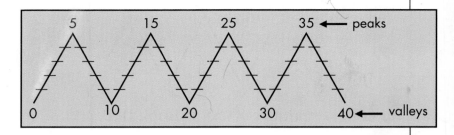

1. What number is halfway between 10 and 20?

2. What number is halfway between 20 and 30?

3. How are all the halfway numbers alike?

If you put a marble on 24 and let it go, it will roll to 20. That is because 24 is closer to 20 than to 30.

4. Write the number the marble will roll to if you put it on:
   a. 6   b. 14   c. 23   d. 37

5. Name every number that you can place a marble at so it will roll to 30.

6. Is 13 closer to 10 or 20?

7. Is 36 closer to 30 or 40?

Instead of saying 36 is closer to 40, you can say 36 **rounds** to 40. So, 36 **rounded to the nearest ten** is 40.

8. Does 33 round to 30 or 40?

9. Does 19 round to 10 or 20?

You round halfway numbers to the larger ten. So, you round 15 to 20.

10. Round each number to the nearest ten.
    a. 22   b. 38   c. 35   d. 14

This number line shows numbers in the hundreds.

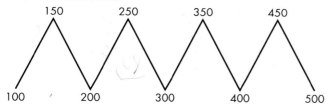

150   250   350   450

100   200   300   400   500

11. How are the halfway numbers alike?

12. If you put a marble at 237, to which number will it roll?

13. Is 185 closer to 100 or 200?

14. Does 361 round to 300 or 400?

15. Does 150 round to 100 or 200?

16. Round each number to the nearest hundred.
    a. 236   b. 307   c. 190   d. 475

SUMMING IT UP

17. On the two number lines, how are all the halfway numbers alike? How are they different?

18. Explain how you use a halfway number to round 23 to the nearest ten.

19. Explain how you use a halfway number to round 156 to the nearest hundred.

20. Think of all the numbers in the twenties.
    a. What numbers round to 20?
    b. What numbers round to 30?

MATH LOG

Think of ways you use rounded numbers. Write 3 examples. Share your ideas with another group.

COMPARING AND ORDERING

▶ The chart at the right shows the weight of some animals at birth. Which weighs more, the giraffe or the rhinoceros?

The birth weight of the giraffe is 150 pounds. The weight of the rhinoceros is 165 pounds.

ANIMAL	NEWBORN'S WEIGHT
Elephant	330 pounds
Giraffe	150 pounds
Rhinoceros	165 pounds

One way to compare numbers is to use a number line. You see that 165 is to the right of 150. So, 165 is greater than 150.

Remember:
< means "is less than"
> means "is greater than"

$$165 > 150 \text{ and } 150 < 165$$

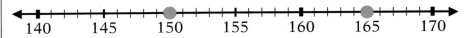

140	145	150	155	160	165	170

The rhinoceros weighs more.

Think

- Which animal in the chart has the greatest birth weight? How do you know?

▶ Which is higher, Mount Washington or Clingmans Dome?

Another way to compare numbers is to use place-value blocks.

NAME OF MOUNTAIN	HEIGHT IN FEET
Mount Washington	6288
Mount Rogers	5729
Clingmans Dome	6643
Black Mountain	4145

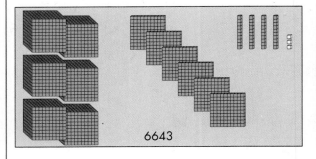

6643

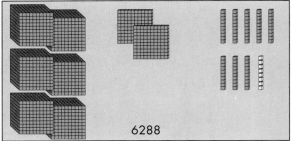

6288

You see that 6288 and 6643 have the same number of thousands, but 6643 has more hundreds. So, 6643 > 6288. Clingmans Dome is higher.

GUIDED PRACTICE

Copy and complete the number sentence.
Write < or >.

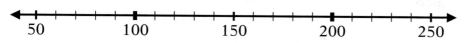

1. 63 ⬤ 59   2. 167 ⬤ 176   3. 134 ⬤ 34   4. 238 ⬤ 127

Copy and complete. Write < or >. Use blocks if you like.

5. 1134 ⬤ 1234   6. 1609 ⬤ 609   7. 1274 ⬤ 1874   8. 1783 ⬤ 1789

Order from least to greatest.

9. 87, 36, 102   10. 1135, 1120, 1129   11. 6043, 5943, 6134

12. How did you get your answer to exercise 11?

INDEPENDENT PRACTICE

Copy and complete. Write < or >. Draw a number line or use blocks if you like.

13. 98 ⬤ 89   14. 162 ⬤ 262   15. 389 ⬤ 308
16. 865 ⬤ 1865   17. 1077 ⬤ 1007   18. 1243 ⬤ 1187

Order from least to greatest.

19. 45, 13, 29   20. 163, 98, 89   21. 352, 523, 235
22. 8442, 7109, 7019   23. 4617, 4716, 4167   24. 6138, 5259, 8135

Problem Solving Use the chart on Giant Trees on page 416 in the Data Book.

25. In what state is the tallest tree located?

26. What kind of tree is the second tallest?

27. Write the names of the trees in order from tallest to shortest.

28. Use the information from the chart to write a problem. Give it to a friend to solve.

PROBLEM SOLVING STRATEGY
USE MODELS

When you act out a problem, the objects you use do not have to be the same as the objects in the problem. You can use objects that are handy and easy to work with.

Kate carries a stack of 15 books. Juanita carries a stack of 9 books. How many books should Kate give to Juanita so that they carry the same number?

Look at these two ways to act out the problem.

A.

B.

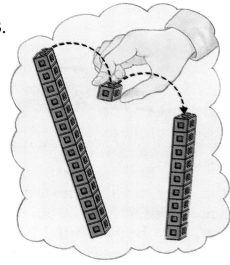

Think

• How is each way used to solve the problem?

• Which would be easier to use? Why?

• What are some other objects you might use to act out the problem?

Act out the problem to solve it.

Use objects that are handy.

Read the problem. Choose the useful way to act out and solve the problem.

1. Olivia has a square sheet of paper. How many times does she need to fold it to get 8 triangles that are all the same size?

A.

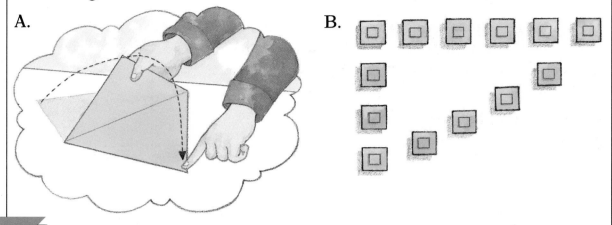

B.

Work in groups to solve each problem. You can use models to help you.

2. Sasha, Paul, and Myra save bottles to use as vases. Sasha has 5 bottles and Paul has 7. Myra had 6 bottles but 3 broke. The children want to share the bottles equally. How many should each child get?

3. Tanya, Matt, and Dan each have 5 baseball cards. Suppose Tanya gives 3 of hers to Matt, and Matt gives 2 of his to Dan. How many cards do they have in all?

4. In art class, Cory plans to make a rectangle pattern with red and blue tiles. His dog chewed his picture of the pattern. How many tiles will be in Cory's pattern?

COINS

Beth, Mario, and Lisa take a bus to the art museum. The bus fare is 50¢. They each have coins ready to give to the driver. Does each of them have the correct fare?

Use the chart to find the value of the coins. Then skip-count.

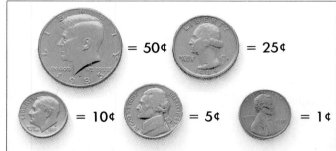

= 50¢ = 25¢ = 10¢ = 5¢ = 1¢

Beth has:

25¢   50¢

Mario has:

25¢   35¢   45¢   50¢

Lisa has:

10¢   20¢   30¢   40¢   45¢   50¢

Yes. Each of them has the correct amount, 50¢.

Think

- The coin machine on the bus does not take pennies. Are there other ways to pay the 50¢ besides the ways shown above?

GUIDED PRACTICE

Write the value of the coins.

1.

2.

3.

4.

5. What other coins could you use to show the amount in exercise 2?

....

INDEPENDENT PRACTICE

Write the value of the coins.

6.

7.

8.

9.

Match the money amount to the item with the same value. Write *a, b,* or *c.*

10.

a.

11.

b.

12.

c.

DOLLARS AND CENTS

You can write the value of bills
and coins in different ways.

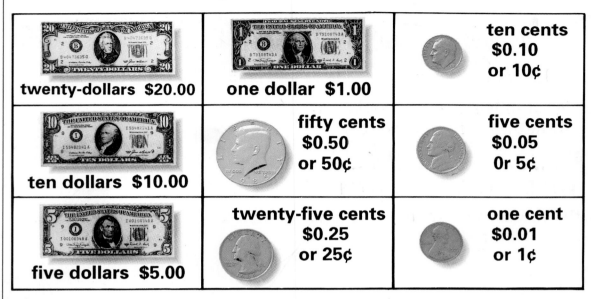

twenty-dollars $20.00	one dollar $1.00	ten cents $0.10 or 10¢
ten dollars $10.00	fifty cents $0.50 or 50¢	five cents $0.05 Or 5¢
five dollars $5.00	twenty-five cents $0.25 or 25¢	one cent $0.01 or 1¢

Think

- What are two ways to write
  "sixty-seven cents"?

Sue Ellen wants to put her money in the
bank. She counts the money she has saved.
How much does she have?

Count the bills and coins from the greatest
value to the least value.

$10.00 $15.00 $16.00 $17.00 $17.25 $17.35

$16.00

Sue

You

thir

the

$17.36

GUIDED PRACTICE

Write the money amount. Use a dollar sign and decimal point.

1.

2.

3. 6 dollars and 48 cents

4. twelve dollars and ten cents

5. What bills and coins could you use to show the amount in exercise 4?

....

INDEPENDENT PRACTICE

Write the money amount. Use a dollar sign and decimal point.

6.

7.

8.

9.

10. 10 dollars and 42 cents

11. sixteen dollars and fifty cents

Problem Solving

12. Ramon has the money shown. Which item can he buy?

13. Ramon's friends have the same amount of money as Ramon. But they have different bills and coins. Jake has 1 bill and 7 coins. Julie has 2 bills and 6 coins. Fred has 2 bills and 7 coins. Write what bills and coins each has.

A. $11.25

B. $1.58

C. $2.29

MAKING CHANGE

Andy buys a race car magazine for $1.83. He pays with 2 one-dollar bills, and receives 17¢ as change. Is 17¢ the correct change?

Here is how you can check:

Count up from the price of the magazine to the amount Andy paid. Start with the coins that have the least value.

$1.84 $1.85 $1.90 $2.00

AMOUNT SPENT

Amount Given

Yes, 17¢ is the correct change.

Think

- With what other coins can you make 17¢?

Other Examples

You paid 50¢.

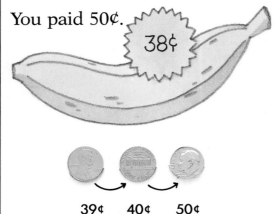

38¢

39¢   40¢   50¢

Your change is 12¢.

You paid $2.00.

Balloons

$1.20

$1.25 $1.50 $1.75 $2.00

Your change is 80¢.

GUIDED PRACTICE

Choose the correct change. Write *a* or *b*.

1. You paid 50¢.   a.   b.

2. You paid $1.75.  a.   b.

3. You paid $2.00.  a.  b.

4. How much is the correct change in exercise 1?

INDEPENDENT PRACTICE

Has the store clerk given the correct change? Write
too much, *too little*, or *correct*.

5. Roy paid $2.00.

6. Pam paid $2.00.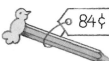

7. Leo paid $1.00.

8. Kim paid 50¢.

....

 • **Number Sense**

Write the missing numbers.

1. 31, 32, ▨, 34, ▨   **2.** 96, ▨, 98, ▨, ▨   **3.** ▨, ▨, 11, 12, ▨

MONEY SENSE

Jody wants to buy 3 apples and 2 oranges. She has $2. Does she have enough money?

The 3 apples cost 98¢. That is less than $1.00. The 2 oranges cost 79¢. That is less than $1.00. So $2.00 is enough. Jody has enough money.

> 2 oranges—less than $1.00

> 3 apples—less than $1.00

Work with a partner. Use the picture above to answer the questions.

1. Pete wants to buy 1 pineapple and 3 apples. He has $4. Does Pete have enough money?

2. Maria has $3. She wants a pineapple and a box of strawberries. Does Maria have enough money?

3. Andy gave the clerk $2. He got 1¢ in change. What did Andy buy?

4. Max gave the clerk $1. He got 2¢ change. What did Max buy?

5. Lisa has 2 quarters, 2 dimes, and 3 nickels. Does she have enough money to buy 3 apples?

6. Joshua has 3 dimes, 1 nickel, and 3 pennies. Can he buy a peach?

7. Use the information in the picture on page 64. Make up a word problem of your own. Exchange papers with another group.

PROJECT • Money

Work with a partner. You will need the amount of play money shown.

1. You can buy any item. You must pay with the exact amount.

2. Keep buying items until you do not have the right change to buy anything else.

3. See how close you can get to spending all your money.

4. Record what you buy and the coins and bills you use. Compare your list with the lists of other groups.

$2.10

PEANUTS $0.39

$1.50

$4.05

$0.60

$0.23

$0.98

TELLING TIME

The short hand is the hour hand.
The long hand is the minute hand.

It takes the minute hand an hour
to go once around the clock.
There are 60 minutes in an hour.
It takes 5 minutes for the minute
hand to go from one number on
the clock to the next number.

5 minutes

2:00

two o'clock

2:15

two-fifteen

2:50

two-fifty

Think

• How many minutes are there between
2:10 and 2:30?

GUIDED PRACTICE

Write the time.

1.

2.

3.

4.

5.

6.

7. In exercise 6, how many minutes will it be
before the clock shows 1:00?

INDEPENDENT PRACTICE

Match the clocks that show the same time.
Write *a, b, c,* or *d.*

8.

9.

10.

11.

a.

b.

c.

d.

Write the time.

12.

13.

14.

15.

16.

17.

Maintain • Mixed Practice

Write the sum. Look for doubles or sums of 10.

1. $\begin{array}{r} 3 \\ 6 \\ +7 \\ \hline \end{array}$	**2.** $\begin{array}{r} 4 \\ 4 \\ +3 \\ \hline \end{array}$	**3.** $\begin{array}{r} 3 \\ 7 \\ +7 \\ \hline \end{array}$	**4.** $\begin{array}{r} 9 \\ 5 \\ +1 \\ \hline \end{array}$	**5.** $\begin{array}{r} 8 \\ 8 \\ +2 \\ \hline \end{array}$	**6.** $\begin{array}{r} 9 \\ 2 \\ +9 \\ \hline \end{array}$

Write the difference.

7. $\begin{array}{r} 14 \\ -\ 7 \\ \hline \end{array}$	**8.** $\begin{array}{r} 15 \\ -\ 7 \\ \hline \end{array}$	**9.** $\begin{array}{r} 16 \\ -\ 9 \\ \hline \end{array}$	**10.** $\begin{array}{r} 20 \\ -10 \\ \hline \end{array}$	**11.** $\begin{array}{r} 13 \\ -\ 0 \\ \hline \end{array}$	**12.** $\begin{array}{r} 17 \\ -\ 8 \\ \hline \end{array}$

A.M. AND P.M.

Julie's mother is going on a business trip. Her plane leaves at 9:20. Does the plane leave at 9:20 in the morning or 9:20 in the evening?

There are 24 hours in a day. The hours from 12:00 midnight to 12:00 noon are labeled **A.M.** The hours from 12:00 noon until 12:00 midnight are labeled **P.M.**

The plane ticket reads 9:20 A.M. So, the plane leaves at 9:20 in the morning.

Think

- How many hours are there from 12:00 noon to 12:00 midnight?

GUIDED PRACTICE

For each exercise, tell whether it is A.M. or P.M.

1.

2.

3.

4. when you go to school

5. when you eat supper

6. Are you awake more during the A.M. or P.M. hours?

INDEPENDENT PRACTICE

For each picture, tell whether it is A.M. or P.M. Look at the clock.

7.  **8.**  **9.**

Tell what time it is when you do each.
Write *A.M.* or *P.M.* in your answer.

10. get up

11. go to school

12. go out for recess

13. eat lunch

14. leave school

15. go to bed

Problem Solving Be sure to write *A.M.* or *P.M.*

16. Paul's favorite TV program starts at 7:30 P.M. It lasts for one-half hour. What time does it end?

17. The soccer game on Saturday started at 11:00 A.M. It lasted for 2 hours. What time did it end?

18. Ms. Chavez works for 8 hours a day. She starts work at 9:00 A.M. When does she finish?

....

PROJECT • Time

Make a list of 5 things that you did yesterday. Write the time that you did each. Be sure to write *A.M.* or *P.M.*

What I did yesterday.

1. Got up 6:45 A.M.
2. Ate pancakes 7:20 A.M.

WHEN IS A NUMBER AN ESTIMATE?

Some numbers that you see in newspapers are exact. Other numbers are estimates.

An **estimate** is a number close to an exact amount. An estimate tells you *about* how much.

This newspaper headline says that 5000 people went to the circus. Do you think there were *exactly* 5000 people there? There could have been a few more than 5000 people or a few less. So, 5000 is probably an estimate.

SUN-GAZETTE

CROWD OF 5000 ATTENDS CIRCUS

1. Work with a group. Decide which numbers below are exact and which are estimates. Write *exact* or *estimate*.

a. SUN-GAZETTE
MAN HAS PARTY FOR 100TH BIRTHDAY!

b. SUN-GAZETTE
GORILLA AT ZOO WEIGHS NEARLY 600 POUNDS

c. SUN-GAZETTE
8,000 PEOPLE VISITED GRANT PARK THIS YEAR

d. SUN-GAZETTE
TOP PRIZE AT HORSE SHOW IS $700

e. SUN-GAZETTE
400 FANS CHEER AT THURSDAY'S FOOTBALL GAME

f. SUN-GAZETTE
JO JO THE CLOWN GIVES 50TH SHOW TONIGHT

2. Make up a newspaper headline that uses 500 as an exact number. Then write one that uses 500 as an estimate.

3. Suppose 3213 people went to a baseball game. What would be a good estimate for that number?

SECTION REVIEW

for pages 50–70

Copy and complete. Write < or >.

1. 78 ● 87   **2.** 136 ● 116   **3.** 492 ● 942   **4.** 1065 ● 1603

Write the letter of the correct amount.

5.

a. $0.68   **b.** 65¢
c. 74¢   **d.** 69¢

6.

a. $0.20   **b.** 30¢
c. 25¢   **d.** thirty cents

Write the amount of money. Use a dollar sign and decimal point.

7.

8.

9. fifteen dollars and fifty-one cents

10. seventeen dollars and ninety-five cents

Write the time.

11.

12.

13.

Write whether it is A.M. or P.M. when you do each.

14. go to school   **15.** go to bed   **16.** eat supper

CHAPTER REVIEW

Language Connection

Sometimes you need to count to find how many. Other times, you can estimate. People often estimate when they buy things. Suppose you were planning a picnic. You could **count** how many people were coming. But you would **estimate** how many paper napkins to buy.

Make your own shopping list for a class picnic. When your list is complete, underline all the items you would estimate.

Test ●●●●●●●

Write the number in standard form.

1. 600 + 30 + 7

2. four hundred eighty-one

3. five thousand two hundred ninety

4. 8000 + 500 + 60 + 3

Write the numbers from least to greatest.

5. 57, 157, 75 6. 637, 736, 673 7. 1092, 1029, 1290 8. 4865, 4685, 485

Write the money amount. Use a dollar sign and decimal point.

9. 6 dollars and 21 cents

10. thirteen dollars and five cents

11. eight dollars and fifty-four cents

12. 5 dollars and 73 cents

Write the correct change.

13. $1.00 paid for an apple that cost 39¢

14. $2.00 paid for a plant that cost $1.67

15. $1.50 paid for a brush that cost $1.25

16. $1.25 paid for a candle that cost $1.12

Write the time that is shown on the clock.

17.   **18.**   **19.**   **20.**

PROBLEM SOLVING

21. Lisa has 18 stickers. Chris has 12 stickers. They want to have the same number of stickers. How many stickers should Lisa give to Chris?

22. Roland has 11 postcards, Alana has 7 postcards, and Percy has 3. The children want to share the postcards equally. How many postcards should each child get?

23. The third-grade play on Friday began at 11:30 A.M. It lasted for 1 hour. At what time did the play end?

24. Jackie buys grapes for $1.62. She pays with 2 one-dollar bills. How much change should she receive?

CUMULATIVE REVIEW

Write the answer.

25.
$$\begin{array}{r} 4 \\ 6 \\ +\ 3 \\ \hline \end{array}$$

26.
$$\begin{array}{r} 9 \\ 5 \\ 3 \\ +\ 2 \\ \hline \end{array}$$

27.
$$\begin{array}{r} 11 \\ -\ 4 \\ \hline \end{array}$$

28.
$$\begin{array}{r} 15 \\ -\ 9 \\ \hline \end{array}$$

29.
$$\begin{array}{r} 17 \\ -\ 8 \\ \hline \end{array}$$

EXCURSION

NUMERATION

Roman Numerals

The ancient Romans used letters to stand for numbers. You often see Roman numerals on clock faces and monuments.

Each letter has a value:

$$I = 1 \qquad V = 5 \qquad X = 10$$

The letters are put in order from the greatest to the least value. Then the values of the letters are added together.

For example, here is how to read XXVII.

$$\begin{array}{ccccc} X & X & V & I & I \\ \downarrow & \downarrow & \downarrow & \downarrow & \downarrow \\ 10 \rightarrow & 20 \rightarrow & 25 \rightarrow & 26 \rightarrow & 27 \end{array}$$

So: XXVII = 27

Sometimes a Roman numeral with lesser value is to the left of another Roman numeral. This means you subtract the value.

For example, here is how to read IX and IV.

$$IX = 10 - 1 = 9 \qquad\qquad IV = 5 - 1 = 4$$

For some Roman numerals, you have to add *and* subtract. Here is how to read XXIV.

$$\begin{array}{cccc} X & X & I & V \\ \downarrow & \downarrow & \downarrow & \downarrow \\ 10 \rightarrow & 20 & 4 \leftarrow & 5 \end{array}$$

So: XXIV = 24

Write in standard form.

1.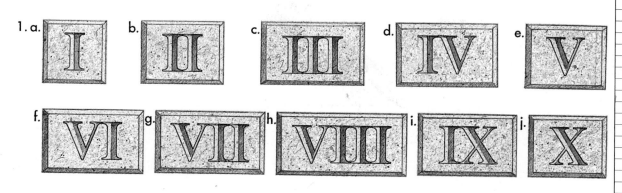
   a. I   b. II   c. III   d. IV   e. V
   f. VI   g. VII   h. VIII   i. IX   j. X

2. XXIII   3. XIX   4. XIV   5. XXXIII

6. XI   7. XXVI   8. XVIII   9. XXIV

Write the time.

10.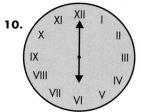

11.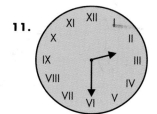

12.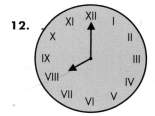

13.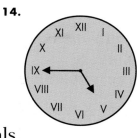

14.

15.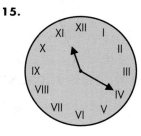

Write in Roman numerals.

16. 10   17. 20   18. 25   19. 13   20. 30   21. 29

MATH LOG

For two weeks, keep track of the Roman numerals you see. You could look at clocks, buildings, and magazines. Copy the Roman numerals and write where you saw them.

CHAPTER 3

ADDITION AND SUBTRACTION

Physical Education

Keeping Score Good dart players can hit the target throw after throw. Their score depends on where each dart lands. A total score is found by adding the number of points for each dart. Players get no points if they miss the target.

Look at the targets on this page. The rings are marked 5, 10, or 25 points. The players used three darts. An *X* marks the spot where each dart landed. Add each player's score and decide who won the match.

Suppose the game used four darts instead of three. How could a player get a score of 40 points? Draw a target to show your answer. Compare answers with your classmates.

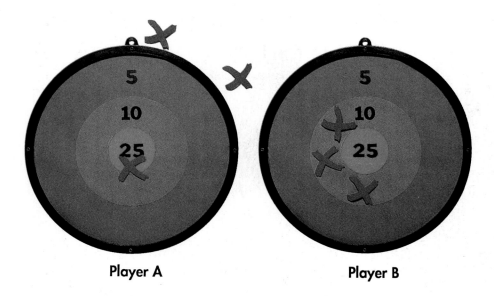

Player A   Player B

REGROUPING AND ADDITION

Play the game Adding to 300.

Groups: partners

You will need:
- 2 number cubes
- place-value blocks
- place-value mat
- recording sheet
- calculator

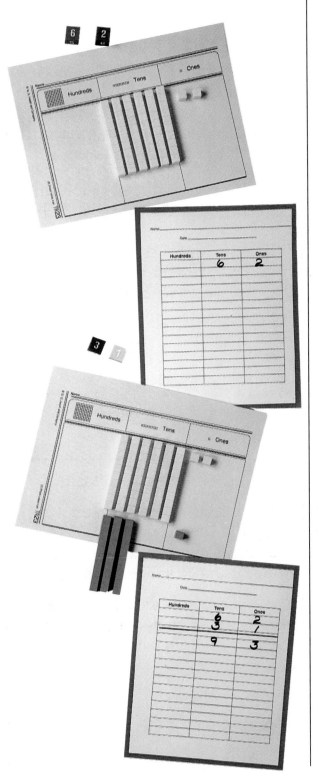

The object of the game is to be the first player to reach 300.

a. Take turns. Toss the number cubes. Put them side by side to make a 2-digit number. Decide which digit is in the ones place and which is in the tens place.

b. Use place-value blocks to show the 2-digit number. Use the fewest blocks. Then write the number on the recording sheet.

c. The next player follows steps a and b. The new blocks are added to the mat and the 2-digit number is put on the recording sheet. The player writes the sum.

d. Keep taking turns. At each turn, join the ones, join the tens, and join the hundreds on the mat. Trade whenever you can. Write the sum on the recording sheet.

e. The first player to reach 300 or more is the winner.

SUMMING IT UP

1. When did you need to trade your blocks?

2. What would happen if you did not trade your blocks at all?

3. How did you decide which number cube stood for tens and which stood for ones?

4. Discuss with your partner a way to play this game without place-value blocks. Compare your ideas with others.

Write the sum. Use your place-value blocks. Be sure to use the fewest blocks to show the sum. Check your answers with a calculator.

5.   20
   + 10

6.   15
   + 9

7.   64
   + 28

8.   39
   + 72

9.   109
   + 91

10.   47
   + 35

11.   470
   + 350

12.   203
   + 40

13.   127
   + 46

14.   245
   + 168

PROJECT • Mental Math

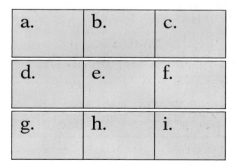

You will need a calculator. Copy the box at the right. Write the sum for each exercise below in the correct space in the box.

Then use your calculator to add all the rows across and all the rows down. What is the sum of each row?

a.	b.	c.
d.	e.	f.
g.	h.	i.

a. 200 + 15 = ▨

b. 25 + 2 = ▨

c. 250 + 28 = ▨

d. 8 + 8 = ▨

e. 400 + 86 = ▨

f. 10 + 8 = ▨

g. 285 + 4 = ▨

h. 4 + 3 = ▨

i. 214 + 10 = ▨

79

ADDING 2-DIGIT NUMBERS

John sold boxes of cookies to raise money for his school. He recorded the number of boxes he sold. How many boxes of cookies did he sell?

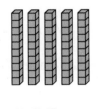

Cookies	Boxes
Oatmeal	47
Vanilla	35

You add to find a total.
Add: 47 + 35

First, write it as:
$$\begin{array}{r} 47 \\ +\ 35 \\ \hline \end{array}$$

● Add the ones.   ● Regroup if you need to.   ● Add the tens.

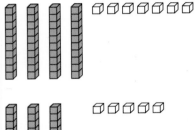
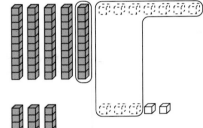
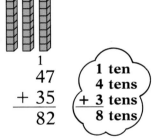

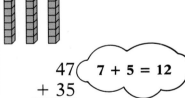
$$\begin{array}{r} 47 \\ +\ 35 \\ \hline \end{array}$$
7 + 5 = 12

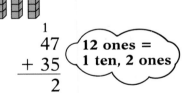
$$\begin{array}{r} \overset{1}{4}7 \\ +\ 35 \\ \hline 2 \end{array}$$
12 ones = 1 ten, 2 ones

$$\begin{array}{r} \overset{1}{4}7 \\ +\ 35 \\ \hline 82 \end{array}$$
1 ten
4 tens
+ 3 tens
8 tens

John sold 82 boxes of cookies.

Think
- Why is there a 1 over the 4?

Other Examples

$$\begin{array}{r} 68 \\ +\ 51 \\ \hline 119 \end{array}$$
$$\begin{array}{r} 42 \\ +\ 35 \\ \hline 77 \end{array}$$
$$\begin{array}{r} \overset{1}{\$0}.71 \\ +\ 0.35 \\ \hline \$1.06 \end{array}$$

GUIDED PRACTICE

Write the sum.

1.

Hundreds	Tens	Ones
	2	5
+	9	2

2.

Hundreds	Tens	Ones
	7	4
+	1	8

3. 26 + 59   4. 90 + 38   5. 53 + 48   6. 75 + 15

7. When can you add without regrouping?
   Give an example.

INDEPENDENT PRACTICE

Write the sum.

8.

Hundreds	Tens	Ones
	6	1
+	9	6

9.

Hundreds	Tens	Ones
	7	7
+	2	7

10.
```
   43
+ 82
```

11.
```
 $0.11
+ 0.79
```

12.
```
   78
+ 21
```

13.
```
   13 miles
+ 28 miles
```

14.
```
   56
+ 82
```

15. 57 + 35   16. $0.48 + $0.94   17. 63 + 52   18. 34 + 34

 • Money

Write the money amount. Use a dollar sign and
decimal point.

1.

2.

3.

4.

81

ADDING 3-DIGIT NUMBERS

Ralph and Chris play a game with a spinner. They each spin twice and add the two numbers. The player with the greater sum wins.

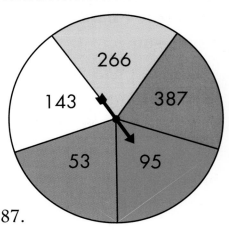

Ralph's first spin lands on white. His second spin lands on red. What is Ralph's score?

To find Ralph's score, you add 143 and 387.
First, write it as:

$$143$$
$$+\ 387$$

● Add the ones. Regroup?

$$\begin{array}{r} 1 \\ 1\,4\,3 \\ +\ 3\,8\,7 \\ \hline 0 \end{array}$$

3 ones
+ 7 ones
10 ones

10 ones = 1 ten, 0 ones

● Add the tens. Regroup?

$$\begin{array}{r} 1\ 1 \\ 1\,4\,3 \\ +\ 3\,8\,7 \\ \hline 3\,0 \end{array}$$

1 ten
4 tens
+ 8 tens
13 tens

13 tens =
1 hundred, 3 tens

● Add the hundreds.

$$\begin{array}{r} 1\ 1 \\ 1\,4\,3 \\ +\ 3\,8\,7 \\ \hline 5\,3\,0 \end{array}$$

1 hundred
1 hundred
+ 3 hundreds
5 hundreds

Ralph's score is 530.

Think

• Why do you add to find Ralph's score?

• What would happen if you needed to regroup hundreds?

Ralph's Score

$$143$$
$$+387$$

Other Examples

$\begin{array}{r}1\ 1\\ \$6.89\\ +\ 1.86\\ \hline \$8.75\end{array}$	$\begin{array}{r}1\,1\\ 276\\ +\ 84\\ \hline 360\end{array}$	$\begin{array}{r}1\\ 421\\ +\ 693\\ \hline 1114\end{array}$	$\begin{array}{r}275\ \text{feet}\\ +\ 722\ \text{feet}\\ \hline 997\ \text{feet}\end{array}$

GUIDED PRACTICE

Use the numbers below to answer exercises 1 and 2.

102   387   490   213   124

1. Write a number sentence with regrouping. Use 387 and another number from above.

2. Write a number sentence that uses no regrouping. Use 490 and another number from above.

3. When do you need to regroup in number sentences?

INDEPENDENT PRACTICE

Write the sum. Use mental math when you can.

4. 116 + 133	5. 732 + 159	6. $358 + 57	7. 675 + 225	8. $6.75 + 2.25
9. 174 + 15	10. $3.00 + 0.36	11. 477 + 31	12. $4.56 + 3.87	13. 289 miles + 46 miles

14. 439 + 333   15. 440 + 332   16. 726 + 434   17. 300 + 500

18. 182 + 35   19. 279 + 63   20. 150 + 50   21. 913 + 485

Problem Solving

22. Ralph's score is 225. Chris spins a purple and a pink. Whose score is higher?

23. Chris needs a score of 500 or more to win. His first spin lands on orange. Which color does he hope to land on next?

24. Ralph scored 268 in two spins. Which colors did he land on?

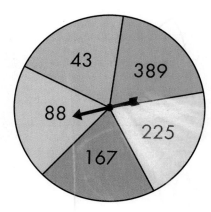

25. What is the greatest possible score for two spins? (HINT: It is greater than 614.)

ESTIMATING SUMS

David and Sandra sold lemonade at a fair. They had hoped to sell at least 500 glasses during the two days. Did they reach their goal?

You do not need an exact answer to decide. You can estimate using a method called **front-end estimation.**

Lemonade Sales

Sat.	234 glasses
Sun.	286 glasses

● **Add the digits in the hundreds place.**

$$234 \rightarrow \quad 2 \text{ hundred}$$
$$+\ 286 \rightarrow +\ 2 \text{ hundred}$$
$$\quad\quad\quad\quad\quad 4 \text{ hundred}$$

● **Adjust your estimate. Look at the other digits.**

$$\begin{aligned} 2\,&3\,4 \\ +\ 2\,&8\,6 \end{aligned} \leftarrow \text{ about 100}$$

rough estimate: 400   **adjusted** estimate: 400 + 100 = 500

Since 34 + 86 is greater than 100, the sum is greater than 500. Yes, David and Sandra reached their goal.

Think

• Suppose Sandra and David only hoped to sell 350 glasses. Is your rough estimate enough to decide if they had sold 350 glasses? Explain.

Other Examples

$$\begin{aligned} 4\,&3\,6 \\ +\ 2\,&2\,7 \end{aligned} \leftarrow \text{ about 50}$$
rough estimate: 600
adjusted estimate:
600 + 50 = 650

$$\$2.95 \leftarrow \text{ about } \$1.00$$
$$3.76 \leftarrow \text{ about } \$1.00$$
$$+\ 1.39$$
rough estimate: $6.00
adjusted estimate: $6 + $1 + $1 = $8

Make a rough front-end estimate.

1. 327 + 458   2. $2.42 + $3.18   3. 236 + 167 + 308

Make a rough front-end estimate. Then adjust.

4.	483	5.	532	6.	$3.34	7.	352	8.	127
	+ 219		+ 238		+ 2.78		258		428
							+ 197		+ 249

9. Is the exact sum in exercise 6 greater than or less than $6? How can you tell?

Make a rough front-end estimate. Then adjust.

10.	164	11.	$5.21	12.	432	13.	$1.97	14.	110
	+ 348		+ 2.34		+ 275		2.56		346
							+ 1.52		+ 259

Estimate. Which two numbers in the box have a sum of:

15. about 600?   16. about 500?

17. about 700?   18. about 900?

355 137 529 603

Estimate. Write *yes* or *no*.

19. Were at least 300 glasses of lemonade sold on Monday and Tuesday?

20. Were at least 500 glasses sold on Tuesday and Wednesday?

21. Were at least 550 glasses sold in all 3 days?

Lemonade Sales	
Day	**Number of Glasses**
Monday	225
Tuesday	167
Wednesday	345

THREE OR MORE ADDENDS

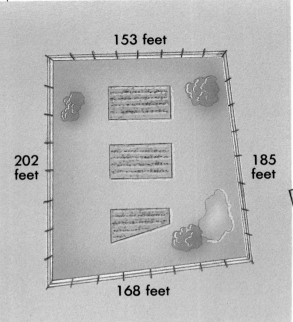

153 feet

202 feet

185 feet

168 feet

Mr. Hopkins wants to donate 600 feet of fencing to go around the community gardens. Will that be enough fencing?

To find the distance around the garden, you add the lengths of the 4 sides.

Think

• Can you answer this question by estimating? Explain.

No, 600 feet of fencing will not be enough.

How much fencing is needed to go around the gardens?

Add: 185 feet + 153 feet + 202 feet + 168 feet

● Add the ones. Regroup?	● Add the tens. Regroup?	● Add the hundreds.	● Check the sum.
1 185 feet 153 feet 202 feet + 168 feet 8	2 1 185 feet 153 feet 202 feet + 168 feet 08	2 1 185 feet 153 feet 202 feet + 168 feet 708 feet	168 feet 202 feet 153 feet + 185 feet 708 feet

One way to check is to add in a different order.

So, 708 feet of fencing is needed.

GUIDED PRACTICE

Write the sum.

1.	2.	3.	4.	5.
33	639	83 feet	12	$1.53
11	146	62 feet	34	3.21
+ 182	+ 127	+ 541 feet	11	2.64
			+ 21	+ 1.76

6. 216 + 545 + 189   7. 63 + 112 + 41 + 813

8. How can you check the sum in exercise 4?

....

INDEPENDENT PRACTICE

Write the sum.

9.	10.	11.	12.	13.
23	47 miles	52	88	$1.50
14	82 miles	123	97	1.39
+ 131	+ 99 miles	+ 481	+ 539	+ 6.27

14. 36 + 48 + 13   15. 19 + 219 + 176   16. $214 + $163 + $412

17. $0.98 + $4.25 + $2.63 + $0.36   18. 61 + 135 + 47 + 182

Problem Solving The picture shows the size of each garden plot.

19. How many feet of fencing does Rita need?

20. Look at Jack's and Gail's plots. Who needs more fencing? How can you tell without adding?

21. Jack and Gail want to make their plots into one big garden. They will use the space between their plots. The space is 4 feet wide. How many feet of fencing is needed to go around their new garden?
(HINT: Draw a picture.)

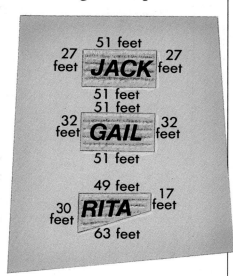

DOES THE ANSWER FIT THE PROBLEM?

If you get stuck, remember...

Tips for Problem Solving

on pages 426–427

When you solve a problem, make sure your answer fits the problem.

Anna has $5. She saves $3 each week. In how many weeks will she have enough money to buy the radio?

Which choice correctly answers the problem?

a. She saves $6 in 2 weeks.
b. She needs $8 more to buy the radio.
c. She will have enough money in 3 weeks.

The answer is c because it tells in how many weeks Anna can buy the radio.

Think

- Are choices a and b true?

- Why do choices a and b not solve the problem?

Write the letter of the choice that correctly answers the question.

1. Burt ran the 400-meter dash three times. His first try took 54 seconds. His second try took 44 seconds, and his third try took 60 seconds. How many meters did he run in all?

   a. Burt ran 1200 meters.

   b. He ran 158 seconds in all.

   c. His second race was the fastest.

2. Sheila wants to buy two blank tapes that cost $2.50 each and a tape rack that costs $12. She has $20. Does she have enough money?

   a. She will get $3 back.

   b. Yes, $20 is enough.

   c. The rack costs $7 more than the tapes.

SECTION REVIEW
for pages 78–88

Write the letter of the correct answer.

1. 28 + 375
   - a. 655
   - b. 393
   - c. 403
   - d. 3913

2. 563 + 28
   - a. 591
   - b. 581
   - c. 5811
   - d. 681

3. 653 + 428
   - a. 10,711
   - b. 1071
   - c. 1171
   - d. 1081

4. 77 + 528
   - a. 595
   - b. 605
   - c. 1298
   - d. 5915

5. 43 + 25 + 124
   - a. 282
   - b. 201
   - c. 192
   - d. 292

6. 34 + 23 + 856
   - a. 1003
   - b. 913
   - c. 81,013
   - d. 803

7. 227 + 45 + 348
   - a. 800
   - b. 710
   - c. 1025
   - d. 620

8. 845 + 23 + 676
   - a. 1544
   - b. 1751
   - c. 1571
   - d. 141,314

9. 25 + 213 + 184
   - a. 647
   - b. 422
   - c. 312
   - d. 431

Solve each problem.

10. At the movies, 93 people see the show at 1:00. At 3:00, 124 people see the show. How many people see the show in the afternoon?

11. Becky earns $5.00 for baby-sitting and the same amount for feeding the cat. She earns 55¢ for returning bottles. How much money does she earn?

REGROUPING AND SUBTRACTION

Play the game Subtracting from 200.

Groups: partners

You will need:

- 2 number cubes
- place-value blocks
- place-value mat
- recording sheet
- calculator

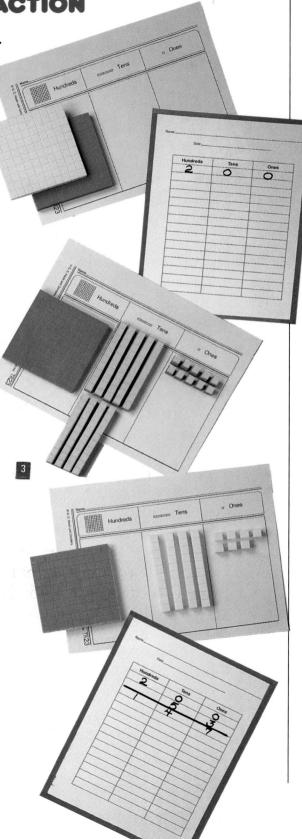

The object of the game is to be the first to reach zero.

a. Show 200 on the mat with the place-value blocks. Write 200 on the recording sheet.

b. Take turns. Toss the number cubes. Put them side by side to make a 2-digit number. Decide which digit is in the ones place and which is in the tens place.

c. Take away that number of blocks from the blocks on the mat. Trade if you need to. Then write the 2-digit number on the recording sheet and subtract. Write the difference.

d. The next player follows steps b and c. At each player's turn, more blocks are taken away from the mat and the 2-digit number is subtracted on the recording sheet.

e. The player to remove all the blocks from the mat wins.

SUMMING IT UP

1. When did you need to trade your blocks?

2. What would happen if you did not trade your blocks?

3. How did you decide which number cube stood for tens and which stood for ones?

4. Discuss with your partner a way to play this game without place-value blocks. Compare your ideas with others.

Write the difference. Use your place-value blocks. Be sure to use the fewest blocks to show the difference. Check your answers with a calculator.

5. $\begin{array}{r} 20 \\ -\ 3 \\ \hline \end{array}$	**6.** $\begin{array}{r} 63 \\ -\ 9 \\ \hline \end{array}$	**7.** $\begin{array}{r} 52 \\ -\ 12 \\ \hline \end{array}$	**8.** $\begin{array}{r} 45 \\ -\ 17 \\ \hline \end{array}$	**9.** $\begin{array}{r} 125 \\ -\ 89 \\ \hline \end{array}$
10. $\begin{array}{r} 70 \\ -\ 30 \\ \hline \end{array}$	**11.** $\begin{array}{r} 58 \\ -\ 8 \\ \hline \end{array}$	**12.** $\begin{array}{r} 100 \\ -\ 25 \\ \hline \end{array}$	**13.** $\begin{array}{r} 153 \\ -\ 76 \\ \hline \end{array}$	**14.** $\begin{array}{r} 285 \\ -\ 48 \\ \hline \end{array}$
15. $\begin{array}{r} 200 \\ -\ 100 \\ \hline \end{array}$	**16.** $\begin{array}{r} 245 \\ -\ 123 \\ \hline \end{array}$	**17.** $\begin{array}{r} 407 \\ -\ 25 \\ \hline \end{array}$	**18.** $\begin{array}{r} 300 \\ -\ 150 \\ \hline \end{array}$	**19.** $\begin{array}{r} 231 \\ -\ 147 \\ \hline \end{array}$

MATH LOG

Imagine you and your partner had to explain how to subtract two 3-digit numbers. Write in words how you would explain this.

SUBTRACTING FROM 2-DIGIT NUMBERS

The scoreboard shows the halftime score in a basketball game. By how many points are the Hawks behind?

To compare the scores, you subtract 37 from 53.

Write it as:
$$\begin{array}{r} 53 \\ -\ 37 \end{array}$$

● **Do you have enough ones to subtract?**

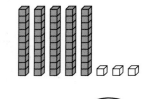

$$\begin{array}{r} 5\ 3 \\ -\ 3\ 7 \end{array}$$
(7 ones > 3 ones)

● **Regroup 1 ten as 10 ones.**

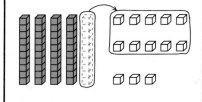

$$\begin{array}{r} {}^{4}\ {}^{13} \\ \cancel{5}\ \cancel{3} \\ -\ 3\ 7 \end{array}$$
(5 tens, 3 ones = 4 tens, 13 ones)

● **Subtract the ones. Then subtract the tens.**

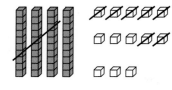

$$\begin{array}{r} {}^{4}\ {}^{13} \\ \cancel{5}\ \cancel{3} \\ -\ 3\ 7 \\ \hline 1\ 6 \end{array}$$

The Hawks are behind by 16 points.

Think

- Why did you have to regroup before subtracting?

- Why is there a 4 over the 5 and a 13 over the 3?

You can check subtraction by adding.

$$\begin{array}{r} 53 \\ -\ 37 \\ \hline 16 \end{array} \qquad \begin{array}{r} {}^{1} \\ 16 \\ +\ 37 \\ \hline 53 \end{array}$$

Write the difference. Use mental math when you can.

1. 85
  − 23

2. 41
  − 18

3. 41
  − 28

4. 64 miles
  − 5 miles

5. 75
  − 38

6. $0.75
  − 0.37

7. For which exercises did you use mental math? Why?

INDEPENDENT PRACTICE

Write the difference. Use mental math when you can.

8. 34
  − 18

9. 36
  − 20

10. 74
   − 46

11. $0.38
   − 0.25

12. 63 feet
   − 17 feet

13. 72 − 8

14. 86 − 49

15. 87 − 50

16. 50 − 49

17. 58 − 37

18. 70 − 40

19. 24 − 8

20. 43 − 39

Problem Solving

21. Here is the final score. By how many points did the Eagles win the game?

22. How many points did the Eagles score in the second half? Look at the scoreboard on page 92.

23. Did the Hawks score more points in the first half or the second half? How many more points?

CHALLENGE • Number Sense

a. What patterns do you see in the number sentences at the right?

b. Continue the patterns until you write an addition sentence with a sum of 90.

c. How did the patterns help you write the addition sentence?

80 + 1 = 81

79 + 3 = 82

78 + 5 = 83

77 + 7 = 84

SUBTRACTING FROM 3-DIGIT NUMBERS

The Children's Museum is giving origami classes. There are enough supplies for 250 children. So far, 87 children have signed up. How many more children can sign up for the classes?

To find how many more, you subtract 87 from 250.

Write it as:
$$\begin{array}{r} 250 \\ -\ 87 \end{array}$$

● Regroup? Subtract the ones.

$$\begin{array}{r} {}^{4}\ {}^{10} \\ 2\ \cancel{5}\ \cancel{0} \\ -\ \ \ 8\ 7 \\ \hline 3 \end{array}$$

5 tens, 0 ones = 4 tens, 10 ones

● Regroup? Subtract the tens. Then subtract the hundreds.

$$\begin{array}{r} {}^{14} \\ 1\ \cancel{4}\ {}^{10} \\ \cancel{2}\ \cancel{5}\ \cancel{0} \\ -\ \ \ 8\ 7 \\ \hline 1\ 6\ 3 \end{array}$$

2 hundreds, 4 tens = 1 hundred, 14 tens

So, 163 more children can sign up for the classes.

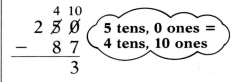

- Why do you regroup twice in the tens place?

Other Examples

$$\begin{array}{r} {}^{3}\ {}^{17} \\ \cancel{4}\ \cancel{7}\ 5 \\ -\ 1\ 8\ 2 \\ \hline 2\ 9\ 3 \end{array}$$

$$\begin{array}{r} {}^{12} \\ 4\ \cancel{2}\ {}^{11} \\ \$\cancel{5}\ .\ \cancel{3}\ \cancel{1} \\ -\ 4\ .\ 5\ 2 \\ \hline \$0\ .\ 7\ 9 \end{array}$$

$$\begin{array}{r} 679 \\ -\ 245 \\ \hline 434 \end{array}$$

94

GUIDED PRACTICE

Write the difference. Use mental math when you can.

1. 388 − 163
2. 249 feet − 57 feet
3. 100 − 98
4. 543 − 345
5. 654 − 456

6. 764 − 127
7. 160 − 60
8. 217 − 139
9. 371 − 91

10. For which exercises did you use mental math? Why?

....

INDEPENDENT PRACTICE

Write the difference. Use mental math when you can.

11. 777 − 369
12. 542 miles − 21 miles
13. 919 − 86
14. $8.47 − 2.58
15. $4.32 − 1.74

16. 140 − 70
17. 637 − 365
18. $3.21 − 1.98
19. 432 − 198
20. 472 − 187

21. 178 − 169
22. $600 − $200
23. 248 − 58
24. $8.21 − $0.93

Problem Solving The museum staff asked children which activity they liked best. The table shows the result.

25. Which activity did most children choose? How many more children chose this activity than chose jewelry?

26. Look at the table. Did more children choose origami than painting and pottery combined? Explain how you decided.

Activity	Number of Children
Jewelry	209
Painting	282
Pottery	216
Origami	310

USING STRATEGIES

If you get stuck, remember...

Tips for Problem Solving

on pages 426–427

Susan was given this map of her summer camp. Use the map to answer each question. Work with a partner.

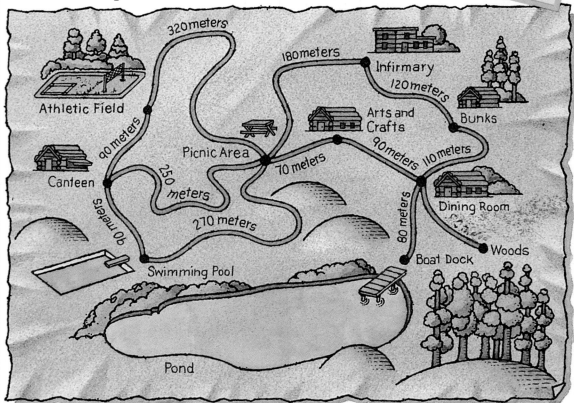

1. Susan is at the Arts and Crafts building. What is the length of the shortest path to the canteen?

2. Which is closer to the picnic area, the athletic field or the swimming pool? How much closer?

3. Susan spilled water on her map and smudged the distance between the dining room and the woods. Choose the best estimate for this distance.
   a. 200 meters   b. 100 meters   c. 60 meters

4. What is the shortest way from the picnic area to the bunks?

5. Are there more than 1000 meters of paths in the camp? How can you tell?

6. Susan is in the dining room and cannot find her glasses. She is not sure if she left them in the picnic area, the athletic field, the canteen, or at the swimming pool.
   a. What is the shortest route she can take to check all four places?
   b. What is the length of that route?

7. A group of campers plans to put markers on the path from the canteen to the athletic field. They will put a marker every 10 meters but not at the canteen or the athletic field. How many markers will they need?

8. Pam ran all the way around the pond. Which is the best estimate for the distance she ran?
   a. 157 meters   b. 200 meters   c. 700 meters

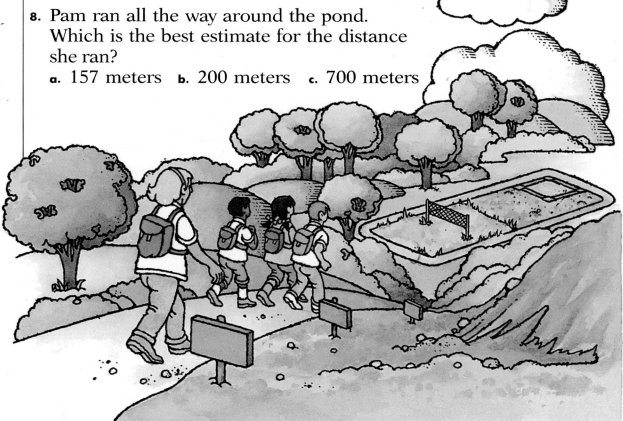

ESTIMATING DIFFERENCES

The largest known tiger weighed 857 pounds. A tiger usually weighs about 425 pounds. About how many pounds heavier was the largest known tiger?

You do not need an exact answer. The question only asks you to find *about* how many more pounds the largest tiger weighed.

You can estimate by looking at the digits in the hundreds place.

$$\begin{array}{r} 857 \text{ pounds} \longrightarrow 8 \text{ hundreds} \\ - 425 \text{ pounds} \longrightarrow 4 \text{ hundreds} \\ \hline 4 \text{ hundreds} \end{array}$$

A **front-end estimate** of this difference is 400 pounds.

The largest known tiger was about 400 pounds heavier.

Think

• Is the actual difference more than or less than 400 pounds? How do you know?

Anne has $9.25 to spend for her brother's birthday. A book on tigers costs $6.76. If she buys the book, about how much money will she have left?

$$\begin{array}{r} \$9.25 \longrightarrow \$9 \\ - 6.76 \longrightarrow - 6 \\ \hline \$3 \end{array}$$

Anne's estimate is $3. She will have about $3 left.

GUIDED PRACTICE

Estimate. Which two numbers have a difference of:

1. about 100?   2. about 300?

3 about 200?   4. about 500?

5. Think of two numbers whose difference is about 600.

....

INDEPENDENT PRACTICE

Write the letter of the closest estimate.

6.   637
     − 249

   a. 100
   b. 400
   c. 800

7.   586
     − 475

   a. 10
   b. 100
   c. 1000

8. 721 − 346

   a. 100
   b. 250
   c. 400

9. $5.42 − $3.27

   a. $2
   b. $4
   c. $8

Estimate. Which exercise has a difference of:

10. about 50?   11. about 500?

a.   85
     − 37

b.   8387
     − 3469

c.   827
     − 348

12. Estimate to find the four errors Anne made. Write the letter of each incorrect answer.

Name: _____Anne_____

a.   49
     − 26
     75

b.   847
     − 239
     68

c. $5.86
     − 3.57
     $ 2.29

d. 87 − 33 = 34

e. 974 − 659 = 315

f. $3.27 − $1.19 = $2.08

g. $9.71 − $6.23 = $6.48

SUBTRACTING WITH ZEROS

Melissa is riding to camp with her family. They are driving from White Plains to Buffalo. After 137 miles, they stop for lunch. How many more miles do they need to travel?

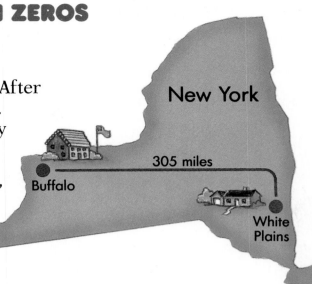

New York

305 miles

Buffalo

White Plains

To find how many more miles, you subtract 137 miles from 305 miles.

Write it as:
$$\begin{array}{r} 305 \text{ miles} \\ -\ 137 \text{ miles} \end{array}$$

● **Enough ones to subtract? No. And no tens to regroup. So, regroup hundreds.**

$$\begin{array}{r} {}^{2}\ {}^{10} \\ \cancel{3}\ \cancel{0}\ 5 \text{ miles} \\ -\ 1\ 3\ 7 \text{ miles} \end{array}$$

● **Regroup the tens. Then subtract the ones.**

$$\begin{array}{r} {}^{9} \\ {}^{2}\ \cancel{10}\ {}^{15} \\ \cancel{3}\ \cancel{0}\ \cancel{5} \text{ miles} \\ -\ 1\ 3\ 7 \text{ miles} \\ \hline 8 \end{array}$$

● **Subtract the tens. Then subtract the hundreds.**

$$\begin{array}{r} {}^{9} \\ {}^{2}\ \cancel{10}\ {}^{15} \\ \cancel{3}\ \cancel{0}\ \cancel{5} \text{ miles} \\ -\ 1\ 3\ 7 \text{ miles} \\ \hline 1\ 6\ 8 \text{ miles} \end{array}$$

They need to travel 168 miles more.

Think

• Would you have to regroup twice in the tens place if the subtraction problem were 307 − 135? Explain.

Other Examples

$$\begin{array}{r} {}^{8}\ {}^{10} \\ \cancel{9}\ \cancel{0}\ 8 \text{ miles} \\ -\ 4\ 8\ 7 \text{ miles} \\ \hline 4\ 2\ 1 \text{ miles} \end{array}$$

$$\begin{array}{r} {}^{9} \\ {}^{4}\ \cancel{10}\ {}^{16} \\ \cancel{5}\ \cancel{0}\ \cancel{6} \\ -\ \ \ 6\ 8 \\ \hline 4\ 3\ 8 \end{array}$$

$$\begin{array}{r} {}^{9} \\ {}^{6}\ \cancel{10}\ {}^{10} \\ \$\cancel{7}.\cancel{0}\ \cancel{0} \\ -\ \ 4.3\ 9 \\ \hline \$2.6\ 1 \end{array}$$

Remember to check subtraction by adding.

$$\begin{array}{r} \$2.61 \\ +\ \ 4.39 \\ \hline \$7.00 \end{array}$$

Write the difference. Use mental math when you can.

1. 305	2. 400	3. 603 miles	4. 704	5. $\$200$
-191	-350	-496 miles	-32	-72

6. $405 - 67$ 7. $\$9.20 - \$0.20$ 8. $240 - 39$ 9. $\$8.04 - \$6.23$

10. For exercises 1–5, show how you can check your answers by adding.

Write the difference. Use mental math when you can.

11. 320	12. $\$7.06$	13. 900 feet	14. 403	15. $\$2.00$
-119	-5.45	-417 feet	-94	-0.50

16. $608 - 29$ 17. $320 - 0$ 18. $489 - 145$ 19. $\$5.00 - \$0.81$

20. $807 - 7$ 21. $\$6.98 - \$6.90$ 22. $309 - 28$ 23. $\$7.05 - \$5.46$

Problem Solving Use the mileage table on page 421 in the Data Book.

24. Mr. and Mrs. Ling are driving from Louisville to Detroit. How far is it between the 2 cities?

25. The Ruiz family is driving from Detroit to Chicago. They have driven 150 miles. Are they halfway there yet?

26. Use the table to write your own word problem. Give it to a friend to solve.

Maintain • **Mixed Practice**

Write the answer.

1. 9	2. 15	3. 6	4. 8	5. 16	6. 15
$+3$	-7	$+5$	$+9$	-9	-5

USING ADDITION AND SUBTRACTION

Title	List Price
Aesop's Fables	$42.00
Charlotte's Web	21.95 ✓
Curious George	11.95 ✓
Horton Hears a Who!	10.95
Mary Poppins	21.90 ✓
Just So Stories	32.90 ✓

▶ Ms. Patel, the school librarian, has $75 to spend on videos. She wants to buy the ones she has checked. Will she have enough money?

Think

- Could you estimate to answer the question? Explain.

▶ Ms. Patel does not have enough money. So, she decides not to order *Mary Poppins*. She wants to pay by check. For what amount should she make the check?

She uses a calculator to add the costs of the videos.

The sum 66.8 on the calculator is the same as $66.80. The calculator does not show zeros at the end of a number after a decimal point. It does not show dollar signs, either.

Think

- How could you estimate to check if the calculator answer is reasonable?

▶ Ms. Patel decides to see how much more money she would need to buy all four videos. She finds the total on her calculator: $88.70.

To find out how much more she would need, she subtracts: $88.70 − $75.00. Her calculator shows: 13.7.

So, she would need $13.70 more.

INDEPENDENT PRACTICE

Problem Solving Use the price list on page 102.
You may use pencil and paper, a calculator,
or mental math.

1. If *Aesop's Fables* is one of the videos Ms. Patel buys with the $75, how much money will she have to spend on other videos?

2. Suppose Ms. Patel decides to buy 2 videos and spend only $25. Which two on the price list can she buy?

3. How did you decide whether to add or subtract to solve the problems?

. . . .

PROJECT • Problem Solving

Ms. Patel has $100 to spend on books.
Decide which books she should buy.
Work with a partner. You may use
pencil and paper or a calculator.

a. Make a list of your choices.
   How much do the books cost
   altogether? How much money
   is left over?

b. What is the greatest number
   of books you could buy for $100?
   (Count each book of a set.)
   Which books are they?

c. Compare your list with
   another group's list. Discuss
   how you made your decisions.

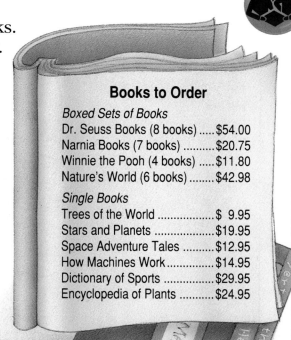

Books to Order

Boxed Sets of Books
Dr. Seuss Books (8 books) $54.00
Narnia Books (7 books) $20.75
Winnie the Pooh (4 books) $11.80
Nature's World (6 books) $42.98

Single Books
Trees of the World .... $ 9.95
Stars and Planets $19.95
Space Adventure Tales $12.95
How Machines Work $14.95
Dictionary of Sports $29.95
Encyclopedia of Plants $24.95

PROBLEM SOLVING
USING STRATEGIES

 Animal Actors, Inc., trains animals to act in movies. You may use a calculator.

Deer: 390 pounds

Llama: 373 pounds

Bear Cub: 53 pounds

Sheep: 150 pounds

Seal: 187 pounds

1. For one movie, Animal Actors, Inc., must move the animals shown on this page to the studio. The company has two trucks. Each truck can carry 600 pounds but not any more. Choose the animals that could go in each truck.

2. As the trucks are about to leave, the trainers get a call from the studio. They do not need a bear cub after all! Instead, they need a small alligator. The trainers have one that weighs 75 pounds. If they use the alligator in place of the bear cub, will the truck still be carrying less than 600 pounds? How do you know?

Otter: 13 pounds

Fox: 14 pounds

Cat: 11 pounds

SECTION REVIEW

for pages 90–104

Write the letter of the correct answer.

1. 75 − 28

  a. 103

  b. 53

  c. 47

  d. 50

2. 563 − 34

  a. 531

  b. 597

  c. 223

  d. 529

3. 653 − 45

  a. 612

  b. 608

  c. 698

  d. 203

4. $5.00 − $1.92

  a. $3.18

  b. $3.08

  c. $3.07

  d. $2.10

5. 800 − 314

  a. 496

  b. 485

  c. 386

  d. 486

6. 900 − 714

  a. 196

  b. 185

  c. 86

  d. 186

7. 502 − 341

  a. 843

  b. 241

  c. 161

  d. 261

8. 712 − 568

  a. 144

  b. 256

  c. 254

  d. 244

9. 205 − 194

  a. 399

  b. 11

  c. 111

  d. 191

Solve each problem.

10. Harry wants to buy a bicycle that costs $142. He has $85 saved. How much more money does he need to save?

11. Patty had $131 saved. Then she earned $27 and got $15 for her birthday. How much money does she have now?

CHAPTER REVIEW

Language Connection

Here are two games you and a partner can play. Look at sale items in newspapers or flyers. Choose as many as you can that will total less than $100. Use front-end estimation. When you both agree on the choices, add the exact costs together. How close were you?

A palindrome is a number that reads the same from left to right and from right to left, such as 2662. Words can be palindromes, too. *Wow* and *Hannah* are palindromes. Find as many palindromes as you can.

Test ●●●●●●●●

Write the sum.

1.
$$\begin{array}{r} 49 \\ 63 \\ + 582 \\ \hline \end{array}$$

2.
$$\begin{array}{r} \$2.61 \\ 3.04 \\ + 1.97 \\ \hline \end{array}$$

3.
$$\begin{array}{r} 54 \\ 79 \\ 146 \\ + 278 \\ \hline \end{array}$$

4.
$$\begin{array}{r} \$0.35 \\ 1.37 \\ 2.21 \\ + 1.02 \\ \hline \end{array}$$

5. $41 + 79$ 6. $\$5.43 + \$0.96$ 7. $613 + 284$ 8. $\$3.62 + \$4.19$

Write the difference.

9.
$$\begin{array}{r} 96 \\ - 39 \\ \hline \end{array}$$

10.
$$\begin{array}{r} 548 \\ - 97 \\ \hline \end{array}$$

11.
$$\begin{array}{r} 777 \\ - 358 \\ \hline \end{array}$$

12.
$$\begin{array}{r} \$6.11 \\ - \$2.45 \\ \hline \end{array}$$

13. $72 - 38$ 14. $\$3.46 - \$0.59$ 15. $653 - 219$ 16. $\$9.42 - \$4.35$

17. $408 - 113$ 18. $\$8.03 - \$7.46$ 19. $600 - 237$ 20. $\$9.00 - \$2.00$

PROBLEM SOLVING

Solve each problem.

21. Terry wants to buy a stereo that costs $279. He has $159 saved. How much more does he need to save?

22. Dina had $192 in her savings account. Then she earned $21 and got $15 for her birthday. How much does she have now?

23. The craft store is giving art lessons. There are enough supplies for 123 children. So far, 65 children have signed up. How many more children can sign up for the lessons?

24. The Santos family needs to drive 200 miles to reach the beach. They travel 75 miles. Then they stop for 45 minutes to eat breakfast. How many more miles do they need to travel?

CUMULATIVE REVIEW

Write the number in standard form.

25. $400 + 60 + 7$

26. six thousand eight hundred fifty-two

27. $5000 + 400 + 9$

28. four thousand two hundred thirty

Write the correct change.

29. $1.00 paid for a ruler that cost 67¢

30. $2.00 paid for a notebook that cost $1.39

Write the number sentence that is missing from the fact family.

31. $9 + 4 = 13$
$4 + 9 = 13$
$13 - 4 = 9$

32. $13 - 5 = 8$
$13 - 8 = 5$
$8 + 5 = 13$

33. $15 - 7 = 8$
$15 - 8 = 7$
$8 + 7 = 15$

EXCURSION

USING TECHNOLOGY

Calculator Patterns

One kind of number pattern is a palindrome.
A **palindrome** is a number that reads the
same from left to right and from right
to left.

Numbers like 636, 22, 989 and 1551 are
palindromes.

Here is how you can use your calculator to
make palindromes.

• Enter a 3-digit number on your calculator.

• Think of the new number you would make
if you reversed the digits. Find the sum of
this new number and the first number.

• If the sum is not a palindrome, then
reverse the digits and add again.

The new sum, 2332, reads the same from
left to right and from right to left.

So, 2332 is a palindrome.

Use a calculator. Match each number to its palindrome.

1. 152   **a.** 1991

2. 25   **b.** 707

3. 347   **c.** 484

4. 49   **d.** 868

5. 731   **e.** 77

 Use a calculator. Make a palindrome from each number.

6. 65   **7.** 235   **8.** 48   **9.** 15

10. 621   **11.** 82   **12.** 651   **13.** 227

14. 165   **15.** 742   **16.** 102   **17.** 456

Problem Solving Three of the five numbers in the box below have the same palindrome.

| 18 | 45 | 14 | 125 | 36 |

18. What is the palindrome?

19. Which numbers have the same palindrome?

20. How many times do you have to add to make a palindrome from 736? What is the palindrome?

CHAPTER 4

COLLECTING AND ORGANIZING DATA

Connections

Social Studies

Interpreting a Graph Building a new school is a big project. It is also expensive. A large elementary school costs millions of dollars.

The graph shows how much money is in the school building fund. Study the graph and answer these questions.

- What is the cost of the new building?

- About how much money has been raised so far?

- About how much more money is needed to pay for the project?

Perhaps you can learn something about your school. When was the school built? How much did it cost? How long did the project take? You may find some answers in your school library.

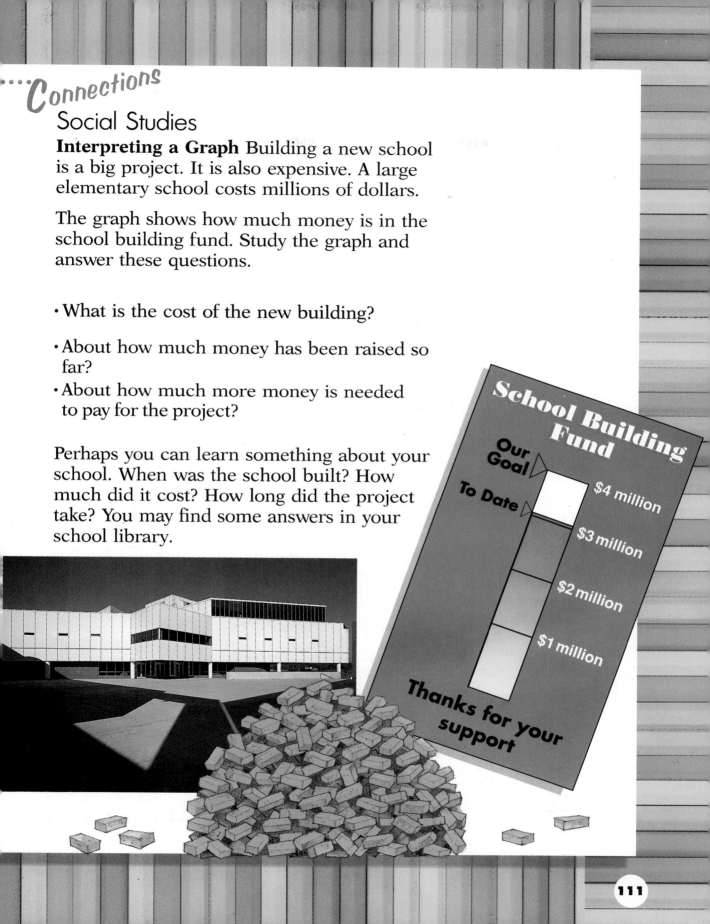

School Building Fund

Our Goal — $4 million

To Date

$3 million

$2 million

$1 million

Thanks for your support

MAKING EQUAL SETS

Groups: partners

You will need:
- 24 counters
- recording sheet

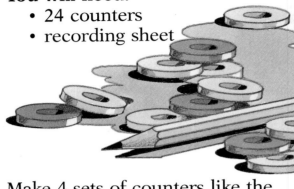

▶ Make 4 sets of counters like the ones shown. Then arrange the counters so there is the same number in each set. Now your sets of counters are equal.

1. How did you make your sets of counters equal?

2. How many counters are in each set now?

Record the results in the table on your recording sheet.

Total Number of Counters	Number of Equal Sets	Number of Counters in Each Set
24	4	

▶ Make 6 sets of counters like the ones shown. Now make the 6 sets equal.

3. How many counters are in each set?

Record your results in the table.

▶ Make 3 sets of counters like the ones shown. Then make the 3 sets equal. Record your results.

Make 8 equal sets with the 24 counters. Record your results.

4. Name some ways you can make unequal sets of counters equal.

5. Suppose you separate 36 counters into 6 equal sets. Then you separate the 36 counters into 3 equal sets. Would there be more counters in each set the first time or the second time? How do you know?

....

PROJECT • Application

Suppose your school is having a book drive. Three grades have collected the number of books shown.

BOOK DRIVE	
Grade	**Books Collected**
2	33
3	40
4	29

The school wants to give the books to the school library, the local hospital, and the senior-citizen center. Each place will get the same number of books.

Work with your partner to figure out how many books each place will get. Use counters, drawings, or a calculator. When you have finished, discuss these questions with other groups.

• How many books will each place get?

• How did you get your answer?

• Are some methods easier than others? Which ones?

113

COLLECTING AND RECORDING DATA

In Mrs. Atwood's science class, the students are studying the solar system. Each student must do a report on one planet. Mrs. Atwood asks the students, one at a time, which planet they will study.

She uses tally marks to record their answers. Each tally mark stands for one student.

Groups: partners

You will need: recording sheet

Find out how many students in Mrs. Atwood's class want to study each planet. Complete the table at the right. Use your recording sheet.

Use your completed table to answer each question.

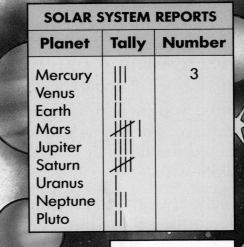

SOLAR SYSTEM REPORTS		
Planet	**Tally**	**Number**
Mercury	|||	3
Venus	||	
Earth	||	
Mars	⑷|	
Jupiter	||||	
Saturn	⑷	
Uranus			
Neptune	|||	
Pluto	||	

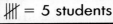

⑷ = 5 students

1. How is the Tally column different from the Number column? How is it the same?

2. Why did Mrs. Atwood use tally marks to record her students' answers?

3. Which is the most popular planet to study? How many students want to study this planet?

4. Which is the least popular planet to study? How many students want to study this planet?

5. How many more students want to study Saturn than want to study Earth?

6. How many students will be writing a report?

SUMMING IT UP

7. Why is there both a Number column and a Tally column on the table?

8. Why do you think Mrs. Atwood asked her students which planets they would study?

PROJECT • Collecting Data

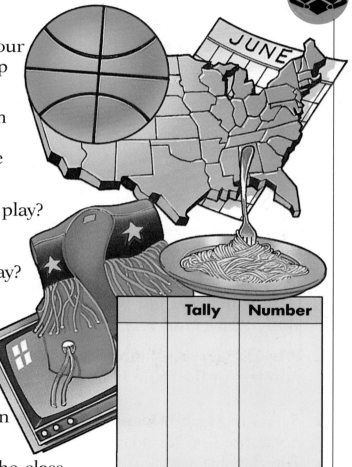

With your partner, choose one of the questions below to ask your classmates. Or you can make up your own question.

Ask each classmate the question and record the results on your recording sheet. Be sure to give your table a title.

- What is your favorite sport to play?

- In what state were you born?

- In what month is your birthday?

- What is your favorite color?

- Are you right-handed or left-handed?

- What is your favorite food?

- What is your favorite television show?

Show your table to the rest of the class. Discuss the results with your classmates.

	Tally	Number

If you get stuck, remember...

Tips for Problem Solving

on pages 426–427

Ms. Vernon owns the V.V. Video store. She keeps track of the movies people rent. The table shows some of her movies and for how many days each one was rented last week. She has 1 copy of each movie. Videos are rented for 1 day only.

MOVIE RENTALS LAST WEEK—SUNDAY TO SATURDAY	
Name of Movie	**Number of Days Rented**
The Circle with 2 Sides	6
Galaxy Getaway	7
Skip and Scott Go Hiking	1
King of the Dragons	4
Secret of Murky Mountain	5
Wally Walrus	4

Work in groups. Help Ms. Vernon by solving each problem.

1. Which of the movies was most popular last week at V.V. Video?

2. How many days last week was *Wally Walrus* not rented?

3. Why do you think the highest number in the table is only 7?

4. *Secret of Murky Mountain* was not rented on Monday or Tuesday last week. Was it rented on Wednesday? How do you know?

This table shows how often the movies were rented each week in February. Some of the numbers are missing. Help complete the table by solving each problem.

V.V. VIDEO MOVIE RENTALS—FEBRUARY					
Name of Movie	**Number of Days Rented**				
	First week	**Second week**	**Third week**	**Fourth week**	**Total**
The Circle with 2 Sides	1	3	5	6	15
Galaxy Getaway	0	4	6	7	17
Skip and Scott Go Hiking	4	2		1	7
King of the Dragons	7		5	4	21
Secret of Murky Mountain	7	7	5	5	
Wally Walrus	6	7	5	4	

5. How many days was *Skip and Scott Go Hiking* rented in the third week?

6. How many days was *King of the Dragons* rented in the second week?

7. Which movie was most popular in February at V.V. Video?

8. Which movies kept getting more popular during the month?

9. Which movies were rented more than 20 days during the month?

10. If you owned V.V. Video, which movie would you buy another copy of? Why?

PICTOGRAPHS

Mr. Clark took his class to the aquarium. They counted the fish in 4 of the small tanks.

In school they made a **pictograph** of the number of fish in the tanks. Each picture stands for more than 1 fish. The **key** tells us that each picture stands for 5 fish.

How many fish did they see in Tank 1?

The pictograph shows 3 pictures of a fish for Tank 1. Each picture stands for 5 fish. Since 5 + 5 + 5 = 15, then 15 fish were in Tank 1.

Fish We Counted
Tank 1 ⋖⋗ ⋖⋗ ⋖⋗
Tank 2 ⋖⋗ ⋖⋗ ⋖⋗ ⋖⋗ ⋖⋗ ⋖⋗
Tank 3 ⋖⋗ ⋖⋗ ⋖⋗ ⋖⋗
Tank 4 ⋖⋗ ⋖⋗ ⋖⋗ ⋖⋗ ⋖⋗
Key : ⋖⋗ = 5 fish

Think

- How many fish would have been in Tank 1 if each picture had stood for 10 fish? How do you know?

GUIDED PRACTICE

Use the pictograph above to answer each question.

1. How many fish were in Tank 2?

2. Which tank had the most fish?

3. How many more fish were in Tank 4 than in Tank 3?

4. How many fish did the class count in all?

5. How did you find the answer to exercise 4?

INDEPENDENT PRACTICE

Use the pictograph to solve each problem.

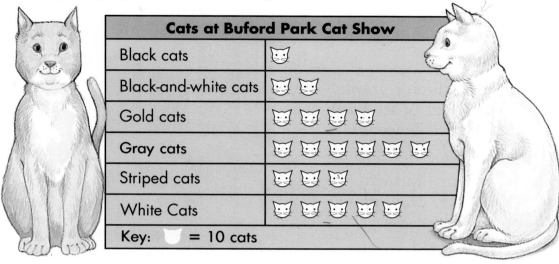

Cats at Buford Park Cat Show	
Black cats	🐱
Black-and-white cats	🐱 🐱
Gold cats	🐱 🐱 🐱 🐱
Gray cats	🐱 🐱 🐱 🐱 🐱 🐱
Striped cats	🐱 🐱 🐱
White Cats	🐱 🐱 🐱 🐱 🐱
Key: 🐱 = 10 cats	

6. How many kinds of cats are at the cat show?

7. Which kind of cat is there the most of at the show?

8. How many more white cats than gold cats are there?

9. How many cats in all are at the cat show?

10. Which two kinds of cats would you combine to equal the number of striped cats?

PROJECT • Making a Graph

Use the Data Book to make a pictograph. Turn to Life Span of Animals on page 417.

a. Choose 5 animals from the table.
b. Make a pictograph of the number of years these 5 animals usually live. Draw a birthday candle to stand for 2 years. (If there is an odd number of years, draw half a candle.)
c. Make a key and give your graph a title.
d. Write two word problems about your graph. Give them to a friend to solve.

119

BAR GRAPHS

Reuben asks his classmates to name their favorite dinosaur. He records the results on a **bar graph.**

The bars in Reuben's graph show the number of students who named each dinosaur as their favorite.

Which dinosaur did most students choose? How many of them named this as their favorite?

The longest bar on the graph is for *Tyrannosaurus rex.* So most students named this dinosaur as their favorite.

The bar for *Tyrannosaurus rex* ends at the 9 mark. This is the mark between the 8 and the 10. So 9 students named that dinosaur as their favorite.

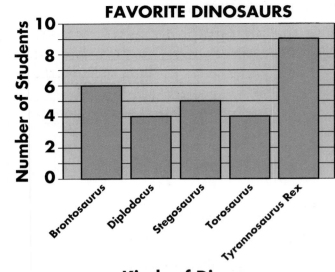

FAVORITE DINOSAURS

Number of Students

Kinds of Dinosaur

Think

- How is a bar graph like a pictograph? How is it different?

Here is another way Reuben can make his bar graph.

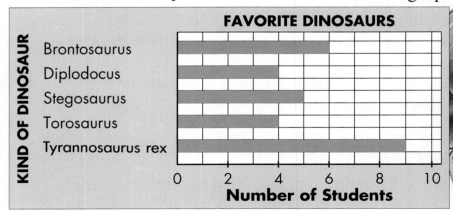

FAVORITE DINOSAURS

KIND OF DINOSAUR

Brontosaurus
Diplodocus
Stegosaurus
Torosaurus
Tyrannosaurus rex

Number of Students

GUIDED PRACTICE

Use the data in the table to copy and complete the graph.
The first bar is done for you. Use squared paper.

1.

Students' Favorite Field Trips	
Where We Went	**Number of Students**
Aquarium	~~HHt~~ III
Art Museum	IIII
Park	III
Zoo	~~HHt~~ I

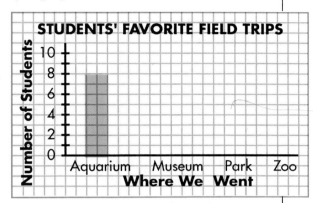

2. How did you know how long to make each bar in the graph?

INDEPENDENT PRACTICE

Use the bar graph to solve each problem.

3. Which subject was the most popular?

4. How many students named Art as their favorite subject?

5. Which subjects were named by the same number of students?

6. Use the data in the table about dinosaurs on page 417 in the Data Book. Use squared paper to make a bar graph.

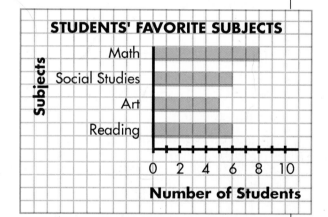

Maintain • Mixed Practice

Write the answer.

1.
$$637 + 124$$

2.
$$\$0.85 + 0.15$$

3.
$$703 - 549$$

4.
$$24 \\ 16 \\ + 36$$

5.
$$\$5.00 - 0.01$$

LINE GRAPHS

Betty is a forest ranger in the state of Maine. In the winter, she records how much snow falls. Then she makes a line graph of the information.

A **line graph** shows changes over time. The points on Betty's graph tell the amount of snow that fell every month.

In which month did the most snow fall? How many inches fell?

The highest point on the graph is shown above January. The point is on the line marked 19. So the most snow—19 inches—fell in January.

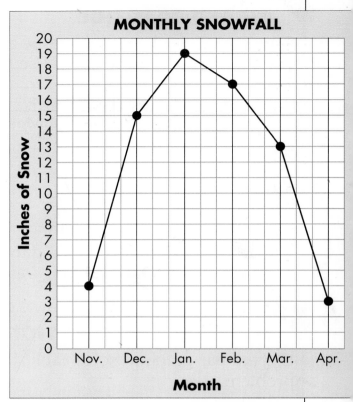

MONTHLY SNOWFALL

Think

- Between which two months was there the greatest change in snowfall? How do you know?

GUIDED PRACTICE

Use the graph above to answer each question.

1. In which month did the least snow fall? How many inches fell?

2. In how many months did more than 10 inches of snow fall? Which months were they?

3. Did more snow fall in December or in March? How much more?

Betty also records the temperature each morning. The graph below shows the temperature during one week in August. Use the graph to solve each problem.

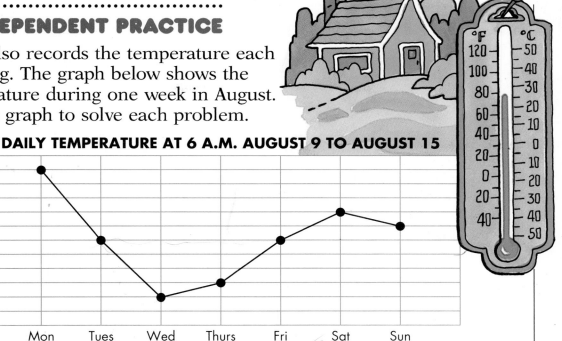

DAILY TEMPERATURE AT 6 A.M. AUGUST 9 TO AUGUST 15

Temperature (°): 69°, 68°, 67°, 66°, 65°, 64°, 63°, 62°, 61°, 60°, 59°, 58°, 57°

Mon 68°, Tues 63°, Wed 59°, Thurs 60°, Fri 63°, Sat 65°, Sun 64°

Day of the Week

4. Which day had the highest temperature? What was the temperature?

5. Which day had the lowest temperature? What was the temperature?

6. Which two days had the same temperature?

7. How much cooler was it on Tuesday than on Monday?

CHALLENGE • Using Data

Use the data in the table to copy and complete the line graph. Use squared paper.

Monthly Rainfall in Tropical Rain Forest	
Month	**Rain (in inches)**
March	12
April	16
May	18
June	14
July	17
August	10

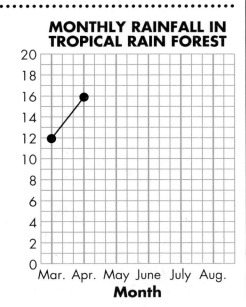

MONTHLY RAINFALL IN TROPICAL RAIN FOREST

Inches of Rain: 20, 18, 16, 14, 12, 10, 8, 6, 4, 2, 0

Mar. Apr. May June July Aug.

Month

RECORDING TEMPERATURES

Every day, newspapers print information about the temperature in cities all around the world.

This table shows the temperatures during a week in the city of Chicago, Illinois. **High** means the highest temperature that day. **Low** means the lowest temperature that day.

DAILY TEMPERATURES
WEEK OF JANUARY 22

	Mon.	Tues.	Wed.	Thurs.	Fri.	Sat.	Sun.
High	42°	48°	45°	37°	33°	50°	38°
Low	32°	28°	33°	25°	12°	36°	21°

Think

- Was the temperature ever 40 degrees on Wednesday? How can you tell?

- Was the temperature ever 40 degrees on Thursday? How can you tell?

GUIDED PRACTICE

Use the table above to answer each question.

1. How would you find the difference between the high and low temperatures on Monday?

2. Write the difference between the high and low temperatures for each day of the week.

3. Which day had the greatest difference in temperature?

INDEPENDENT PRACTICE

The table below shows the high temperatures for two cities, St. Paul and São Paulo. Use the information from the table to answer each question.

**DAILY HIGH TEMPERATURES
WEEK OF JANUARY 22**

	Mon.	Tues.	Wed.	Thurs.	Fri.	Sat.	Sun.
St. Paul	40°	37°	34°	29°	33°	33°	39°
São Paulo	86°	88°	84°	90°	90°	86°	86°

4. Was it warmer in St. Paul or in São Paulo during the week of January 22?

5. What was the highest temperature in St. Paul? What was the lowest temperature?

6. What was the highest temperature in São Paulo? What was the lowest temperature?

7. What was the difference between the highest temperature in São Paulo and the highest temperature in St. Paul?

Problem Solving

8. A newspaper headline read "Temperature Drops 25 Degrees in 2 Hours!" If the temperature was 43 degrees, what was the temperature 2 hours later?

9. The difference between the high and low temperatures one day was 16 degrees. If the low was 21 degrees, what was the high temperature?

USING MATH SENSE

Solve each problem. If there is not enough information, tell what you need to know.

1. José was born in 1984. Ricardo was born in 1982. Who is older?

2. Keisha is 2 years older than her brother. In 5 years, how much older than her brother will Keisha be?

3. Mary Beth walks 3 miles to school. How many miles would it be if she ran?

4. Aaron plans to buy a notebook for $2.19 and a marker for 79¢. How much change will he get back?

5. There are 7 people waiting in line. Adele is the last one in line. Then 4 more people get on the end of the line. What place is Adele in now?

6. Keri is sending a 3-page letter to her grandmother in St. Paul, Minnesota. She is also sending a 4-page letter to her aunt in Atlanta, Georgia. How many envelopes does she need?

7. Ernie buys an eraser for 58¢. He pays for it with a dollar bill. What is the least number of coins he can get as change? What coins are they?

8. Teresa has 5 pencils. Laura has 8 pencils. Marcus has 2 pencils. They want to share the pencils so that they each have the same number. How many will each of them have?

SECTION REVIEW

for pages 112–126

The third grade is collecting cans to help clean up their neighborhood. Use the pictograph to answer each question.

1. How many cans were collected on Wednesday?

2. How many more cans did the class collect on Monday than on Tuesday?

3. On which day were the most cans collected?

4. On which day were the fewest cans collected?

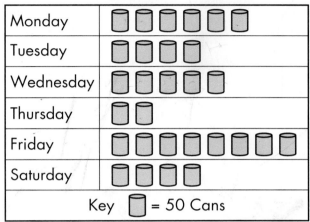

CAN COLLECTION CLEAN-UP

Monday	
Tuesday	
Wednesday	
Thursday	
Friday	
Saturday	

Key [= 50 Cans

Jack asks each of his classmates in which month they were born. He makes a bar graph of the results.

Use the graph to answer each question.

5. In which month were the most classmates born?

6. How many classmates were born in January?

7. In which month were the fewest classmates born?

8. How many more classmates were born in September than August?

9. In which months were 5 classmates born?

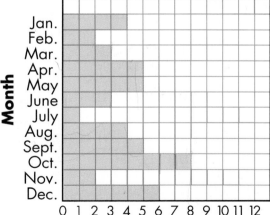

BIRTHDAYS

Number of Students

10. Were there any months in which none of Jack's classmates were born? Explain.

EXPERIMENTING WITH CHANCE

Groups: partners

You will need:
- 5 red cubes
- 5 blue cubes
- small paper bag
- recording sheet

▶ Put 2 red cubes and 1 blue cube into the paper bag. You will pick 1 cube out of the bag 25 times.

1. Which color cube do you think you will pick more often, red or blue? Why?

Follow these steps.

   a. Pick one cube from the bag.

   b. Mark the color of the cube on the recording sheet. Use tally marks.

   c. Put the cube back in the bag.

Color	Tally	Total
Red		
Blue		

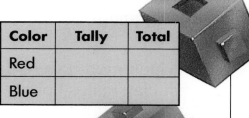

Now repeat steps a–c 24 times. Take turns with your partner.

2. How many times did you pick a red cube?

3. How many times did you pick a blue cube?

4. Which color did you pick more often, red or blue?

5. Was that the color you thought you would pick more often?

For a second experiment, put 5 red cubes and 1 blue one into the bag.

6. Which color do you think you will pick more often this time? Why?

Now repeat steps a–c 25 times.

7. How many times did you pick a red cube?

8. How many times did you pick a blue cube?

9. Which color cube did you pick more often?

10. Was that the color you thought you would pick?

For your third experiment, put 5 red cubes and 5 blue cubes into the bag.

11. Which color do you think you will pick more often?

Now repeat steps a–c 25 times.

12. Did the color you picked more often turn out to be the one you thought it would be? Explain.

SUMMING IT UP

13. Compare your results with those of your classmates. What do you see?

14. If you did the experiment with 4 red cubes and 4 blue ones, which color do you think you would pick more often? Why?

MATH LOG

How are the experiments in this lesson like calling "heads" or "tails" when you flip a coin?

PROBABILITY

Groups: partners

You will need:
- 2 spinner boards like the ones here
- paper clip
- recording sheet

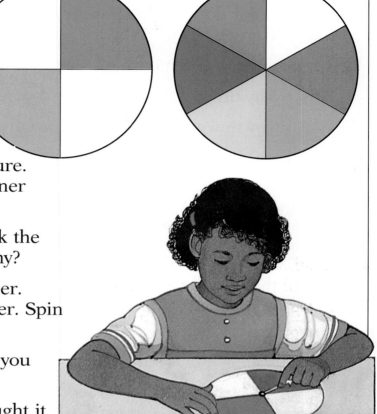

Look at the girl in the picture. Suppose she spins the spinner once.

1. Which color do you think the spinner will land on? Why?

Use the same kind of spinner. Take turns with your partner. Spin the spinner once.

2. Which color did each of you spin?

3. Was it the color you thought it might land on?

Take turns so that each of you spins the spinner 10 times.

4. Use the recording sheet to keep track of the colors the spinner lands on. Use tally marks.

Color	Tally	Total
Red		
White		
Blue		

5. Which color did the spinner land on the most?

Look at the spinner at the right.

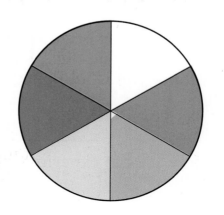

6. Suppose you spin it 20 times. Which color do you think the spinner would land on most? Why?

7. Use the same kind of spinner. Take turns with your partner. Spin the spinner 20 times and see what happens. Record the number of times the spinner lands on each color.

Color	Tally	Total
White		
Red		

8. What happened? Did you get the results you thought you would?

SUMMING IT UP

Look at the three spinners below. Suppose you could spin each one only once. Is there an equal chance of the spinner landing on blue as on red? Write *yes* or *no*.

9.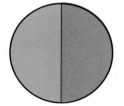

10.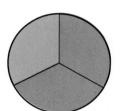

11.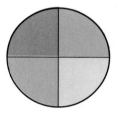

12. Suppose you were playing a spinner game and landing on red meant you were a winner. Which of the above spinners would you like to play with?

Look at the three spinners below.

a.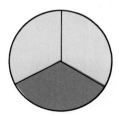

b.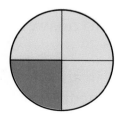

c.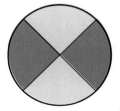

13. If a game is won by spinning yellow, which spinner would you like to play with?

14. If a game is won by spinning green, which spinner would you like to play with?

MAKING PREDICTIONS

You have used colored cubes and spinners to make predictions. When you say what you think will happen, you are making a **prediction.**

You can make predictions about how often letters of the alphabet appear in words.

Group: partners

You will need: recording sheet

Read the poem below titled "Dogs," by Marchette Chute. Use the recording sheet to record how many times each letter appears. Use tally marks.

Letter	Tally	Total	Letter	Tally	Total
A			N		
B			O		
C			P		
D			Q		
E			R		

The dogs I know
Have many shapes.
For some are big and tall,
And some are long,
And
some
are thin,
And some are fat and small.

And some are little bits of fluff
And have no shape at all.

Use the completed recording sheet to answer each question.

1. Which letter appears most often in the poem? How many times does it appear?

2. Which letter appears the second most often? How many times does it appear?

3. Which letters do not appear at all?

Now use your results to make a prediction about how often letters will appear in other words. Look at the first paragraph on page 132.

4. Which letter do you think will appear most often?

5. Which letter do you think will appear the second most often?

6. Which letters do you think will not appear at all?

Read the paragraph. Use your recording sheet to record how many times each letter appears.

Letter	Tally	Total	Letter	Tally	Total
A			N		
B			O		
C			P		
D			Q		
E			R		
F			S		
G			T		
H			U		
I			V		
J			W		
K			X		
L			Y		
M			Z		

SUMMING IT UP

7. Were your predictions correct? Explain.

8. Which letters do you think appear most often in our language?

9. Which letters do not appear very often?

Maintain • Mixed Practice

Write the time.

1.    **2.**    **3.**    **4.**    **5.**

Write the number in standard form.

6. four hundred thirty-one

7. two thousand five hundred

8. 8000 + 300 + 60 + 4

9. 5 hundreds + 7 ones

USING STRATEGIES

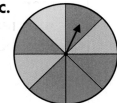

A.

Julie's class made 4 different spinners. They spun each one many times and made graphs of the results. The graphs got mixed up. Can you help Julie sort them out?

D.

B.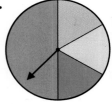

C.

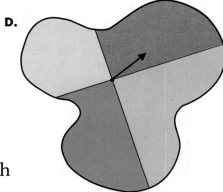

Write the letter of the spinner that goes with the graph. Work with a partner.

1.

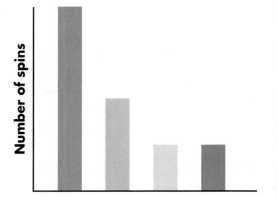

2.

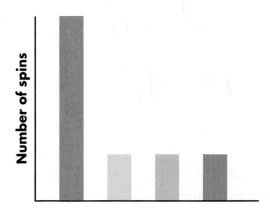

3.

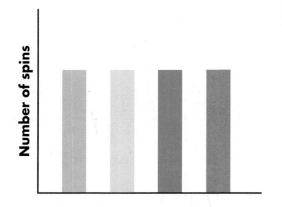

4.

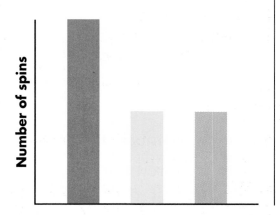

SECTION REVIEW

for pages 128–134

Write the letter of the correct answer.

1. There are 10 red cubes and 3 blue cubes in a bag. Suppose you pick 1 cube out of the bag 20 times. Which color do you think you would pick more often?

  a. red, because there are fewer

  b. blue, because there are fewer

  c. red, because there are more

  d. blue, because there are more

2. There are 5 red cubes and 6 blue cubes in a bag. Suppose you pick out 1 cube 20 times. Which color do you think you would pick more often?

  a. red, because there are fewer

  b. blue, because there are fewer

  c. red, because there are more

  d. blue, because there are more

Is there a greater chance of the spinner landing on red, white, or blue? Write the color.

3.
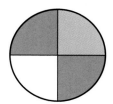

4.
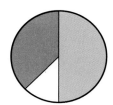

5.
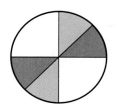

Read the poem below. Make a tally to find how many times each letter appears.

There was a little turtle.
He lived in a box.
He swam in a puddle.
He climbed on rocks.

Use your tally to answer each question.

Letter	Tally	Total	Letter	Tally	Total
A			N		
B			O		
C			P		
D			Q		
E			R		
F			S		

6. Which letters do not appear in the poem?

7. Which letter appears most often?

CHAPTER REVIEW

Language Connection

Memory hints help people remember things. For example: "Keys let you in."

Make up your own memory hints for the following words: *data, pictograph, tally, chance,* and *prediction.*

These tips also might help. The root **graph** means "write" or "writing"; the root **picto** means "drawing"; the root **dict** means "say"; and the prefix **pre-** means "before".

data
pictograph

tally

chance
prediction

Test ● ● ● ● ● ● ●

Use the pictograph to find the answer.

1. How many eggs are there in Basket 2?

2. Which basket has the most eggs?

3. How many more eggs are there in Basket 4 than in Basket 3?

4. How many eggs are there in all?

Eggs in Baskets

Basket 1	⬯⬯⬯⬯⬯⬯⬯⬯
Basket 2	⬯⬯⬯⬯
Basket 3	⬯⬯⬯
Basket 4	⬯⬯⬯⬯⬯⬯

Key: ⬯ = 2 eggs

Use the bar graphs to find the answers.

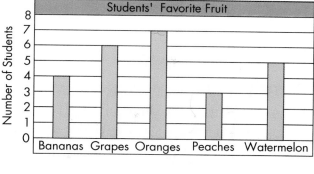
Students' Favorite Fruit

5. Which fruit was the most popular?

6. How many students named watermelon as their favorite fruit?

7. Which activities were chosen by the same number of campers?

8. How many campers voted?

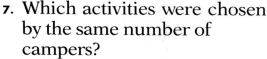
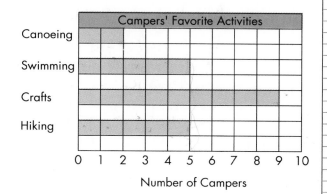
Campers' Favorite Activities

PROBLEM SOLVING

Use the line graph to find the answers.

9. In which month did the team win the most games?

10. In how many months did the team win more than 4 games?

11. How many more games were won in May than in April?

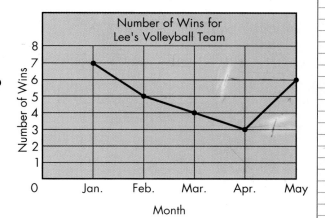
Number of Wins for Lee's Volleyball Team

CUMULATIVE REVIEW

Write the numbers from least to greatest.

12. 98, 101, 89   13. 3261, 1263, 3621   14. 48, 24, 44   15. 601, 603, 600

Write the answer.

16.   37
      + 65

17.   61
      − 35

18. $4.48
     + 0.59

19.   824
      + 96

20. $6.44
     − 2.95

21. $3.27
     + 4.56

EXCURSION

PROBABILITY

NUMBER CUBE EXPERIMENT

In this experiment, you will roll 2 number cubes several times. Each time, you will find the sum of the numbers that turn up.

You will need:

- 2 different colored number cubes, such as a red cube and a white cube

Before you begin, make a chart like the one at the right.

Which sums do you predict will appear most often?

Roll the number cubes. Write a number sentence to show the sum of the two numbers you rolled.

	Red + White = Sum
1.	5 + 2 = 7
2.	

Continue to roll the cubes. Write a number sentence for each roll until you have written 25 number sentences.

	Red + White = Sum
1.	
2.	
3.	
4.	
5.	
6.	
7.	
8.	
9.	
10.	
11.	
12.	
13.	
14.	
15.	
16.	
17.	
18.	
19.	
20.	
21.	
22.	
23.	
24.	
25.	

Now make a table like the one below.
Record the number of times you rolled each
sum. Use tally marks. Then write the tally
number in the Total column.

Sum	Tally	Total
2		
3		
4		
5		
6		
7		
8		
9		
10		
11		
12		

Use your chart and your table to answer each
question.

1. Which sum did you roll
most often?

2. How many ways did you roll
this sum?

3. Which sum did you roll
least often?

4. How many ways did you roll
this sum?

5. What do you notice about the
number of ways you can roll
a sum and how often that sum
is rolled?

6. How do your results compare
with the prediction you made?

CHAPTER 5

MULTIPLICATION AND DIVISION TO 5

Number Sense

Quintuplets Is your house a busy place in the morning? You have to dress, eat breakfast, and maybe catch a bus. If you have brothers and sisters, your house is very busy.

The children in the pictures may have a busier morning than yours. In fact, you could say they are 5 times as busy. They are quintuplets.

Quintuplets are 5 children that were born at the same time. Think of what it would be like to be a quintuplet. Imagine having 5 third-graders living in your house. How do you think your life would be different? Discuss your ideas with your classmates.

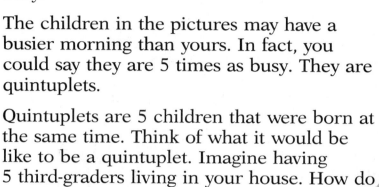

UNDERSTANDING MULTIPLICATION

Groups: partners

You will need: 35 counters

▶ Make 2 sets of counters with 5 counters in each set. The 2 sets are the same size because they have the same number of counters.

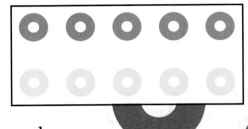

1. Write an addition sentence to show the total number of counters.

▶ Use counters to show 4 sets of 3 counters.

2. Write an addition sentence to show the total number of counters.

3. How many times is the addend repeated in the number sentence?

▶ Now use counters to show 5 sets of 7 counters.

4. Write an addition sentence to show the total number of counters.

5. How many times is the addend repeated in the number sentence?

▶ You can also skip-count to find the total number of counters in sets of the same size. To find the total in 6 sets of 5, skip-count by 5's.

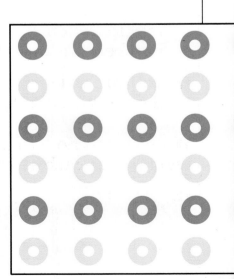

6. How many counters are there in 6 sets of 5?

7. When you skip-counted by 5's, how many number words did you say?

When you need to find the total number in sets of the same size, you can:

- add. 5 + 5 + 5 + 5 + 5 + 5 = 30
- skip-count. 5, 10, 15, 20, 25, 30

You can also **multiply:** $6 \times 5 = 30$.

The multiplication sentence $6 \times 5 = 30$ means *6 sets of 5 equals 30.* You say "6 times 5 equals 30."

8. What do you notice about the number of addends in the addition sentence and the number of sets shown in the multiplication sentence?

9. What do you notice about the number of times you skip-counted and the number of sets shown in the multiplication sentence?

10. In the multiplication sentence $6 \times 5 = 30$, what does the number 6 mean? What does the number 5 mean?

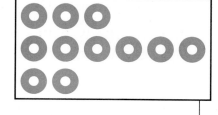

SUMMING IT UP

11. Look at these counters. Can you write a multiplication sentence to show the total number of counters? Why or why not?

12. Can you write an addition sentence for the set? Why or why not?

Write an addition sentence and a multiplication sentence for each set.

13.
14.
15.
16.

MULTIPLYING BY 2

Monica, Jesse, Peter, and Rita want to go on a bicycle ride. All their bicycle tires need air. How many tires do they need to fill?

To find the answer, you can:

- use counters. ⊙⊙ ⊙⊙ ⊙⊙ ⊙⊙

- draw a picture. 🚲 🚲 🚲 🚲

- add. 2 + 2 + 2 + 2 = 8

- skip-count. 2, 4, 6, 8

- multiply. 4 × 2 = 8

You read 4 × 2 = 8 as "four times two equals eight."

$$4 \quad \times \quad 2 \quad = \quad 8$$

factor   factor   product

> The **factors** are the numbers you multiply.
> The **product** is the answer.

They need to fill 8 tires.

Think

- What do the 4 and 2 stand for in the multiplication sentence?

- What would the multiplication sentence be if 3 bicycles needed their tires filled? What would the addition sentence be?

Multiplying by 2 is just like using doubles.

3 + 3 = 6	5 + 5 = 10	4 + 4 = 8
2 × 3 = 6	2 × 5 = 10	2 × 4 = 8
The double of 3 is 6.	The double of 5 is 10.	The double of 4 is 8.

GUIDED PRACTICE

Write the product. Use the picture if you like.

1. 2×2

2. 1×2

3. 2×5

4. 0×2

5. How is multiplying with 2 like adding doubles?

INDEPENDENT PRACTICE

Write the product.

6. How many flowers?

2×3

7. How many chicken legs?

4×2

8. 2×2 **9.** 5×2 **10.** 3×2 **11.** 2×1

Write a multiplication sentence for the addition sentence.

12. $3 + 3 = 6$ **13.** $5 + 5 = 10$ **14.** $1 + 1 = 2$

Problem Solving

15. The children ride 5 miles to the park and then back again. How many miles do they ride in all?

16. Peter and Rita each take 3 fig bars with them on the bicycle ride. They each eat 1. How many fig bars are left?

 • **Mixed Practice**

Write the answer.

1.   54
       $+ 16$

2.   369
       $+ 84$

3. $4.41
       $- 1.18$

4.   777
       $+ 222$

5.   121
       $- 65$

GUESS AND CHECK

> Sometimes you can keep making guesses and checking them until your problem is solved.

> One time, we guessed and checked to help set up a contest for our scout troup.

map $3.00

canvas $6.50

bug spray $4.75

canteen $5.25

stove $5.50

OUR PROBLEM

We wanted first prize to be a box with 2 camping items worth a total of $10.00. We needed to know which of these items to put in the box.

OUR SOLUTION

We started with a guess that was easy to add. Then we checked our guess to see if it was too high, too low, or just right.

So $9.50 was too low. We made another guess to make the total larger. Then we checked our guess. We did not have to find the exact sum. We knew it was too high.

So we made another guess. This time it was just right.

We put the canteen and bug spray in the box for first prize.

> **First guess: canvas and map**
>
> Check: canvas $6.50
>   map   + $3.00
>   total $9.50

> **Second guess: canvas and stove**
>
> Check: canvas $6.50
>   stove   + $5.50
>   total   over $10.00

> **Third guess: canteen and bug spray**
>
> Check: canteen $5.25
>   bug spray   + $4.75
>   total $10.00

GUIDED PRACTICE

Solve the problem. The first guess is done for you.

1. The numbers 1 and 2 come one after another and add up to 3. What two numbers that come one after another add up to 33?

   First guess: 10 and 11
   Check: 10 + 11 = 21

....

APPLICATION

Work in groups. Solve each problem.

2. Ted bought 3 different snacks. He spent 80 cents. What did he buy?

   First guess:
   apple, raisins, popcorn

   Check:
apple	10¢
raisins	25¢
popcorn	+ 40¢
total	75¢

3. Sara has 9 dollars. Each game costs 2 dollars. How many games can she buy?

   First guess: 5 games
   Check: 5 × $2 = $10

4. John paid for 2 slices of pizza with a five-dollar bill. He got $2.60 back in change. How much did each slice cost?

   First guess: $1.00

   Check: $1.00
            1.00
         + 2.60
           $4.60

5. If you add 5 to this mystery number or multiply it by 2, you get the same answer. What is the mystery number?

   First guess: 4
   Check: 4 + 5 = 9
   Does 4 × 2 = 9?

UNDERSTANDING DIVISION

Groups: partners

You will need:
- 30 counters
- recording sheet

One meaning of **division** is sharing.

▶ Suppose you have some peanuts and want to share them equally with a friend. You would separate the peanuts into two equal sets.

Use counters as make-believe peanuts.

1. Separate 12 peanuts into 2 equal sets. How many are in each set?

2. Separate 12 peanuts into 3 equal sets. How many are in each set?

3. Can you separate 12 peanuts into 5 equal sets? Explain.

▶ You will practice separating counters into equal sets. Use your recording sheet. Write the number in each set.

You can show this kind of separating with a division number sentence.

So, **12 ÷ 2 = 6** can mean *12 peanuts separated into 2 equal sets makes 6 peanuts in each set.*

4. Write a division sentence for each row of numbers in the table.

Total number of counters	Number of equal sets	How many in each set?
30	2	
30	3	
30	6	
16	2	
16	4	
16	8	
21	3	
21	7	

Division can also mean grouping.

► Suppose you have saved a lot of pennies and you want to trade them for nickels. You would have to separate all the pennies into sets of 5 pennies. Every set would be equal in value to one nickel.

Use counters as make-believe pennies.

5. How many nickels could you get with 20 pennies?

6. How many nickels could you get with 30 pennies?

7. How many nickels could you get with 27 pennies?

► You will practice separating counters into equal sets. Use your recording sheet. Write the number of equal sets.

You can also show this kind of separating with a division number sentence.

So, **20 ÷ 5 = 4** can mean *20 pennies separated into sets of 5 makes 4 sets.*

8. Write a division sentence for each row of numbers in the table.

Total number of counters	Number in each set	How many equal sets?
30	5	
30	10	
24	4	
24	8	
24	12	
18	3	
18	6	
18	9	

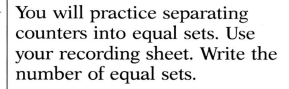

SUMMING IT UP

9. Write in your own words what dividing means to you.

DIVIDING BY 2

There are 10 children at Emma's birthday party. They form groups of 2 to play a game. How many pairs of children are there?

To find the answer, you can:

• use counters.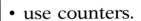

• draw a picture.

• divide. 10 ÷ 2 = 5

You read 10 ÷ 2 = 5 as
"10 divided by 2 equals 5."

| 10 | ÷ | 2 | = | 5 |

dividend · divisor · quotient

There are 5 pairs of children.

> The **dividend** is the number you divide.
> The **divisor** is the number you divide by.
> The **quotient** is the answer.

Think

• What do you think the children would have done if 11 children were at the party?

Half of the 10 children have ice cream with their cake and the other half do not. How many children have ice cream?

When you divide something into 2 equal sets, each set is one half of what you started with.

Divide: 10 ÷ 2 = 5

One half of 10 is 5.

So, 5 children have ice cream with their cake.

GUIDED PRACTICE

Write the quotient.

1. How many bananas in each bunch?

6 ÷ 2

2. How many sets of counters?

10 ÷ 2

3. 8 ÷ 2   4. 2 ÷ 2   5. 4 ÷ 2   6. 2 ÷ 1

7. Draw a picture to show 8 ÷ 2.

INDEPENDENT PRACTICE

Write the quotient.

8. 4 ÷ 2   9. 10 ÷ 2   10. 6 ÷ 2   11. 8 ÷ 2

   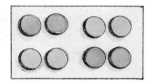

Write a division sentence. Draw a picture if you like.

12. 10 apples shared equally between 2 people

13. 6 socks put into pairs

Problem Solving

14. At Emma's party, 6 of the 10 children want grape juice. Is this more than or less than half of the children?

15. There are 6 children who want to play checkers at the same time. How many checkerboards do they need?

CHALLENGE • Operation Sense

Write a division sentence for the picture. Then write a multiplication sentence for it. Explain what your number sentences mean.

PROBLEM SOLVING

USING STRATEGIES

Ms. Marker is making up a game called Chickers for the Ton-of-Fun Company. It is like checkers but there are fewer squares and the game pieces look like baby chicks.

Help Ms. Marker by solving these problems. Use squared paper.

1. The board for Chickers is 4 squares across and 2 squares down. How many squares are on the whole board?

2. Ms. Marker places two Chickers boards end to end to make a game called Big Chickers.
   a. How many squares across and how many squares down is the Big Chickers board?
   b. How many squares are on the whole board?

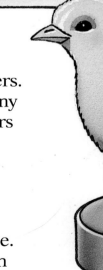

3. Ms. Marker wants to make a Super Chickers game. She decides to make it twice as long and twice as wide as Chickers.
   a. How many squares across and how many squares down is this new Super Chickers board?
   b. How many squares are on the whole board?

4. Ms. Marker wants to make a board with 24 squares. The board must be a rectangle. Draw some of the different boards she can make. Draw as many as you can.

SECTION REVIEW
for pages 142–152

Write the product. Use the picture if you like.

1. 2×3

2. 4×2

3. 2×5

Write the quotient. Use the picture if you like.

4. $8 \div 2$

5. $6 \div 2$

6. $4 \div 2$

Write the answer.

7. 1×2 **8.** $10 \div 2$ **9.** 2×2 **10.** 3×2

Write the letter of the exercise with the same answer.

11. 2×4 **a.** 2×1

12. $1 + 1$ **b.** $6 - 3$

13. $0 + 0 + 0 + 0$ **c.** $5 + 5$

14. $6 \div 2$ **d.** 4×0

15. $10 - 5$ **e.** $4 + 4$

16. 5×2 **f.** $10 \div 2$

Solve each problem.

17. Sam has 8 crackers. He wants to give half of them to Todd. How many crackers should he give to Todd?

18. Maria, Bob, and Carl each pick 2 flowers for their teacher, Mrs. Carter. How many flowers will the children give to Mrs. Carter?

MULTIPLYING AND DIVIDING BY 3

The circus is planning new acts. Each of the 3 trained dogs will need 4 costumes. How many costumes must be made?

You can draw a picture to help you find the answer. The picture below shows 3 sets of 4.

You can also multiply. Multiply the number of dogs times the number of costumes for each dog.

You can write multiplication two ways.

$3 \times 4 = 12$ or

$$\begin{array}{r} 4 \leftarrow \text{factor} \\ \underline{\times\ 3} \leftarrow \text{factor} \\ 12 \leftarrow \text{product} \end{array}$$

So, 12 costumes must be made.

Think

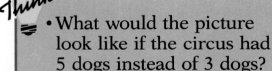

- What would the picture look like if the circus had 5 dogs instead of 3 dogs?

The picture above also fits these division problems.

The circus has 3 tiger cages and 12 tigers. They want to put the same number of tigers in each cage. How many tigers will go in each cage?

$$12 \div 3 = 4$$

There are 12 monkeys dressed as Western settlers. Only 4 monkeys can fit in one stage coach. How many stage coaches are needed for the monkeys?

$$12 \div 4 = 3$$

Write the answer. Use objects or draw a picture if you like.

1. 3 × 2   2. 5 × 3   3. 3 × 3   4. 3 × 1

5. 15 ÷ 3   6. 9 ÷ 3   7. 12 ÷ 3   8. 6 ÷ 3

9. How are exercises 2 and 5 alike?

INDEPENDENT PRACTICE

Write the answer. Use objects or draw a picture if you like.

10. 3 × 3   11. 3 × 4   12. 2 × 3   13. 2 × 2

14. 3   15. 5   16. 3   17. 4   18. 2
   × 1   × 3   × 2   × 3   × 4

19. 12 ÷ 3   20. 6 ÷ 3   21. 15 ÷ 3   22. 9 ÷ 3

Problem Solving

23. At the circus, clowns will squeeze into little cars. Each car will hold 5 clowns. How many cars are needed for 15 clowns?

24. There are 3 clowns that juggle hoops. Each clown juggles 3 hoops. How many hoops do the clowns need for their act?

PROJECT • Arrays

Use squared paper and crayons.

a. Color 3 rows of 4 squares red.
b. Color 4 rows of 2 squares blue.
c. Color 2 rows of 3 squares green.
d. Write a multiplication sentence and a divison sentence for each set of colored squares.

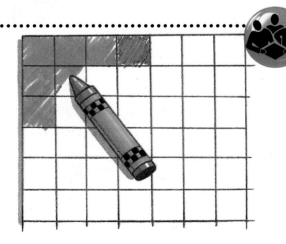

Multiplying and Dividing by 4

▶ The ice show is coming to town. Stella wants to buy a ticket. She plans to save $3 every week for 4 weeks. What is the most expensive ticket she can buy?

You can use repeated addition to find the answer:
$3 + $3 + $3 + $3 = $12.

You can also multiply: 4 × $3.

One way to multiply with 4 is to use doubles two times.

First, double $3: **2** × $3 = $6 or $3 + $3 = $6.

Then double $6: **2** × $6 = $12 or $6 + $6 = $12.

So, **4** × $3 = $12.
Stella can buy a $12 ticket.

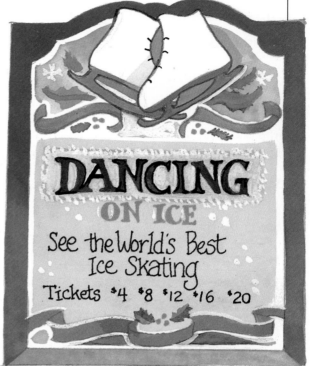

Think

- • How would you use repeated addition to find 4 × 5?

- • How would you use doubles to find 4 × 5?

▶ One way to divide by 4 is to find halves two times.

Divide: 12 ÷ 4

First, find half of 12: 12 ÷ **2** = 6. (You know 6 + 6 = 12.)

Then find half of 6: 6 ÷ **2** = 3. (You know 3 + 3 = 6.)

So, 12 ÷ **4** = 3.

GUIDED PRACTICE

Write the answer.

1. 4×2 2. 5×4 3. 1×4 4. 4×4

5. $8 \div 4$ 6. $16 \div 4$ 7. $20 \div 4$ 8. $12 \div 4$

9. Draw a picture to show 4×4.

INDEPENDENT PRACTICE

Write the answer. Watch the signs.

10. $\begin{array}{r} 4 \\ \times\ 4 \\ \hline \end{array}$ 11. $\begin{array}{r} 5 \\ \times\ 4 \\ \hline \end{array}$ 12. $\begin{array}{r} 5 \\ \times\ 2 \\ \hline \end{array}$ 13. $\begin{array}{r} 2 \\ \times\ 4 \\ \hline \end{array}$ 14. $\begin{array}{r} 3 \\ \times\ 5 \\ \hline \end{array}$

15. $20 \div 4$ 16. $12 \div 4$ 17. $16 \div 4$ 18. $8 \div 4$

Write a multiplication sentence for the addition sentence.

19. $3 + 3 + 3 + 3 = 12$ 20. $5 + 5 + 5 + 5 = 20$ 21. $3 + 3 + 3 = 9$

Problem Solving Remember, some problems
may not have enough information.

22. Mr. Abrams has a $20 bill. He
wants to buy 4 tickets to the
ice show for his family. Which
tickets can he buy? (Look at
the sign on page 156.)

23. Hal is sitting in a section with
5 rows of seats. There are
3 empty seats in the section.
How many seats are filled?

Maintain • Using a Graph

Answer each question. Use the bar graph about ski
tickets on page 419 in the Data Book.

1. What is the greatest cost of a
ski ticket? What is the lowest
cost?

2. What is the difference
between the highest and
lowest costs?

MULTIPLYING AND DIVIDING BY 5

There are 4 teams in the swimming contest. Each team has 5 swimmers. How many swimmers are in the contest?

There are 4 sets of 5. So you can multiply to find the answer: 4×5.

You can use skip-counting to help you multiply.

To find 4×5, skip-count by 5's four times: 5, 10, 15, 20. So, $4 \times 5 = 20$.

There are 20 swimmers in the contest.

You also can use skip-counting to help you divide.

To find $20 \div 5$, skip-count by 5's until you reach 20: 5, 10, 15, 20. You said 4 numbers. So, $20 \div 5 = 4$.

Think

- To what number would you skip-count to find the product of 5×5?

Knowing 1 number sentence can help you know 3 other number sentences.

Since you know: $4 \times 5 = 20$

Then you know: $5 \times 4 = 20$

$20 \div 4 = 5$

$20 \div 5 = 4$

Notice that each number sentence has the same 3 numbers.

The 4 related number sentences are called a **fact family.**

GUIDED PRACTICE

Write the answer. Skip-count if you like.

1. 3×5 **2.** 5×5 **3.** 4×5 **4.** 5×2

5. $25 \div 5$ **6.** $10 \div 5$ **7.** $20 \div 5$ **8.** $15 \div 5$

9. Write a fact family for exercises 4 and 5. What do you notice about the number sentences in exercise 5?

INDEPENDENT PRACTICE

Write the answer.

10.
$$\begin{array}{r} 3 \\ \times\ 5 \\ \hline \end{array}$$

11.
$$\begin{array}{r} 5 \\ \times\ 5 \\ \hline \end{array}$$

12.
$$\begin{array}{r} 5 \\ \times\ 1 \\ \hline \end{array}$$

13.
$$\begin{array}{r} 4 \\ \times\ 2 \\ \hline \end{array}$$

14.
$$\begin{array}{r} 3 \\ \times\ 4 \\ \hline \end{array}$$

15. $20 \div 4$ **16.** $10 \div 5$ **17.** $25 \div 5$ **18.** $16 \div 4$

Copy and complete each fact family.

19. $5 \times 4 = 20$
$4 \times 5 = 20$
$20 \div 4 = 5$

20. $3 \times 5 = 15$
$15 \div 3 = 5$
$5 \times 3 = 15$

21. $16 \div 4 = 4$

22. $12 \div 3 = 4$
$3 \times 4 = 12$
$12 \div 4 = 3$

Problem Solving

23. A diver made 4 dives and scored a total of 20 points. He got the same score on each dive. What was that score?

24. Another diver made 4 dives and scored 20 points. He got a different score on each dive. What could those scores have been?

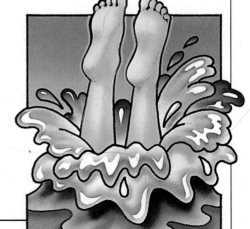

MATH LOG _____

What do you notice about the products when you multiply 5 and an even number? When you multiply 5 and an odd number?

GUESS AND CHECK

Our dinosaur party will be great. I listed the jobs we still have to do.

write name cards — 25 minutes
set table — 10 minutes
wrap favors – 15 minutes
frost cake – 30 minutes
decorate room — 45 minutes
make sandwiches – 35 minutes

When you use guess and check to solve a problem, learn from your guesses. If a guess turns out to be too low, make your next guess higher.

Alan and Amanda want to divide the jobs so they will each spend the same amount of time on them.

The two children decide to use guess and check. They start with this guess:

Jobs for Alan		Jobs for Amanda	
set table	10 minutes	wrap favors	15 minutes
write name cards	25 minutes	frost cake	30 minutes
make sandwiches +	35 minutes	decorate room +	45 minutes
total	70 minutes	total	90 minutes

Look at the 2 ways below to make the next guess.

A. Make Alan's total smaller and Amanda's total greater.	B. Make Alan's total greater and Amanda's total smaller.

Think

- Which way would you use to make the next guess?

- How would you make those changes?

Finish using guess and check to solve the problem.

Read the problem and the first guess. Choose
one of the second guesses. Use it to help you
solve the problem.

1. What 3 numbers that come
   one after another have a sum
   of 33?

   First guess: 7, 8, and 9
   Check: 7 + 8 + 9 = 24, too low

   A. Second guess: 5, 6, and 7   B. Second guess: 10, 11, and 12

APPLICATION

Work in pairs to solve each problem. You can use
guess and check to help you.

2. John bought 3 different items.
   He paid with a $10 bill and
   got $1 in change. What did he
   buy?

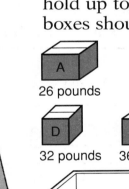

A. $1.25
B. $2.75
C. $4.50
D. GAME
E. $3.25
BOOK $5.25

3. The 6 boxes must be mailed
   in 2 cartons. Each carton can
   hold up to 80 pounds. Which
   boxes should go in each carton?

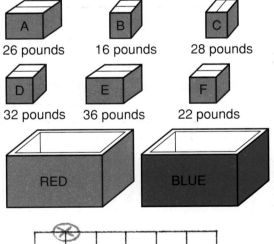

A 26 pounds   B 16 pounds   C 28 pounds

D 32 pounds   E 36 pounds   F 22 pounds

RED   BLUE

4. Mandy puts up posters for the
   circus. The map shows where
   she will put them up. Copy the
   map on squared paper. Show
   the shortest way for Mandy to
   go from the circus to all 3
   places and back to the circus.
   How many blocks is that?

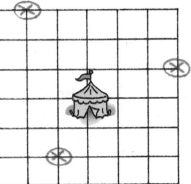

PROPERTIES OF MULTIPLICATION

Groups: partners

You will need:
- 20 counters
- calculator

▶ Show 5 sets of 4 with your counters.

1. Write a multiplication sentence for 5 sets of 4.

Now use the counters to show 4 sets of 5.

2. Write a multiplication sentence for 4 sets of 5.

3. What do you notice about the factors in the two multiplication sentences? What do you notice about the products?

Your results show that *changing the order of the factors does not change the product.* This is called the **order property.**

▶ Use your counters to show 8 sets of 1.

4. Write a multiplication sentence for 8 sets of 1.

Now use your counters to show 1 set of 12.

5. Write a multiplication sentence for 1 set of 12.

6. What do you notice about the factors and the product in each multiplication sentence?

Your results show that *if 1 is a factor, the product always equals the other factor.* This is called the **property of one.**

You do not need counters for the next property. Use a calculator instead. Find each product. Write a multiplication sentence to record your results.

7. 3 × 0   **8.** 0 × 90   **9.** 284 × 0

10. What do you notice about the factors and product in each multiplication sentence?

Your results show that *if 0 is a factor, the product is always equal to 0.* This is called the **zero property.**

Test the multiplication properties. Find the products. Use a calculator for the large numbers.

11. 3 × 2 2 × 3	**12.** 4 × 3 3 × 4	**13.** 9 × 12 12 × 9	**14.** 14 × 25 25 × 14
15. 5 × 1	**16.** 1 × 56	**17.** 1 × 798	**18.** 1842 × 1
19. 0 × 8	**20.** 99 × 0	**21.** 850 × 0	**22.** 0 × 5879

23. Do the properties work?

SUMMING IT UP

24. If 16 × 24 = 384, what is the product of 24 × 16? How do you know?

25. Do you need a calculator to multiply 947 × 1? Why or why not?

26. Without using a calculator, what is the product of 8249 × 0? How do you know?

27. Could you use counters to show 8249 × 0? Explain.

MATH LOG _____

How can the multiplication properties help you multiply?

PROBLEM SOLVING
USING MATH SENSE

If you get stuck, remember...
Tips for Problem Solving
on pages 426–427

Solve each problem. If there is not enough information, tell what you need to know.

1. Avery has $57. Can she buy both the roller skates and the bicycle basket? How do you know?

2. Mrs. Porter is making a quilt with 5 rows. She will sew 5 squares of cloth in each row. Every other square will be red. How many red squares will be in the quilt?

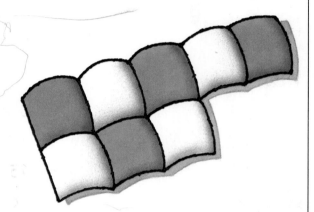

$39

$15

3. Adam has 4 stamps from Canada and 8 stamps from Mexico. How many pages in his stamp book will he need for these stamps?

4. There are 5 rows of seats for people to watch the class play. There are 8 seats in each row. Only 3 of the seats are empty. How many people are watching the play?

Solve each problem. Use the table about the 1988 Olympics on page 419 in the Data Book.

5. Hockey teams get 2 points for each game they win and 1 point for each game they tie. How many points did Sweden get in the 1988 Olympics?

6. How many more points did the first-place team get than the second-place team?

SECTION REVIEW

for pages 154–164

Write the product for each exercise. Draw a picture if you like.

1. 3×4
2. 4×1
3. 5×3
4. 3×5
5. 1×5
6. 2×4
7. 3×3
8. 2×2

Write the multiplication sentence for each exercise.

9. $3 + 3 + 3$
10. $5 + 5 + 5$
11. $2 + 2 + 2 + 2 + 2$
12. $4 + 4 + 4$
13. $1 + 1 + 1$
14. $0 + 0 + 0 + 0$

Write the answer.

15. 4×4
16. 3×5
17. $10 \div 2$
18. 0×5
19. 1×1
20. $20 \div 4$
21. 5×3
22. $15 \div 3$
23. 0×5
24. $8 \div 2$
25. $16 \div 4$
26. $25 \div 5$

Solve each problem.

27. Judy's class is selling pencils at the school fair. They have 15 pencils and they plan to put 3 pencils in each set. How many pencil sets can the class make?

28. Jay sold records at the school fair for $4.00 each. How much money did Jay make if he sold 5 records?

29. Mrs. Dean wants to sell cookies at the fair. She baked 25 cookies and will put 5 in each bag. How many bags will she need?

30. At the fair, 4 rows of seats were set up for a show. There are 5 seats in each row. All the seats are filled except 1. How many seats are filled?

CHAPTER REVIEW

Language Connection

Play Flashlight with your vocabulary words. Here is how to play. One person silently chooses a word. Then the person makes up a sentence with the word in it. The person says the sentence aloud, but says "flashlight" instead of the vocabulary word.

Other students may ask questions if they cannot guess the word. (Their questions must have *yes* or *no* as their answers.)

VOCABULARY WORDS
- factor
- product
- dividend
- divisor
- quotient
- fact family
- order property
- property of one
- zero property

There are only two number sentences in the *flashlight*.

Test ● ● ● ● ● ● ●

Write the product.

1.   5
   × 2

2.   2
   × 3

3.   4
   × 3

4.   3
   × 1

5. 4 × 5

6. 2 × 4

7. 5 × 1

8. 3 × 5

Write the quotient.

9. 8 ÷ 2

10. 4 ÷ 2

11. 15 ÷ 3

12. 9 ÷ 3

13. 4 ÷ 4

14. 12 ÷ 4

15. 20 ÷ 5

16. 10 ÷ 5

Complete each fact family.

17. 2 × 5 = 10
    5 × 2 = 10
    10 ÷ 2 = 5

18. 20 ÷ 4 = 5
    20 ÷ 5 = 4
    5 × 4 = 20

19. 12 ÷ 4 = 3
    3 × 4 = 12
    12 ÷ 3 = 4

20. 2 × 3 = 6
    6 ÷ 3 = 2
    3 × 2 = 6

PROBLEM SOLVING

Solve each problem.

21. Marcia and Pat each take 3 cans of juice to their picnic. They each drink 1 can of juice. How many cans of juice are left?

22. Diego buys 3 rulers with a five-dollar bill. He gets $2.00 in change. How much does each ruler cost?

23. At the circus, clowns ride in wagons. Each wagon holds 2 clowns. How many wagons are needed for 10 clowns?

24. There are 4 shelves in Sandy's bookcase. Each shelf has 4 books. How many books are in the bookcase?

CUMULATIVE REVIEW

Write the difference.

25.　$4.05
　　− 2.65

26.　808
　　− 279

27.　499
　　− 269

28.　$7.83
　　− 5.90

29. $9.07 − $6.31　　30. 600 − 193　　31. $8.01 − $4.79　　32. 700 − 138

Use the pictograph to find the answer.

33. How many apples are there in Bowl 3?

34. Which bowl has the most apples?

35. How many more apples are there in Bowl 1 than in Bowl 2?

36. How many apples are there in all?

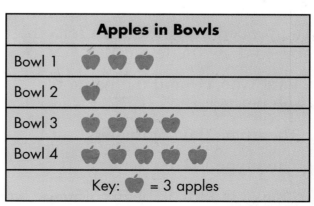

EXCURSION
USING TECHNOLOGY

LOGO

You will need Logo software, a computer, and squared paper.

You use special commands to tell the Logo turtle how to move. Here are some of these commands.

Logo Command	What you type	What the turtle will do	
FORWARD 5	FD 5	move forward 5 steps	↑
BACK 9	BK 9	move back 9 steps	
RIGHT 45	RT 45	turn this far to the right	
RIGHT 90	RT 90	turn this far to the right	
LEFT 45	LT 45	turn this far to the left	
LEFT 90	LT 90	turn this far to the left	

You can write a procedure to tell the turtle what to draw. **A procedure** is a list of commands that tells the turtle how to move. The procedure at the right tells the turtle how to draw the letter *Y*.

- First type TO and the name of the procedure.

- Then type the commands.

- Then type END.

To make the turtle begin drawing, you must type DRAW and the name of the procedure.

TO Y

FD 15 ↑

RT 45

FD 10

BK 10

LT 90

FD 10

END

DRAW Y

1. Look at the procedure at the right. Predict what the turtle will draw. Draw your prediction on squared paper. Type in the procedure. Tell the turtle to DRAW PICTURE to check your prediction.

```
TO PICTURE
FD 70
RT 90
FD 30
RT 90
FD 20
RT 90
FD 30
END
```

2. Look at the turtle drawing below. Type in the procedure. Fill in the commands that are missing. Then tell the turtle to DRAW ZIGZAG.

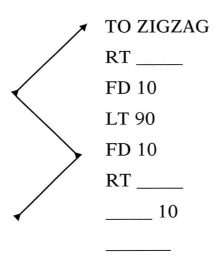

```
TO ZIGZAG
RT _____
FD 10
LT 90
FD 10
RT _____
_____ 10
_____
```

3. Write a procedure to draw a square. Call the procedure BOX. Make the sides of the square 40 turtle steps long. Then tell the turtle to DRAW BOX.

4. Think of another shape. Write a procedure to draw that shape. Type in your procedure. Tell the turtle to draw the shape.

MULTIPLICATION AND DIVISION TO 9

Connections

Physical Education

Baseball Numbers A baseball game uses lots of numbers. The game lasts 9 innings. There are 9 players on the field at one time. Players wear numbers on their shirts. Umpires count balls and strikes. The scoreboard keeps track of all these numbers.

A game lasts about 3 hours. Each team gets 3 outs in an inning. How many outs does each team get in a 9-inning game?

Sometimes a game lasts more than 9 innings. In fact, the game may go on and on until there is a winner. The scoreboard below shows a game that lasted for 18 innings. It was twice as long as a normal game. How many outs did each team get in the game? How long do you think it took to finish the game?

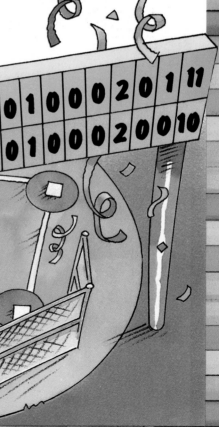

| VISITORS | 0 | 1 | 1 | 0 | 2 | 0 | 1 | 2 | 0 | 0 | 0 | 1 | 0 | 0 | 0 | 2 | 0 | 1 | 11 |
| HOME | 0 | 0 | 0 | 0 | 1 | 0 | 0 | 1 | 2 | 3 | 0 | 1 | 0 | 0 | 0 | 2 | 0 | 0 | 10 |

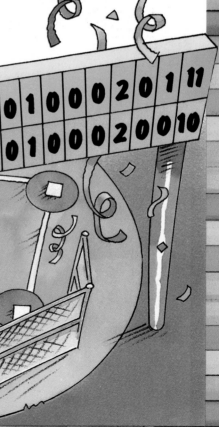

MULTIPLICATION AND DIVISION

At a picnic, Melissa sees 5 tables. Every table has the same number of pitchers of lemonade. There are 20 pitchers in all. How many pitchers of lemonade are on each table?

You can think of this division problem as a multiplication sentence with a **missing factor.**

$$20 \div 5 = \blacksquare$$

asks the same question as

$$5 \times \blacksquare = 20$$

$$\uparrow$$

missing factor

The multiplication fact $5 \times 4 = 20$ helps you solve the division problem. So, $20 \div 5 = 4$.

There are 4 pitchers of lemonade on each table.

Think

• Do you think $20 \div 5 = \blacksquare$ asks the same question as $\blacksquare \times 5 = 20$? Why or why not?

Other Examples

$$16 \div 4 = \blacksquare$$

asks the same question as

$$\blacksquare \times 4 = 16$$

or

$$4 \times \blacksquare = 16$$

$$2 \times \blacksquare = 18$$

asks the same question as

$$18 \div 2 = \blacksquare$$

GUIDED PRACTICE

Write the missing factor.

1. ■ × 4 = 8 **2.** 3 × ■ = 12 **3.** 5 × ■ = 25

Write a multiplication sentence that asks the same question.

4. 12 ÷ 2 = ■ **5.** 20 ÷ 4 = ■ **6.** 4 ÷ 2 = 2

7. Does it matter if the missing factor is written first or second in the multiplication sentence? Why or why not?

INDEPENDENT PRACTICE

Write the missing factor.

8. 2 × ■ = 10 **9.** ■ × 3 = 6 **10.** 4 × ■ = 12

Write a multiplication sentence that asks the same question.

11. 8 ÷ 4 = ■ **12.** 9 ÷ 3 = ■ **13.** 15 ÷ 3 = ■

Problem Solving

14. Melissa is helping to set the 5 tables. She will put 3 baskets of bread on each table. How many baskets of bread does she need?

15. There are 16 people who want to play badminton. If 4 people play at each net, how many nets will they need to set up?

CHALLENGE • Problem Formulation

Write a word problem about the children at the table. Write either a multiplication or division sentence to solve the problem. Then give your problem to a friend to solve.

RULES FOR DIVISION

These division rules may help you divide more easily and quickly.

Groups: partners

You will need: calculator

> **Remember:**
> The quotient is the answer when you divide.

▶ Use a calculator to divide. Record the quotient.

1. $1 \div 1$
2. $5 \div 5$
3. $17 \div 17$
4. $999 \div 999$

5. What do you notice about the quotients?

6. What do you notice about the numbers in each example?

The pattern you see shows the rule about *dividing a number by itself.*

▶ Use a calculator to divide. Record the quotient.

7. $3 \div 1$
8. $8 \div 1$
9. $56 \div 1$
10. $100 \div 1$

11. What do you notice about each quotient?

The pattern you see shows the rule about *dividing a number by 1.*

▶ Use a calculator to divide. Record the quotient.

12. $0 \div 2$
13. $0 \div 7$
14. $0 \div 22$
15. $0 \div 401$

16. What is the quotient each time you divide zero by a number?

The pattern you see shows the rule about *dividing zero by a number.*

You cannot divide a number by zero. Use a calculator to see what happens when you try. Look carefully at the calculator display.

17. $9 \div 0$ **18.** $13 \div 0$ **19.** $42 \div 0$ **20.** $834 \div 0$

21. What do you notice about the calculator display? Did other students get the same display?

SUMMING IT UP

22. What do you know about dividing a number by itself? Give an example.

23. What do you know about dividing a number by 1? Give an example.

24. What do you know about dividing zero by a number? Give an example.

25. What do you know about dividing a number by zero?

Predict the quotient. Then use a calculator to check your prediction.

26. $25 \div 25$ **27.** $629 \div 1$ **28.** $0 \div 18$ **29.** $234 \div 0$

30. $17 \div 0$ **31.** $0 \div 2$ **32.** $543 \div 1$ **33.** $709 \div 709$

MATH LOG
How can the division rules help you divide?

MAKING A MULTIPLICATION TABLE

Groups: small groups

You will need: recording sheet for each student

Look at the multiplication table at the right. The blue numbers are factors. The squares in the middle are for products.

	1	2	3	4	5	6	7	8	9	10
1										
2					10					
3										
4										
5		10								
6										
7										
8										
9										
10										

▶ Find the 2 in the top row of factors. With your finger, trace down the 2's column until you reach the 5's row. You will see a 10 in the square. This is because $5 \times 2 = 10$.

1. What are the factors for the other product of 10 on the table?

2. Are there any other squares which should have a 10 written in them? Which ones?

▶ Fill in as much of the multiplication table as you can. The following questions may help you.

3. What is the product of 1 and any number?

4. How does knowing the product of 2×3 help you find the product of 3×2?

5. How can skip-counting help you find a product? Give an example.

6. How can adding help you find a product? Give an example.

▶ Look at your table when you have filled in as much as you can. Read the numbers across. Then read them down.

7. What patterns do you see when reading across? What patterns do you see when reading down?

8. Can these patterns help you fill in more of the table? Explain.

Now try to fill in some more of the missing products.

SUMMING IT UP

Compare your tables with another group's tables. Discuss how you found the products.

9. Were you able to fill in any squares with a product greater than 25? How were you able to do it?

10. Describe two patterns you found in the table.

11. Which columns or rows were easier to fill in?

12. Which columns or rows were more difficult? How did you fill in the more difficult ones?

PROJECT • Operation Sense

Choose three products from your multiplication table. Write them down. Trade papers with a friend.

Write all the pairs of factors you can think of for each of the three products. Compare these pairs of factors and their products to the ones on your multiplication table. Do they match? Explain.

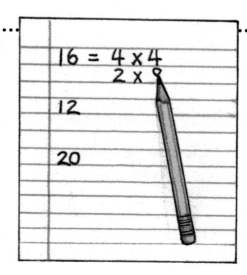

MAKE A PLAN

Sometimes it takes more than one step to solve a problem. You can make a plan to help you keep track of the steps.

One time, we made a plan to get ready for a class party

OUR PROBLEM

We had 3 full packages of party hats. Each package had 5 hats. We also had one open package with 4 hats in it. We wanted to know how many hats we had.

OUR SOLUTION

We thought of a plan. It had 2 steps.

Step 1: Find how many hats are in the full packages. Multiply: $3 \times 5 = 15$.

Step 2: Find how many hats there are altogether. Add: $15 + 4 = 19$.

So, we had 19 hats altogether.

Complete the plan and use it to solve the problem.

1. Lucy has 3 sheets of baseball stickers. Each sheet has 4 stickers on it. She gives 2 of the stickers to Meg. How many stickers does Lucy have left?

   Step 1: Find how many stickers Lucy has before she gives 2 away.
   Multiply: $3 \times 4 = 12$.

   Step 2:

....

APPLICATION

Complete the plan and solve each problem.
Work in groups.

2. Pam has 9 pennies and 3 nickels. How much money will she have left if she buys a pencil for 17¢?

   Step 1: Find how much money Pam has now.
   Multiply: $3 \times 5¢ = 15¢$.
   Add: $15¢ + 9¢ = 24¢$.

   Step 2:

3. Luis needs to make 6 puppets for a class show. He can make 2 puppets in 1 hour. If he starts at 2:00, when will he finish making the 6 puppets?

   Step 1: Find how many hours it will take Luis to make 6 puppets.

   Step 2:

4. Tickets to the zoo cost $5 for each adult and $2 for each child. How much will tickets cost for Ms. Beane and 4 children?

   Step 1: Find the cost of 4 children's tickets.

   Step 2:

MULTIPLYING AND DIVIDING BY 6

At the Old Toy Museum, Toby sees the rag doll collection. There are 6 shelves with 5 rag dolls on each shelf. How many rag dolls are there?

You can count or skip-count to find out how many rag dolls there are.

To save time, you can multiply. Multiply the number of shelves times the number of dolls on each shelf: $6 \times 5 = 30$.

Another way to multiply with 6 is to use doubles: 6 is the double of 3.

Use what you know: **$3 \times 5 = 15.$**

Then double 15: $15 + 15 = 30$.

So, **$6 \times 5 = 30$**.

There are 30 rag dolls.

> **Remember, another way to write this is:**
> $$\begin{array}{r} 5 \\ \times\, 6 \\ \hline 30 \end{array}$$

Think

- How can knowing the product of 3×4 help you find the product of 6×4?

Since you know: $6 \times 5 = 30$

Then you know: $5 \times 6 = 30$

$30 \div 6 = 5$

$30 \div 5 = 6$

> **These four number sentences are related. They belong to the same fact family.**

Write the answer.

1. 6×2
2. 4×6
3. 6×6
4. 9×6
5. $18 \div 6$
6. $42 \div 6$
7. $48 \div 6$
8. $6 \div 6$

9. Write a fact family for exercises 4 and 5.

INDEPENDENT PRACTICE

Write the answer.

10. $\begin{array}{r} 1 \\ \times\ 6 \\ \hline \end{array}$
11. $\begin{array}{r} 6 \\ \times\ 5 \\ \hline \end{array}$
12. $\begin{array}{r} 6 \\ \times\ 8 \\ \hline \end{array}$
13. $\begin{array}{r} 3 \\ \times\ 6 \\ \hline \end{array}$
14. $\begin{array}{r} 7 \\ \times\ 6 \\ \hline \end{array}$

15. $12 \div 6$
16. $6 \div 1$
17. $36 \div 6$
18. $54 \div 6$

Write the missing factor.

19. $3 \times \blacksquare = 18$
20. $6 \times \blacksquare = 0$
21. $6 \times \blacksquare = 36$

22. Fill in your multiplication table with any new facts you have learned. If your table is filled, check the products.

Problem Solving

23. On Tuesday, 36 third-graders visit the Old Toy Museum. They get into 6 equal groups. Can there be 7 third graders in each group? Why or why not?

24. At the museum, Toby buys 3 packs of postcards. There are 6 postcards in each pack. How many postcards did Toby buy?

Maintain • Mixed Practice

Write the answer. Use mental math when you can.

1. $72 + 19 + 33$
2. $\$3.04 + \$6.29 + \$4.81$
3. $500 + 200 + 100$
4. $\$9.00 - \$0.50$
5. $408 - 129$
6. $653 - 53$

MULTIPLYING AND DIVIDING BY 7

The Heels and Toes Dance School is getting ready to put on a show. All the tap dancers are practicing the cakewalk on stage. There are 7 rows of dancers. In each row there are 9 dancers. How many tap dancers are there?

You can multiply to find the answer.

Multiply the number of rows times the number of dancers in each row:
$$7 \times 9 = 63.$$

There are 63 tap dancers.

Think

- If you know that $6 \times 7 = 42$, how can you use addition to find the product of 7×7?

There are two ways to show division.

$$63 \div 7 = 9 \quad \text{or} \quad 7\overline{)63}$$

dividend   divisor   quotient   divisor

quotient   dividend

GUIDED PRACTICE

Write the answer.

1. 3×7
2. 7×7
3. $14 \div 7$
4. $28 \div 7$

5. $\begin{array}{r} 5 \\ \times\, 7 \end{array}$
6. $\begin{array}{r} 7 \\ \times\, 8 \end{array}$
7. $\begin{array}{r} 4 \\ \times\, 7 \end{array}$
8. $7\overline{)42}$
9. $7\overline{)63}$

10. Write a fact family for exercise 2. Why are there only two number sentences in the fact family?

INDEPENDENT PRACTICE

Write the answer.

11.   7
       × 2

12.   6
       × 7

13.   7
       × 9

14. 7)56

15. 7)49

16. 6 × 6   **17.** 7 × 0   **18.** 7 ÷ 7   **19.** 24 ÷ 6

Write two division sentences that belong to the same fact family.

20. 7 × 8 = 56   **21.** 7 × 1 = 7   **22.** 4 × 5 = 20

Write a multiplication sentence and a division sentence for the picture.

23.    **24.**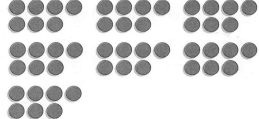

25. Fill in your multiplication table with any new facts you have learned. If your table is filled, check the products.

Problem Solving

26. The dance school has 7 rows of 8 seats on the main floor. All the seats are filled except 1. How many people are seated on the main floor?

27. There are 5 rows of ballet dancers on the stage. There are 4 dancers in each row. One of the rows dances off. How many dancers are left?

28. Curtis had 20 tickets for the dance show. He sold 7 to his family and some to friends. He has 5 left. How many did he sell to friends?

29. There are 3 dancers who face the audience. They each turn all the way around 4 times. Which way are they facing now?

CALCULATOR OR MENTAL MATH

The calculator is a great tool to help you compute. But sometimes it is faster and easier to compute mentally.

Before you solve a problem, think about whether to use a calculator or mental math.

Here are some questions to ask yourself:

• Can I quickly compute in my head?

• Will entering the problem into a calculator take too much time?

....

INDEPENDENT PRACTICE

Write the answer. Write whether you used a calculator or mental math.

1. $600 + 300$ 2. 125×4 3. 50×2 4. $479 + 368$ 5. 78×1

6. $400 - 100$ 7. $350 \div 1$ 8. $348 \div 4$ 9. $400 \div 2$ 10. $189 \div 9$

Problem Solving Use a calculator or mental math.

11. Dan works 2 hours a day mowing lawns. He worked 10 days last month. How many hours did he work?

12. Mitzi buys supplies for a party. She buys paper plates for $2.78, napkins for $1.86, and cups for $1.53. How much money does she spend?

13. Jenny buys Ted a set of cars for $12. She also buys a birthday card for $1. How much does Jenny spend?

14. Which problems did you solve with a calculator? Which did you solve using mental math?

SECTION REVIEW

for pages 172–184

Write the answer. Draw a picture if you like.

1. 9×6

2. 7×8

3. 7×3

4. 6×5

5. $35 \div 5$

6. $18 \div 6$

7. $28 \div 4$

8. $7 \div 1$

9. $\begin{array}{r} 6 \\ \times\ 6 \\ \hline \end{array}$

10. $\begin{array}{r} 9 \\ \times\ 7 \\ \hline \end{array}$

11. $\begin{array}{r} 2 \\ \times\ 6 \\ \hline \end{array}$

12. $\begin{array}{r} 6 \\ \times\ 7 \\ \hline \end{array}$

13. $\begin{array}{r} 6 \\ \times\ 8 \\ \hline \end{array}$

14. $7\overline{)14}$

15. $6\overline{)48}$

16. $7\overline{)49}$

17. $3\overline{)18}$

18. $7\overline{)56}$

Write a multiplication sentence that asks the same question.

19. $63 \div 7 = \blacksquare$

20. $42 \div 6 = \blacksquare$

21. $54 \div 6 = \blacksquare$

22. $18 \div 6 = \blacksquare$

23. $14 \div 2 = \blacksquare$

24. $35 \div 7 = \blacksquare$

Complete. Write the missing factor.

25. $4 \times \blacksquare = 28$

26. $\blacksquare \times 5 = 30$

27. $\blacksquare \times 3 = 21$

28. $6 \times \blacksquare = 0$

29. $7 \times \blacksquare = 63$

30. $7 \times \blacksquare = 56$

Solve each problem.

31. Josie's grandmother plans to travel for 35 days. How many weeks will she be traveling?

32. Mona wants to sell stickers for 7¢ each. How much will 9 stickers cost?

33. Danny collects 54 eggs. He wants to put them in boxes that hold 6 eggs. How many boxes will he need for the eggs?

34. Allen needs 50¢ in stamps to mail a letter to his pen pal. He has only 6¢ stamps. How many of the stamps will he need to mail the letter?

MULTIPLYING AND DIVIDING BY 8

The 8 members of the Model
Spaceship Club display their
model spaceships in a show.
Each club member displays
5 models. How many models
does the club display?

You can multiply to find the answer.

Multiply the number of members
times the number of models each
member displays:

$$8 \times 5 = 40$$

Another way to multiply with 8 is
to use doubles: 8 is the double of 4.

Use what you know: **4 × 5 = 20.**

Then double 20: 20 + 20 = 40.

So, **8 × 5 = 40.**

The club displays 40 model
spaceships.

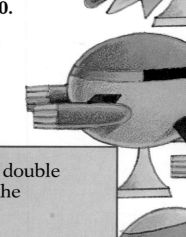

Think

• How many times would you double
the product of 2 × 5 to get the
product of 8 × 5?

GUIDED PRACTICE

Write the answer.

1. 8 × 2   2. 4 × 8   3. 8 × 8   4. 9 × 8

5. 40 ÷ 8   6. 56 ÷ 8   7. 24 ÷ 8   8. 8 ÷ 1

9. Write a fact family for exercises 4 and 6.

INDEPENDENT PRACTICE

Write the answer.

10. $\begin{array}{r} 3 \\ \times\ 8 \\ \hline \end{array}$
11. $\begin{array}{r} 8 \\ \times\ 7 \\ \hline \end{array}$
12. $\begin{array}{r} 1 \\ \times\ 8 \\ \hline \end{array}$
13. $\begin{array}{r} 8 \\ \times\ 6 \\ \hline \end{array}$
14. $\begin{array}{r} 8 \\ \times\ 8 \\ \hline \end{array}$

15. $5\overline{)40}$
16. $8\overline{)64}$
17. $2\overline{)16}$
18. $8\overline{)72}$
19. $8\overline{)32}$

20. 5×8
21. 5×7
22. $25 \div 5$
23. $24 \div 3$

Copy and complete.

24. $8 \times 6 = \blacksquare$
$\blacksquare \times 8 = 48$
$48 \div \blacksquare = 6$
$\blacksquare \div 6 = 8$

25. $9 \times 8 = \blacksquare$
$8 \times \blacksquare = 72$
$\blacksquare \div 9 = 8$
$72 \div \blacksquare = 9$

26. $3 \times 8 = \blacksquare$
$8 \times 3 = \blacksquare$
$24 \div \blacksquare = 8$
$24 \div \blacksquare = 3$

27. $8 \times \blacksquare = 0$
$\blacksquare \times 8 = 0$
$0 \div 8 = \blacksquare$
$\blacksquare \div 8 = 0$

Draw a picture for the number sentence.

28. $8 \times 4 = 32$

29. $16 \div 8 = 2$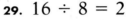

30. Fill in your multiplication table with any new facts that you have learned. If your table is filled, check the products.

Problem Solving

31. The members of the Model Spaceship Club go to the Air and Space Museum. The 8 tickets cost $32. How much does each ticket cost?

32. Rajiv built a model space station. He worked 2 hours each day from Monday to Friday. He worked 5 hours on Saturday. How many hours did he work?

....

Maintain • Place Value

Write the value of the digit 8.

1. 18
2. 802
3. 387
4. 6283
5. 8096

MULTIPLYING AND DIVIDING BY 9

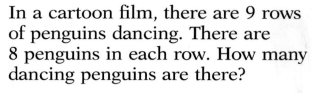

In a cartoon film, there are 9 rows of penguins dancing. There are 8 penguins in each row. How many dancing penguins are there?

You can multiply to find the answer.

Multiply the number of rows times the number of penguins in each row:
$$9 \times 8 = 72.$$

There are 72 dancing penguins.

Think

• How could you use the fact $10 \times 7 = 70$ to find the product of 9×7?

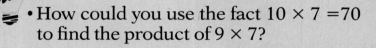

GUIDED PRACTICE

Write the answer.

1. 9×1 2. 4×9 3. 9×9 4. 7×9

5. $27 \div 9$ 6. $18 \div 9$ 7. $72 \div 9$ 8. $45 \div 9$

Write a fact family for each set of numbers.

9. 2, 9, 18   10. 4, 9, 36   11. 7, 9, 63   12. 6, 9, 54

13. Fill in your multiplication table with any new facts that you have learned. If your table is filled, check the products.

INDEPENDENT PRACTICE

Write the answer.

14.   3
    × 9

15.   9
    × 6

16.   2
    × 9

17.   8
    × 9

18.   7
    × 8

19. 9)81

20. 9)63

21. 5)45

22. 7)42

23. 9)54

24. 9 × 5

25. 9 × 6

26. 36 ÷ 9

27. 64 ÷ 8

Copy and complete.

28. 9 × 5 = ▧
    5 × ▧ = 45
    45 ÷ 9 = ▧
    ▧ ÷ 5 = 9

29. ▧ × 9 = 27
    9 × 3 = ▧
    ▧ ÷ 9 = 3
    27 ÷ 3 = ▧

30. 9 × ▧ = 9
    1 × ▧ = 9
    9 ÷ ▧ = 1
    9 ÷ ▧ = 9

31. 9 × 9 = ▧
    ▧ × 9 = 81
    81 ÷ 9 = ▧
    ▧ ÷ 9 = 9

Problem Solving

32. It takes 24 pictures to make 1 second of a cartoon film. How many pictures does it take to make 2 seconds of a cartoon?

33. The only colors used to make a cartoon picture are yellow, blue, and red. How many colors are used to make 10 pictures?

34. Use the Meatball Casserole recipe on page 423 in the Data Book. How many potatoes would you need if you were serving 12 people?

•••

PROJECT • Multiplication Patterns

Write multiplication facts using the factor 9. Begin with 1 × 9 and end with 9 × 9.

Add the digits in each product. What pattern do you see?

What pattern do you see in the ones digits of the products?

What other patterns do you see?

$1 × 9 = 9$

$2 × 9 = 18$

$3 × 9$

PROBLEM SOLVING STRATEGY
MAKE A PLAN

Before you make a plan, be sure you understand the problem. Your plan should fit the problem.

Joe wants to buy 3 books that cost $8 each. He has saved $18. How much more money does he need to buy all 3 books?

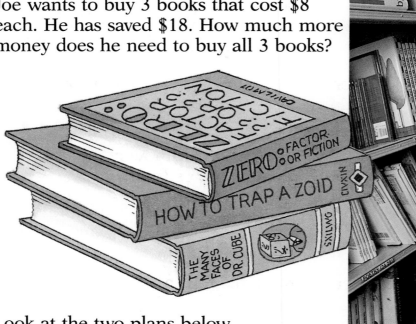

Look at the two plans below.

Plan A	Plan B
Step 1: Find how much money Joe will have if he saves another $8.	**Step 1:** Find how much all 3 books cost.
Step 2: Find how much he will have left after he buys all 3 books.	**Step 2:** Find the difference between the cost of 3 books and $18.

Think

• Which plan would you choose to solve the problem? Why?

Use the plan you chose to solve the problem.

GUIDED PRACTICE

Read the problem. Use one of the plans to solve the problem.

1. The 9 boys in Gerald's scout troop are painting model cars. The boys will paint 15 blue cars and 30 red cars. Each boy will paint an equal number of cars. How many cars will each boy paint?

Plan A

Step 1: Find the total number of cars the boys will paint.

Step 2: Find the number of cars each boy will paint.

Plan B

Step 1: Find how many more red cars than blue cars the boys will paint.

Step 2: Find how many extra cars there will be.

APPLICATION

Work with a group to solve each problem. Make a plan to show your steps.

2. In a two-day contest, Ms. Deng's class scored 77 points on the first day and 21 points on the second day. Ms. Lopez's class scored a total of 85 points in the two days. Which class won the contest? By how many points did they win?

3. Alan plants 5 rows of tomatoes. There are 8 tomato plants in each row. Half of the plants are cherry tomatoes and the other half are large tomatoes. How many cherry tomatoes does he plant?

4. Greg makes jewelry from shells he finds on the beach. He can make 3 shell necklaces in an hour. If he works from 2:00 to 6:00, how many necklaces can he make?

5. Felice had 2 quarters, 3 dimes, and 1 nickel in her pocket. On the way to the store, some of the money fell out of her pocket. She had 40¢ left when she got to the store. How much money did she lose?

PATTERNS IN MULTIPLICATION

Groups: small groups

You will need: place-value blocks

With your ones blocks, make 4 sets of 2 blocks.

1. How many ones in all do you have? Leave the blocks on your work space.

Use your tens blocks and hundreds blocks. Show 4 sets of 2 tens and 4 sets of 2 hundreds.

2. How many tens do you have? Write the number your tens blocks show.

3. How many hundreds do you have? Write the number your hundreds blocks show.

4. Copy and complete these 3 multiplication sentences to show what you have done with your blocks.

$4 \times 2 = $ ▓ $4 \times 20 = $ ▓ $4 \times 200 = $ ▓

5. What is the same about the 3 multiplication sentences? What is different?

Use your blocks to make the sets below. Then copy and complete the multiplication sentences.

6. 3 sets of 4 ones
   3 sets of 4 tens
   3 sets of 4 hundreds

   $3 \times 4 = $ ▓
   $3 \times 40 = $ ▓
   $3 \times 400 = $ ▓

7. 1 set of 3 ones
   1 set of 3 tens
   1 set of 3 hundreds

   $1 \times 3 = $ ▓
   $1 \times 30 = $ ▓
   $1 \times 300 = $ ▓

8. 2 sets of 5 ones
   2 sets of 5 tens
   2 sets of 5 hundreds

   $2 \times 5 = $ ▓
   $2 \times 50 = $ ▓
   $2 \times 500 = $ ▓

9. What patterns do you see in the multiplication sentences in exercises 6–8?

Predict each product. Use the patterns to help you.
Use place-value blocks to check your predictions.

10. $2 \times 2 = $ ▨
$2 \times 20 = $ ▨
$2 \times 200 = $ ▨

11. $5 \times 1 = $ ▨
$5 \times 10 = $ ▨
$5 \times 100 = $ ▨

12. $4 \times 5 = $ ▨
$4 \times 50 = $ ▨
$4 \times 500 = $ ▨

Use the patterns to find each product.

13. 3×20

14. 4×10

15. 3×30

16. 2×400

17. 2×300

18. 4×300

19. 5×20

20. 3×50

21. 6×100

SUMMING IT UP

22. Does the product always have the same number of zeros as the factors? Why or why not?

23. Write a rule that would help someone to multiply tens and hundreds mentally. Share your rule with the class.

PROJECT • Game

Play this game with a partner.

a. Make cards like the ones shown. Make 4 of each.

b. Make money cards like the ones shown. Make 4 of each.

c. Place the 2 decks face down. Each player takes 1 card from each deck and multiplies the 2 amounts.

d. The player with the greater product keeps all 4 cards. If the products are the same, each player keeps the 2 cards.

e. Play until the deck is gone. The player with the most cards wins.

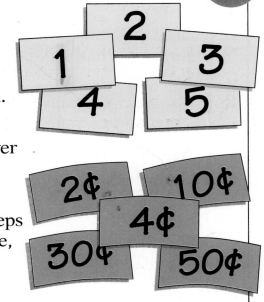

PATTERNS IN DIVISION

Groups: small groups

You will need: place-value blocks

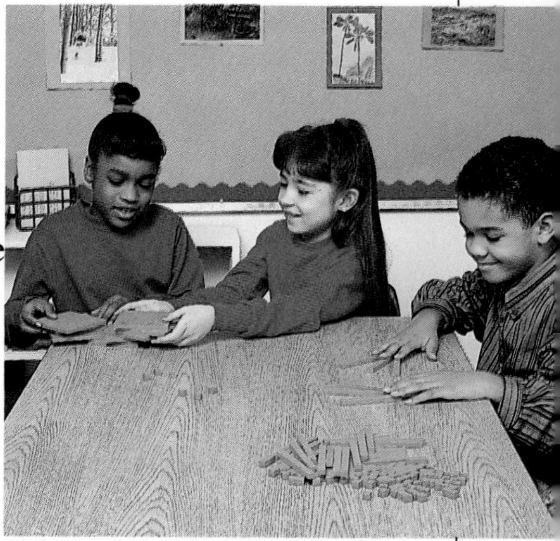

Take 6 ones blocks and separate them into 2 equal sets.

1. How many ones are in each set? Leave the ones on your work space.

Take 6 tens and separate them into 2 equal sets.

2. How many tens are in each set? Write the number your blocks show in each set.

Then take 6 hundreds and separate them into 2 equal sets.

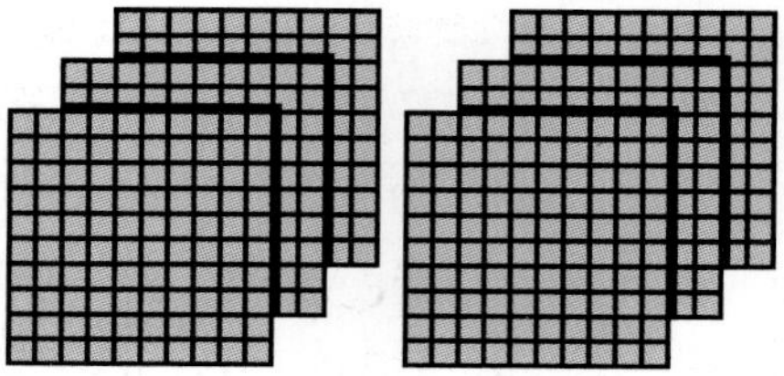

3. How many hundreds are in each set? Write the number your blocks show in each set.

4. Copy and complete these 3 division sentences to show what you have done with your blocks.

   6 ÷ 2 =
   60 ÷ 2 =
   600 ÷ 2 =

5. What is the same about the 3 division sentences? What is different?

Use your blocks to make the sets below. Then copy and complete the division sentences.

6. 12 ones in 2 sets
   12 tens in 2 sets
   12 hundreds in 2 sets
   12 ÷ 2
   120 ÷ 2 =
   1200 ÷ 2 =

7. 2 ones in 1 set
   2 tens in 1 set
   2 hundreds in 1 set
   2 ÷ 1 =
   20 ÷ 1 =
   200 ÷ 1 =

8. 20 ones in 5 sets
   20 tens in 5 sets
   20 hundreds in 5 sets
   20 ÷ 5 =
   200 ÷ 5 =
   2000 ÷ 5 =

9. What patterns do you see in the division sentences in exercises 6–8?

Predict each quotient. Use the patterns to help you.
Use place-value blocks to check your predictions.

10. $6 \div 1 = $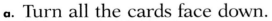
$60 \div 1 = $
$600 \div 1 = $

11. $21 \div 7 = $
$210 \div 7 = $
$2100 \div 7 = $

12. $30 \div 6 = $
$300 \div 6 = $
$3000 \div 6 = $

Use the patterns to find each quotient.

13. $50 \div 5$

14. $60 \div 6$

15. $800 \div 8$

16. $400 \div 4$

17. $60 \div 3$

18. $80 \div 2$

19. $400 \div 2$

20. $100 \div 5$

21. $150 \div 3$

SUMMING IT UP

22. Are there always the same number of zeros in the quotient as there are in the dividend? Why or why not?

> **Remember:**
> dividend ÷ divisor = quotient

23. Write a rule that would help someone to divide tens and hundreds mentally. Share your rule with the class.

PROJECT • Game

Play this game with a partner.
Make a set of cards like the ones shown at the right.

a. Turn all the cards face down.
b. Each player chooses a card and gives the answer.
c. The player with the greater quotient keeps both cards. If the quotients are equal, the players keep their own cards.
d. Repeat steps b and c until all cards are gone. The player with more cards wins.

$40 \div 2$	$80 \div 4$	$100 \div 4$
$120 \div 3$	$70 \div 7$	$60 \div 2$
$300 \div 3$	$350 \div 5$	$150 \div 3$
$80 \div 2$	$90 \div 3$	$240 \div 4$
$600 \div 3$	$160 \div 2$	$800 \div 2$
$50 \div 5$	$900 \div 3$	$120 \div 2$

MULTIPLYING BY 11 AND 12

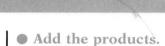

▶ Look at the examples below. What patterns do you see?

11	11	11	11
$\times\ 1$	$\times\ 2$	$\times\ 3$	$\times\ 4$
11	22	33	44

These patterns may help you multiply with 11.

▶ You can multiply with 12 by thinking of 12 as 10 + 2. If you can multiply with 10 and with 2, you can multiply with 12.

For example, multiply: 2 × 12.

● Multiply by 10.	● Multiply by 2.	● Add the products.
$2 \times 10 = 20$	$2 \times 2 = 4$	$20 + 4 = 24$

So, 2 × 12 = 24.

INDEPENDENT PRACTICE

Write the product.

	1.	2.	3.	4.	5.	6.
	11	12	11	11	12	12
	$\times\ 8$	$\times\ 5$	$\times\ 6$	$\times\ 9$	$\times\ 6$	$\times\ 4$

	7.	8.	9.	10.	11.	12.
	12	11	11	12	11	12
	$\times\ 8$	$\times\ 7$	$\times\ 5$	$\times\ 9$	$\times\ 4$	$\times\ 7$

13. 5 × 11   14. 3 × 12   15. 9 × 11   16. 9 × 12

17. Use what you know about patterns to write the products of 10 × 11 and 10 × 12.

SECTION REVIEW

for pages 186–196

Write the answer. Draw a picture if you like.

1. 9×3 2. 4×8 3. 9×2 4. 8×5

5. $40 \div 5$ 6. $54 \div 6$ 7. $8 \div 1$ 8. $64 \div 8$

9. $\begin{array}{r} 0 \\ \times\ 9 \\ \hline \end{array}$ 10. $\begin{array}{r} 2 \\ \times\ 8 \\ \hline \end{array}$ 11. $\begin{array}{r} 9 \\ \times\ 4 \\ \hline \end{array}$ 12. $\begin{array}{r} 6 \\ \times\ 9 \\ \hline \end{array}$ 13. $\begin{array}{r} 8 \\ \times\ 8 \\ \hline \end{array}$

14. $9\overline{)81}$ 15. $3\overline{)27}$ 16. $5\overline{)45}$ 17. $9\overline{)72}$ 18. $8\overline{)56}$

Write a multiplication sentence that asks the same question.

19. $63 \div 9 = $ ▨   20. $40 \div 5 = $ ▨   21. $72 \div 8 = $ ▨

22. $81 \div 9 = $ ▨   23. $16 \div 2 = $ ▨   24. $32 \div 8 = $ ▨

Complete. Write the missing factor.

25. $4 \times$ ▨ $= 36$ 26. ▨ $\times 5 = 45$ 27. ▨ $\times 3 = 24$

28. $8 \times$ ▨ $= 48$ 29. $9 \times$ ▨ $= 9$ 30. $8 \times$ ▨ $= 56$

Solve each problem.

31. There are 36 people who want to play baseball. If 9 people play on each team, how many teams can be formed?

32. Jane's parents bought a new van that can carry up to 8 children. How many trips will it take to drive 32 children to the movies?

33. At the end of the day, Mrs. Tamiko had made $72 selling dolls at a fair. If the price of each doll is $8, how many dolls did Mrs. Tamiko sell?

34. Doug collects old stamps. He plans to save money to buy 3 stamps that cost $9 each. How much money will Doug need to save?

CHAPTER REVIEW

Language Connection

Compare a **missing factor** to something else
that might be missing. First, think about what
factors do. You multiply them together to get a
product. This is a little like mixing colors. When
you mix red and white, you get pink. If you had
red and wanted pink, the missing color would
be white.

What else is a missing factor like? A missing
piece of a puzzle? A clue to a mystery? A key to
a lock? Write your own ideas. Explain why you
think they are like missing factors.

Red   Pink

Missing
Factor

Test ●●●●●●●

Write the product or quotient.

1. $\begin{array}{r} 6 \\ \times\ 3 \\ \hline \end{array}$

2. $\begin{array}{r} 7 \\ \times\ 5 \\ \hline \end{array}$

3. $\begin{array}{r} 9 \\ \times\ 7 \\ \hline \end{array}$

4. $\begin{array}{r} 8 \\ \times\ 2 \\ \hline \end{array}$

5. $7\overline{)56}$

6. $9\overline{)54}$

7. $8\overline{)32}$

8. $9\overline{)81}$

Write the missing factor.

9. $4 \times \blacksquare = 24$ 10. $1 \times \blacksquare = 8$ 11. $3 \times \blacksquare = 27$ 12. $2 \times \blacksquare = 14$

Write a related division sentence.

13. $6 \times 5 = 30$ 14. $7 \times 3 = 21$ 15. $9 \times 6 = 54$

Write a related multiplication sentence.

16. $40 \div 8 = 5$ 17. $49 \div 7 = 7$ 18. $6 \div 6 = 1$

PROBLEM SOLVING

Solve each problem.

19. Anita and Rob plan to travel during the summer for 21 days. For how many weeks will they travel?

20. There are 5 boys and 5 girls in art class. Each student draws 5 pictures. How many pictures are drawn?

21. Bill needs to buy 32 hot dog rolls for a picnic. There are 8 rolls in each package. How many packages of rolls does Bill need to buy?

22. Tickets to a craft show cost $3 for each adult and $2 for each child. How much will tickets cost for Mr. and Mrs. Ross and their 5 children?

CUMULATIVE REVIEW

Use the bar graph to answer each question.

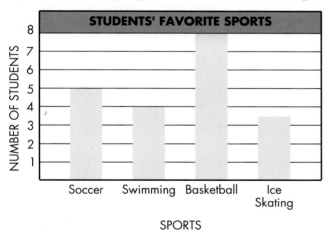

23. Which sport was the most popular?

24. How many students named swimming as their favorite sport?

Write the answer.

25. 2×4

26. 0×2

27. 3×3

28. 5×3

29. $10 \div 2$

30. $6 \div 2$

31. $12 \div 3$

32. $6 \div 3$

33. 4×1

34. $16 \div 4$

35. 4×5

36. $12 \div 4$

EXCURSION

USING TECHNOLOGY

LOGO
You will need:
- Logo software
- computer
- squared paper

Here is a Logo procedure for drawing a square. The turtle follows the same commands for each side of the square.

TO SQUARE

FD 30   RT 90   FD 30   RT 90   FD 30
RT 90   FD 30   RT 90   END

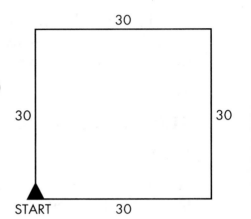

What two commands are repeated? How many times does the turtle repeat these commands?

The turtle repeats FD 30 RT 90 four times.

You can write this procedure another way by using the REPEAT command.

- First type **TO**. Then type the   TO SQUARE
  name of the procedure.
- Type **REPEAT** and the number   REPEAT 4
  of times the turtle repeats its
  steps and turns.
- Inside 2 brackets type the steps   REPEAT 4 [FD 30 RT 90]
  and turns that are repeated.
- Then type **END**.   END

To make the turtle begin drawing,   DRAW SQUARE
type **DRAW** and the name of the
procedure.

200

1. You can tell the turtle how to draw some letters of the alphabet. The procedure below tells the turtle to draw the letter *D*.

   TO D

   REPEAT 2 [LT 90 FD 30 LT 90 FD 50]

   END

   Type in the procedure. Tell the turtle to DRAW D.

2. Predict what letter the procedure below tells the turtle to draw. Draw your prediction on squared paper.

   TO _____

   REPEAT 3 [LT 90 FD 40]

   END

   Name the procedure and type it in. Tell the turtle to draw the letter.

3. Complete this next procedure so that it tells the turtle to draw the letter *B*.

   TO B

   REPEAT 4 [FD 20 RT 90]

   FD 20

   Type in the procedure. Tell the turtle to DRAW B.

4. Write a procedure for a letter in your name. Use the REPEAT command whenever you can. Type in the procedure. Tell the turtle to draw the letter.

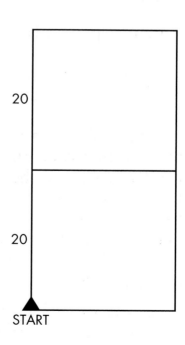

20

20

START

GEOMETRY

Shapes

A square was sitting quietly
Outside his rectangular shack
When a triangle came down—*kerplunk!*—
And struck him in the back.
"I must go to the hospital,"
Cried the wounded square,
So a passing rolling circle
Picked him up and took him there.

by Shel Silverstein

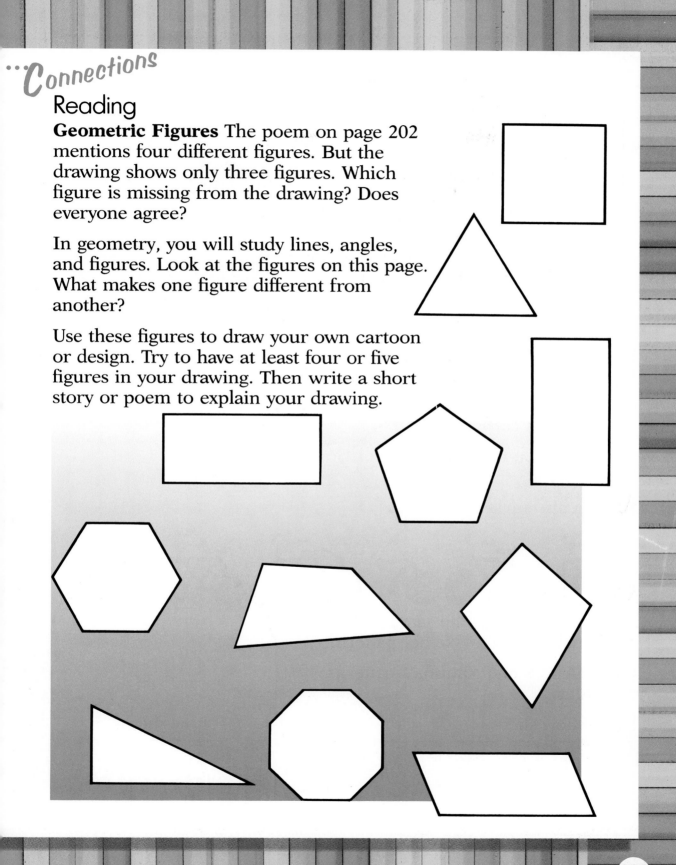

Reading

Geometric Figures The poem on page 202 mentions four different figures. But the drawing shows only three figures. Which figure is missing from the drawing? Does everyone agree?

In geometry, you will study lines, angles, and figures. Look at the figures on this page. What makes one figure different from another?

Use these figures to draw your own cartoon or design. Try to have at least four or five figures in your drawing. Then write a short story or poem to explain your drawing.

SLIDES

You will need a recording sheet.

▶ Miguel uses cutout pictures of cars to make a pattern.

1. How could you move one cutout car to fit on the next car in the row?

2. What do you think Miguel's rule for the pattern is?

▶ Natasha also makes a pattern.

3. Does Natasha use the same rule or a different rule to make her pattern?

Both Miguel's and Natasha's patterns use **slides.**

▶ These show slides.

These do *not* show slides.

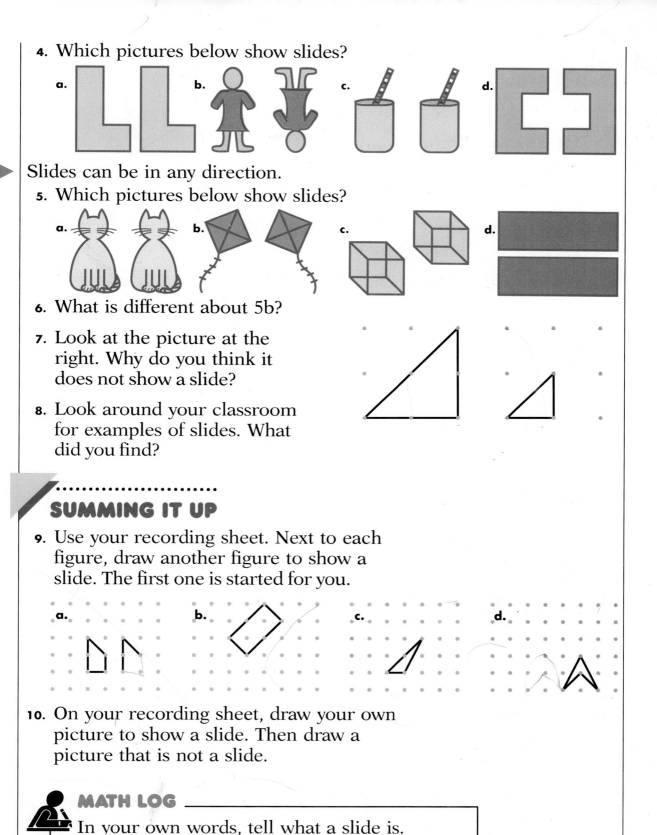

4. Which pictures below show slides?

a.   b.   c.   d.

Slides can be in any direction.

5. Which pictures below show slides?

a.   b.   c.   d.

6. What is different about 5b?

7. Look at the picture at the right. Why do you think it does not show a slide?

8. Look around your classroom for examples of slides. What did you find?

SUMMING IT UP

9. Use your recording sheet. Next to each figure, draw another figure to show a slide. The first one is started for you.

a.   b.   c.   d.

10. On your recording sheet, draw your own picture to show a slide. Then draw a picture that is not a slide.

MATH LOG
In your own words, tell what a slide is.

FLIPS

You will need:
- a recording sheet
- colored paper
- glue
- square dot paper
- scissors

Do you remember Miguel's pattern?

▶ Robert uses cutout cars to make a different pattern.

1. How is Robert's pattern different from Miguel's?

2. How could you move one car to fit on the next car in Robert's pattern?

▶ Belinda made a pattern of houses.

3. Did she use Robert's or Miguel's rule? How can you tell?

Robert and Belinda both used **flips** to make their patterns.

4. Use your recording sheet. Continue the pattern by drawing a figure to show a flip.

a.

b.

c.

▶ Flips can be made in any direction.

5. Which of these show flips?

a.   b.   c.   d.

6. What is different about 5c and 5d?

7. Do you think the picture at the right
   shows a flip? Why or why not?

▶ When you flip a figure, it stays the same size
and shape.

8. Use your recording sheet. Next to each
   figure, draw another figure to show a flip.

a.   b.   c.   d.

9. Look around the classroom for examples
   of flips. What did you find?

10. Which pair of houses shows a flip? What
    does the other pair show?

a.   b.

··

SUMMING IT UP

11. Use square dot paper. Draw
    and cut out two figures that
    are the same size and shape.
    Paste them down on colored
    paper to show a flip.

12. Again, draw and cut out two
    figures that are the same.
    Paste them down to show a
    slide.

TURNS

You will need:

- a recording sheet
- scissors
- colored paper
- glue

This pattern does not use slides or flips.

1. How could you move one tree to fit on the next tree?

The pattern uses **half turns.**

Now make a pattern with half turns.

2. Cut out 6 L-shaped figures from your recording sheet. Then paste them down on colored paper to show a half-turn pattern. Be sure to turn the figures a half turn each time.

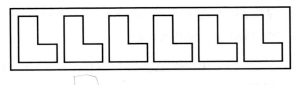

3. Which pairs of figures below show half turns?

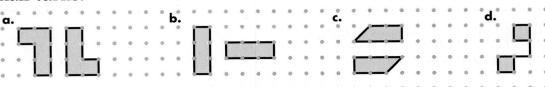

a.   b.   c.   d.

4. Use your recording sheet. Draw another figure to continue the pattern.

a.

b.

5. Use your recording sheet. Next to each figure, draw another figure to show a half turn.

a. b. c. d.

6. With what part of each object could you make a half turn?

a.  b.  c.

7. What examples of half turns can you find in the classroom?

8. Tell whether each figure shows a half turn, a slide, or a flip.

a.   b.   c. d.

Maintain • **Mixed Practice**

Write the answer.

1. 4×4 2. 2×8 3. $30 \div 6$ 4. $7 \div 7$

5. 6×4 6. $56 \div 8$ 7. 4×9 8. $72 \div 8$

9. $27 \div 9$ 10. 5×0 11. $64 \div 8$ 12. 2×1

Order from least to greatest.

13. 87, 58, 78   14. 120, 102, 112   15. 516, 561, 506

16. 194, 914, 149   17. 703, 370, 730   18. 2413, 3214, 1234

MAKE A DIAGRAM

> Making a diagram can help you get a picture of what is going on. It can also help you solve the problem.

> I remember one time we used a diagram to help a railroad company.

OUR PROBLEM

A train had 3 cars. Each car was 20 feet long. The cars were 5 feet apart. We needed to know how long the train was.

OUR SOLUTION

We made a diagram of the train. We did not need a fancy picture. Our diagram helped us see that there were 3 cars, but only 2 spaces between cars.

Next, we marked the length of each car. We also marked the length of the spaces.

Then we found the total of all those lengths.

The train was 70 feet long.

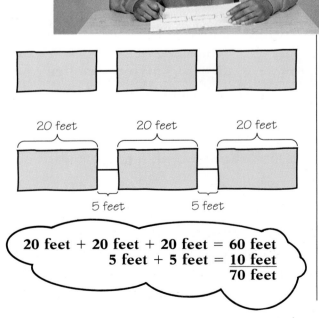

20 feet   20 feet   20 feet

5 feet   5 feet

20 feet + 20 feet + 20 feet = 60 feet
5 feet + 5 feet = 10 feet
70 feet

Copy and finish the diagram to help solve the problem.

1. There were 10 runners that finished a race. Della finished fourth. How many runners finished behind Della?

Work with a partner to solve each problem. Copy and finish the diagrams to help you.

2. The Square-Meal Restaurant has square tables. One person can sit on each side of a table. Sometimes the restaurant pushes two tables together. How many people can sit at two tables pushed together?

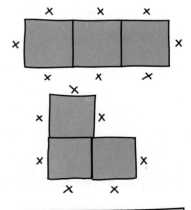

3. The restaurant pushes 3 tables together in a row to seat 8 people. When they move 3 tables to form an L-shape, they can seat only 7 people.

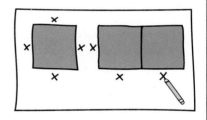

   a. Suppose they push 4 tables together to seat 10 people. Draw a diagram to show how the tables would look.

   b. Draw a diagram to show how 4 tables could be pushed together to seat 8 people.

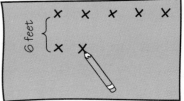

4. Help the Oak-Kay School band plan for the parade. The band has 20 members. There will be 5 band members in each row. The rows will be 6 feet apart. How far apart will the first and last rows be?

ANGLES

You will need two strips of oaktag and a paper fastener.

▶ Jaime, Marcella, and Peter were showing turns with flags they had cut out.

This is Jaime's.   This is Marcella's.   This is Peter's.

> The arrow shows the direction of the turn.

Who turned the flag the most?

If an arrow shows how the turn is made, you can see who turned the flag the most.

                    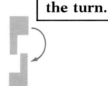

Jaime's   Marcella's   Peter's

Peter turned the flag the most.

An **angle** is a figure that can be used to show a turn.

▶ Connect two strips of oaktag with a paper fastener. Now you have an angle maker that can make different angles and show different turns.

> Angles can show turns in either direction.

a.   b.   c.   d.

Think

- In what order would you arrange the angles to show them from the smallest to the largest?

This page in your book is a rectangle. Use your angle maker to make an angle that matches one corner of the page. This angle is called a **square corner,** or **right angle.** Find other square corners in the classroom.

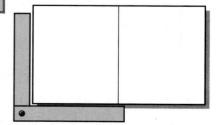

GUIDED PRACTICE

Use the angles below to answer the questions.
You may use your angle maker to check.

a.   b. 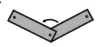   c.   d.

1. Which of the angles is less than a square corner?

2. Which of the angles is greater than a square corner?

3. Are any of the angles square corners? Which ones?

INDEPENDENT PRACTICE

Use the figures below to answer the questions.
You may use your angle maker to check.

a.   b.   c.   d.   e.

4. How many square corners does each figure have?

5. Which figure has the most square corners? Which has none?

6. Which has the most corners of any kind?

CHALLENGE • Problem Solving

Use square dot paper. Draw a figure that has the following number of square corners.

a. only 1 square corner
b. exactly 4 square corners
c. more than 4 square corners

CONGRUENCE

You will need square dot paper.

When you draw slides, flips, or half turns, you draw figures that are the same size and shape.

For example, this drawing shows a flip.

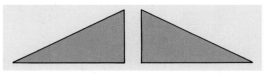

This drawing does not show a flip because the figures are not the same size and shape.

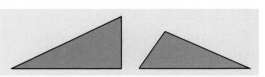

Each figure below is the same size and shape as another figure in the set.

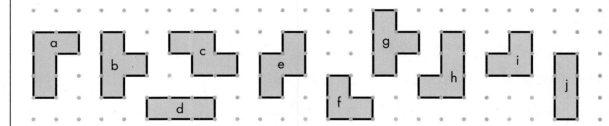

You could show that *a* and *h* are the same size and shape by tracing *a* on another sheet of paper and turning it to match *h*.

What other pairs are the same size and shape?

Think

- How could you show that *b* and *g* have the same size and shape?

- How could you show that *f* and *i* have the same size and shape?

Pairs *b* and *g*, *c* and *e*, *d* and *j*, *f* and *i* are the same size and shape.

GUIDED PRACTICE

Copy each figure on square dot paper. Next to the figure, draw another figure that is the same size and shape. The figures can show a slide, flip, or a half turn. An example is started for you.

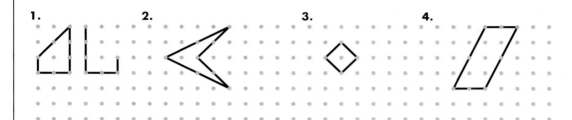

1.   **2.**   **3.**   **4.**

5. Look at the pairs of figures you drew for exercises 1–4. Write whether each pair shows a slide, a flip, or a half turn.

INDEPENDENT PRACTICE

Use two sheets of square dot paper.

6. This figure has 5 sides. Copy it on dot paper. Draw as many other figures as you can that have the same size and shape.

7. On the other sheet of dot paper, mark 3 × 3 squares. Inside the squares, draw as many triangles as you can that are **not** the same size and shape. Here are two to start.

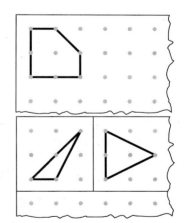

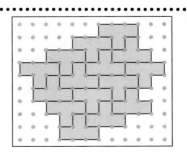

PROJECT • Tiling Patterns

Josh cut out several figures of the same size and shape. Then he fit them together to make a pattern. Copy Josh's pattern on dot paper. Color it so that figures of the same color do not touch each other.

SYMMETRY

Groups: partners

You will need:

- a recording sheet
- geoboard dot paper
- scissors

Mr. McRae's class makes paint designs. They put drops of paint on one side of a sheet of paper. Then they fold the paper in half and carefully smooth it down.

When they open the paper, they see the same design on both sides of the fold line.

1. Which of these designs could have been made this way?

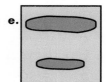  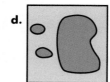 

a.   b.   c.   d.   e.

2. Use your recording sheet. Draw the other half of the design. The first one is started for you.

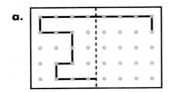   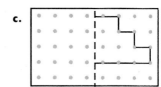

a.   b.   c.

The fold line is called a **line of symmetry.** If you fold a design or a figure on a line of symmetry, the two halves will match.

3. Use your recording sheet. Which of these figures have a line of symmetry? You can cut out a copy of each and fold to check.

a. 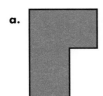 b.  c. d. 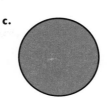 e.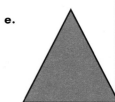

4. Which of the figures in exercise 3 could you fold from top to bottom so the two halves match?

5. Which of the figures in exercise 3 have two or more lines of symmetry?

6. Use geoboard dot paper to make the following kinds of figures.
  a. a figure with one line of symmetry
  b. a figure with two lines of symmetry

SUMMING IT UP

7. From your recording sheet, cut out a copy of each figure. Then find as many lines of symmetry as you can for each. Which figure has the most lines of symmetry?

a.  b. 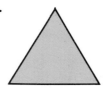 c.  d.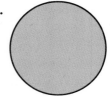

PROJECT • **Symmetry**

Use your recording sheet. Cut out these numbers: 0, 1, 2, 3, 4, 5, 6, 7, 8, and 9.

Which numbers have a line of symmetry?

CIRCLES

Groups: partners

You will need:

- a strip of oaktag
- scissors

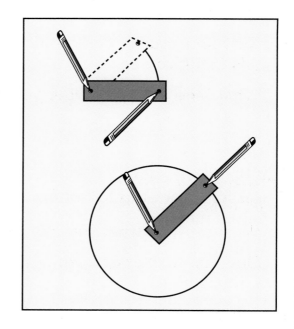

A circle is a special figure. What makes it special?

Follow these steps to make a circle.

1. Make a small hole at each end of the strip.

2. Place the strip on a sheet of paper. Put a pencil point in one hole. Hold it steady. This will be the **center** of the circle.

3. Put the other pencil point in the other hole. With this pencil, turn the strip around.

4. The pencil will trace a circle.

You also can make circles by tracing around such things as mugs, jars, or bottles.

5. Look for circles in the classroom. Make a list of the circles you see.

6. Draw circles of different sizes by tracing around different objects.

7. Cut out one of your circles. Then fold it in half. Is this fold line a line of symmetry? Why or why not?

8. Fold your circle in half another way. Is this fold line also a line of symmetry?

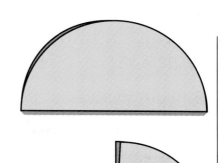

9. How many lines of symmetry can you find with your circle?

10. Now fold your circle in half. Then fold this half circle in half.

11. What kind of corner have you made?

······················

SUMMING IT UP

12. What are two ways you can make circles?

13. How many lines of symmetry does a circle have?

14. Tell one other thing you know about circles.

···

PROJECT • Art

Daniel made a circle design using a card strip.

First, he drew a circle.

Then he drew another circle the same size. The second circle went through the center of the first circle.

Then he drew another circle.

He continued until he had drawn 7 circles altogether.

Use your card strip to draw the same design. Then color it.

Draw some other circle designs.

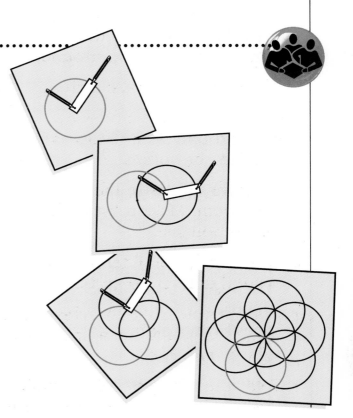

MENTAL MATH OR PAPER AND PENCIL

Sometimes you can use mental math to compute. Other times, you should use paper and pencil. You need to think about which way is easier and faster.

Here are some questions to help you decide:
- Can I group numbers to make them easier to work with mentally?
- Are the numbers basic facts?
- Are the numbers too large for me to compute mentally?

INDEPENDENT PRACTICE

Write the answer. Write whether you used mental math or paper and pencil to find the answer.

1. $15 \div 3$

2.
$$\begin{array}{r} 10 \\ + 14 \\ \hline \end{array}$$

3.
$$\begin{array}{r} 6000 \\ - 3000 \\ \hline \end{array}$$

4.
$$\begin{array}{r} 129 \\ + 111 \\ \hline \end{array}$$

5.
$$\begin{array}{r} 25 \\ 131 \\ + 62 \\ \hline \end{array}$$

6.
$$\begin{array}{r} 800 \\ + 500 \\ \hline \end{array}$$

7.
$$\begin{array}{r} 16 \\ - 9 \\ \hline \end{array}$$

8. 3×20

9.
$$\begin{array}{r} 432 \\ - 268 \\ \hline \end{array}$$

10.
$$\begin{array}{r} 225 \\ - 25 \\ \hline \end{array}$$

Problem Solving Write which method you used.

11. Lynn walks 3 blocks to the shoe store. Next, she walks 7 blocks to the fruit market. Then she walks 2 blocks to the park. How many blocks does Lynn walk?

12. In art class, the third-graders made 127 clay pitchers. The fourth-graders made 193 clay pitchers. How many clay pitchers did both classes make?

13. Randy has 31 model cars. Sally has 46 model cars. How many model cars do they have?

SECTION REVIEW

for pages 204–220

Use the pictures to answer exercises 1–3.
Write the letter of the correct answer.

1. Which two boxes show slides?

2. Which two boxes show flips?

3. Which two boxes show half turns?

4. Which figure below has a square corner?

5. Which two triangles below are the same size and shape?

6. Do the two triangles show a slide, a flip, or a half turn?

7. Which figure below has only two lines of symmetry?

8. Which figure has no lines of symmetry?

9. Which figure has more than two lines of symmetry?

SOLIDS

Match each object with one of the solids. Write the letter.

1.   2.   3.   4.

5.    6.    7.

a.
   cone

b.
   cylinder

c.
   cube

d.
   sphere

e.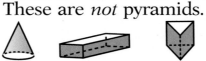
   triangular
   prism

f.
   pyramid

g.
   rectangular
   prism

These are pyramids.

These are *not* pyramids.

8. What is the same about all the pyramids?

9. Look at the pictures of solids below. Write the letters of the solids that are pyramids.

a.   b.   c.   d.   e.

These are prisms.

These are *not* prisms.

10. What is the same about all the prisms?

11. Write the letters of the solids below that are prisms.

a.   b.   c.   d.   e.

The flat part of a solid is called a **face.** Name the shape of the red face on each solid.

12.

13.

14.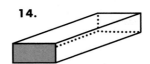

SUMMING IT UP

15. These solids were sorted into two sets. What sorting rule was used?

16. Name some objects that are shaped like prisms. Name some objects that are shaped like pyramids.

SET A

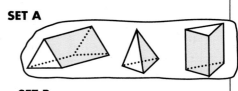

SET B

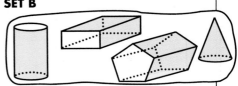

PROJECT • Making Figures

Work with a partner. You will need a recording sheet, toothpicks, and small marshmallows or small balls of clay.

These figures are made from toothpicks and marshmallows.

Use your recording sheet to complete the chart.

cube

square pyramid

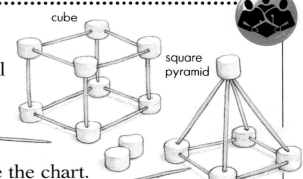

Kind of Solid	Number of Marshmallows	Number of Corners	Number of Toothpicks	Number of Edges
cube			12	
square pyramid	5			

Make a triangular prism with toothpicks and marshmallows or small balls of clay.
How many toothpicks and marshmallows does it take?

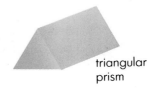

triangular prism

VISUALIZATION

Groups: small groups

You will need: • 24 cubes
• triangle dot paper

A special kind of dot paper makes it easy to draw cubes. The paper is called triangle dot paper.

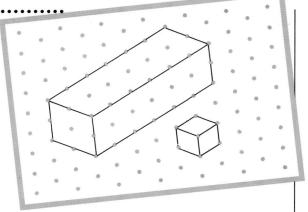

Here are some figures made of cubes drawn on triangle dot paper.

a.   **b.**   **c.**   **d.**

1. How many cubes do you see in each figure above?

2. Could any cubes be hidden behind the figures? If so, which figures?

3. Write the letters of the pairs of figures below that have the same size and shape.

a.   **b.**   **c.**

d.   **e.**   **f.**

4. How many cubes do you think are in each figure?

5. Copy the figures below on triangle dot paper. Draw lines to show the cubes. Write the number of cubes in each figure.

a.   **b.**   **c.**   **d.**

1 cube

6. Use cubes to build figures a and b below.
Fit figures a and b together to make figure c.

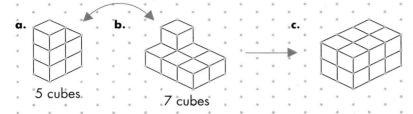

7. Repeat exercise 6 using these figures.

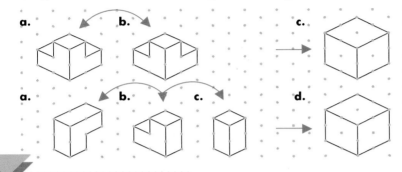

··

SUMMING IT UP

The prisms below are made with cubes.

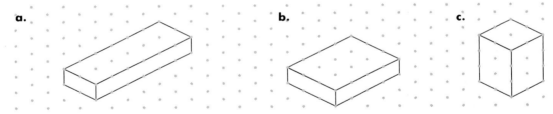

8. How are these prisms alike? How are they different?

···

PROJECT • Problem Solving

Work with your group. You will need
24 cubes and triangle dot paper.

Make as many different rectangular prisms
as you can, using all 24 cubes. Draw each
prism on triangle dot paper.

LINES AND LINE SEGMENTS

You will need square dot paper.

Patterns like these are easy to make with squares or rectangles.

a. 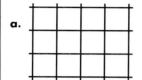   b. 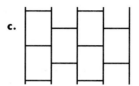   c. 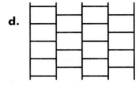   d.

All the patterns can be drawn with lines or line segments. A **line segment** is part of a line. It has two end points. A **line** goes on forever. To show this, you use arrows.

These show lines.

These do *not* show lines.

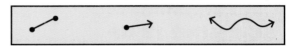

These show line segments.

These do *not* show line segments.

In patterns a and b above, the line segments cross each other.

In patterns c and d, the line segments meet each other.

What is special about the colored lines in each pattern below?

e. 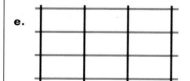   f. 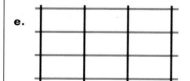   g.

Lines or line segments that are always the same distance apart are **parallel.**

1. Copy these patterns onto dot paper.

a.    b.    c.

2. Color two parallel line segments in each pattern.

3. In each pattern, mark an *X* in three places where the line segments cross.

4. Tell whether each picture below shows a line, a line segment, or neither. Write *line*, *line segment*, or *neither*.

a.    b.   c.   d.   e.   f.

5. Tell whether or not the red parts show parallel line segments. Write *parallel* or *not parallel*.

a.   b. 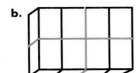   c.    d.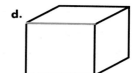

6. On this map, First Street is parallel to Second Street.
   a. Write the names of another pair of streets that are parallel.
   b. Write a pair of streets or avenues that cross.

SUMMING IT UP

Parallel lines, crossing lines, and line segments are all around us.

7. Give three examples of parallel line segments in your classroom.

8. Give three examples of crossing line segments in your classroom.

ORDERED PAIRS

The treasure map has squares that show where things are located. Each square is named with a letter and a number, like C2 or B3.

Find column C. Move up column C to row 2. A tree is in square C2.

What is in square B2? Go across to column B and up to row 2. Safe Bay is in square B2.

Which square is Pirate Pete in? First, find Pete. Then go down that column to find the letter. Go back to Pete. Then go across that row to find the number. Pirate Pete is in square B3.

Think

- Which square is the volcano in?
- Where is the treasure?

Use the map of downtown Everytown to answer each question.

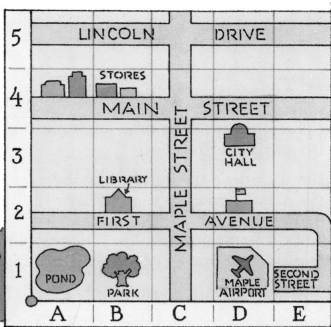

1. Where is the library?

2. What is in square A1?

3. Where do First Avenue and Maple Street cross?

4. In what squares is Main Street?

Use the map of Everytown to answer each question.

5. The school is marked with this symbol:

   Where is the school located?

6. Lincoln Drive runs through B5. What other squares does it run through?

7. Which square is Maple Airport in?

8. Name one street that is in both B2 and C2.

9. Name the street that is completely in E1.

10. Name two streets that are parallel.

Maintain • Comparing and Ordering

Copy and complete. Write < or >.

1. 741 ● 714   2. 1033 ● 1303   3. 2113 ● 987   4. $6.01 ● $5.99

229

You do not have to draw well to make a useful diagram. Just draw enough to help you solve the problem.

Rita is putting tiles on her kitchen floor. She will make 8 rows of tiles. There will be 8 tiles in each row. She will make a checkerboard pattern. Every other tile will be red. How many red tiles will Rita need?

Look at the two diagrams below.

a.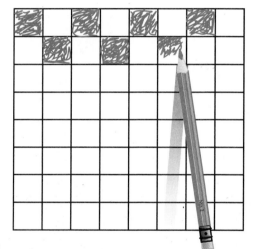

b.

Think

- What does each diagram show about the problem?

- Which diagram would be easier to draw?

- Which diagram would be more helpful when solving the problem?

Copy and finish one of the diagrams. Use it to solve the problem.

GUIDED PRACTICE

Read the problem. Choose a diagram and use it to solve the problem.

1. On Monday at 9:00 A.M., Lex begins making 3 model boats. It takes him 2 hours to finish each boat. He takes an hour for lunch between the first and second boats. What time does Lex finish?

   a.

   First Boat Lunch

   9 10 11 12 1 2 3 4 5 6

   b.

....

APPLICATION

Work in groups to solve each problem. Make a diagram when it helps.

2. In the lunchroom, there are 4 square tables. Each table is 6 feet long. Mrs. Hansen places the tables in a row. She leaves 2 feet of space between tables. How long is the row of tables?

3. The Pine Street Theater has 3 sections. Each section has 5 rows of seats. The middle section has 4 seats in each row. The other sections have 3 seats in each row. How many seats are in the theater?

4. There are 13 children in line waiting to visit the zoo. There are 4 children ahead of Eva. How many children are behind her?

....

Maintain • Using Data

Use the diagram of the Great Lakes on page 418 in the Data Book.

1. Write the depths of the lakes in order from greatest to least.

2. How much deeper is the deepest lake than the second-deepest lake?

AREA

You will need:
- square dot paper
- scissors

▶ Carmen cuts out three figures from dot paper. Then she asks Luis which figure covers the most.

a.  **b.**  **c.**

Luis is not sure because all the figures have different shapes. Do you know?

Luis draws lines to make squares in the figures. Then he counts the squares. He decides that figure a covers the most. Do you agree?

a.   **b.**   **c.**

Copy the figures onto dot paper. Draw lines to make squares. Now count the squares in each figure.

Yes, figure a covers the most.

Which figure below covers the most? Copy the figures onto dot paper. Count the squares.

1. 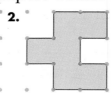 **2.** 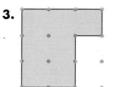 **3.** 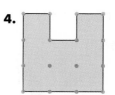 **4.**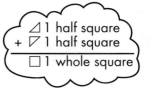

The figures below have some half squares in them. Two half squares equal one whole square.

Copy the figures onto dot paper and find the number of squares in each.

△ 1 half square
+ ▽ 1 half square
□ 1 whole square

5.   **6.**  **7.**   **8.**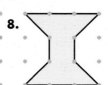

9. On dot paper, draw four different figures that each have 12 squares.

▶ Carmen decides to use one of her figures to make a larger figure. She cuts out five copies of the figure and fits them together.

10. How many squares are in each small cutout?

11. How many squares are in the large figure?

Cut out six copies of this figure from dot paper.

12. How many squares are there in each figure?

13. How many squares are there in all six figures?

14. Use all six figures to make a larger figure of 18 squares. Copy this figure onto dot paper.

15. Can you make another figure of 18 squares? If so, copy it onto dot paper.

SUMMING IT UP

Guess which of these figures covers the most. Then count the squares to check your guess.

16.   17. 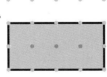 18.  19.

PROJECT • Tiling Designs

Cut out six copies of this figure from dot paper. Make three different figures with 24 squares in each. Copy each of the figures onto dot paper.

AREA OF IRREGULAR FIGURES

Groups: partners

You will need: squared paper

Tina draws a map of Treasure Island on squared paper. She wants to count the number of squares in the island.

● Tina starts by counting all the whole squares.

● Then she counts the "almost whole" squares.

● Then she counts the "about half" squares.

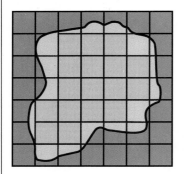 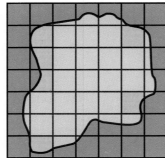 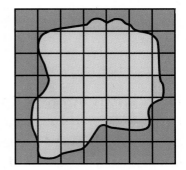

Tina counts 17 whole squares. She counts 6 "almost whole" squares. She counts 6 "about half" squares, or 3 "almost whole" squares. Then she adds: 17 + 6 + 3 = 26.

She thinks, "I don't know exactly how many squares are in my island, but there are about 26. I have estimated."

Use Tina's method to estimate the number of squares in each of these islands.

1.
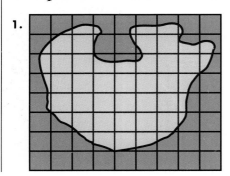

2.
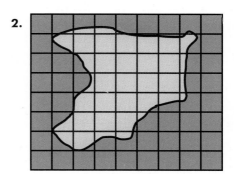

Jackson was comparing animal tracks to see which ones were larger.

3. Count to estimate the number of squares in each.

4. Which animal has the biggest footprint?

5. Which animal has the smallest footprint?

a.

deer

b.
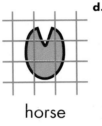
bear

c.
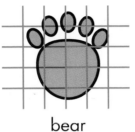
horse

d.
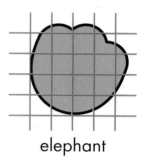
elephant

6. How big is your footprint? Place your foot on a sheet of squared paper and trace around it. Count squares to estimate the size of your footprint.

7. How big is your handprint? Trace around your hand on a sheet of squared paper. Estimate the number of squares in your handprint.

....
SUMMING IT UP

8. Which do you think covers more squares, your math book or your footprint? Use squared paper and check by counting squares. Which was easier to count? Explain.

9. Find something in the room that covers:

   a. more than your footprint.

   b. less than your handprint.

   c. more than your thumbprint but less than your footprint.

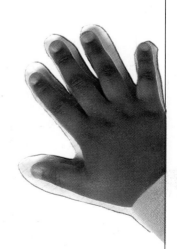

NETS OF SOLIDS

Suppose someone cut apart a box and laid it
flat. Using your imagination, you could
figure out the shape of the box. A flat pattern
that folds into a solid is called a **net.**

Match each net with the correct solid.

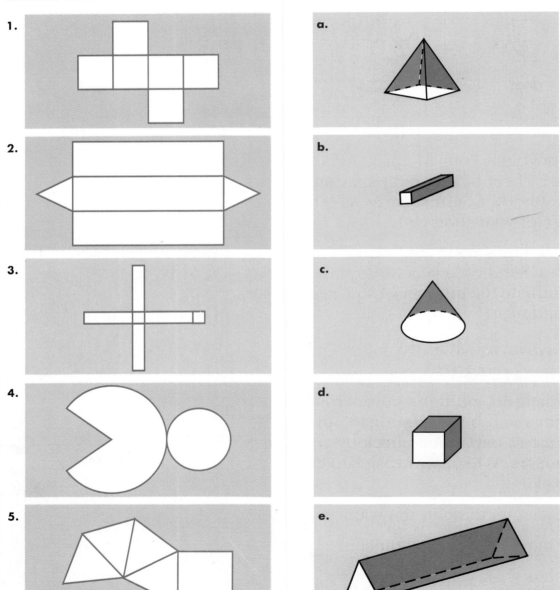

1.

a.

2.

b.

3.

c.

4.

d.

5.

e.

SECTION REVIEW

for pages 222–236

1. Write the pairs of figures that are the same size and shape.

a.

b.

c.

d.

e.

f.

g.

h.

Use the map of Blue Bay to answer each question below.

2. In which square do you find the fishing boat?

3. In which squares do you find the seals and the dolphins?

4. What do you find in square D3?

5. What do you find in squares C3 and C4?

Count to estimate the number of squares in Shark Island.

6. How many whole squares?

7. How many "almost whole" squares?

8. How many "about half" squares?

9. About how many squares are in Shark Island?

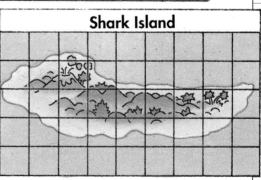

237

CHAPTER REVIEW

Language Connection

Look at each group of words. Each group has words that are alike in some way. Think about how they are alike. Write a sentence or two for each group. Tell how the words are alike. If you want, draw pictures to go with your sentences.

WORD GROUPS
slides • flips • half turns
square corner • right angle
line of symmetry • center
line segment • line • parallel lines

Test ● ● ● ● ● ● ●

Write *slide, flip,* or *half turn* for the set of figures.

1. 　　**2.** 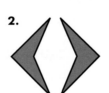　　**3.** 　　**4.**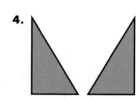

Is the angle greater than, less than, or equal to a square corner? Write >, <, or =.

5. 　　**6.** 　　**7.** 　　**8.**

Find the lines of symmetry. Write the total number.

9. 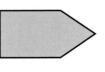　　**10.** 　　**11.** 　　**12.**

Use the map of Sayerville Zoo to answer each question.

13. In what square are the wild birds?

14. Which street is in both A4 and B3?

15. Apple Lane is in what two squares?

16. What is in C4?

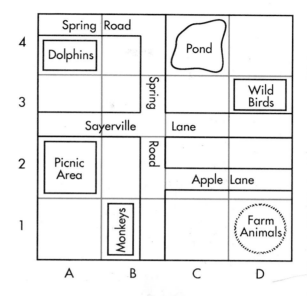

PROBLEM SOLVING

17. Karen has 57 crayons. Dean has 38 crayons. Karen gives 9 crayons to Dean. How many crayons do they have in all?

18. There were 8 runners who finished a race. Carmen finished second. How many runners finished behind Carmen?

19. There are 3 stacks of plates in a cupboard. Each stack is 7 inches wide. There are 2 inches between each pair of stacks. How wide is the row of plate stacks?

20. On Sunday at 1:00 P.M., Clive begins painting 3 signs. It takes him 2 hours to finish each sign. At what time will Clive finish painting the signs?

CUMULATIVE REVIEW

Write the answer.

21. $20 \div 4$

22. $12 \div 4$

23. $10 \div 5$

24. $5 \div 5$

25. 6×4

26. 7×7

27. 9×5

28. 8×3

EXCURSION
NUMBER THEORY

Modeling Square Numbers
Use squared paper and crayons to learn about square numbers.

Take a sheet of squared paper. In pencil, number 2 squares down and 4 squares across.

Color in the squares to make a shape. The picture below shows you how.

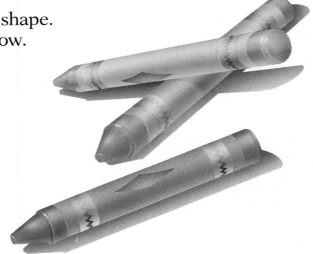

You have just modeled 2 sets of 4 squares.

1. How many squares have you colored?

2. Do the colored squares for 2 sets of 4 squares form a square?

Now number 3 squares down and 3 squares across. Color in the squares to make a shape.

You have now modeled 3 sets of 3 squares.

3. How many squares have you colored?

4. Do the colored squares for 3 sets of 3 squares form a square?

Use your crayons and squared paper to model each set of squares.

5. 1 set of 5 squares

	1	2	3	4	5
1					

6. 2 sets of 4 squares

	1	2	3	4
1				
2				

7. 3 sets of 4 squares

	1	2	3	4
1				
2				
3				

8. 4 sets of 4 squares

	1	2	3	4
1				
2				
3				
4				

9. 3 sets of 5 squares

	1	2	3	4	5
1					
2					
3					

10. 5 sets of 5 squares

	1	2	3	4	5
1					
2					
3					
4					
5					

After you have completed your models, answer each question.

11. Which sets did not form a square?

12. Which sets did form a square?

13. What do you notice about the sets that did form a square?

14. Count the colored squares for each set that formed the shape of a square. You can also multiply to find the total. These totals are **square numbers.** For exercises 5–10, which square numbers did you model?

FRACTIONS

····Connections

Number Sense

Choosing the Right Fraction Have you ever tried to fix your own bike? Nicole's bike had a loose pedal. She found that the nut on the pedal was very loose. So she looked for a wrench to tighten it.

In the toolbox, Nicole found several wrenches of different sizes. Each wrench size was marked with a fraction. The smallest wrench was marked $\frac{1}{4}$, and the largest was marked $\frac{7}{8}$.

Nicole chose the wrench marked $\frac{1}{2}$. But it was too small. The $\frac{5}{8}$ wrench looked a little larger, so she tried it. The $\frac{5}{8}$ wrench fit perfectly. The next time she needs to tighten her bicycle pedal, Nicole will remember which size wrench to use.

Visit a hardware store or check a hardware catalog. Notice the number of different wrenches. You may be surprised by how many you find.

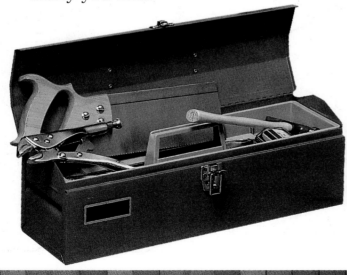

FRACTIONS

In this lesson you will work with pattern blocks and discover some things about fractions.

Groups: partners

You will need:
- pattern blocks
- recording sheet
- crayons

Use your recording sheet.

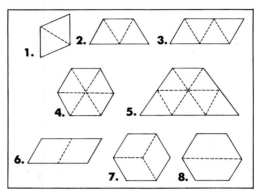

1. Cover figure 1 with green triangles. How many does it take?

One green triangle covers *one half* of figure 1.

2. Cover figure 2 with green triangles. How many does it take?

One green triangle covers *one third* of figure 2.

3. Cover figure 3 with green triangles. How many does it take?

One green triangle covers *one fourth* of figure 3.

4. Cover figure 4 with green triangles. How many does it take?

5. What fractional part of figure 4 is covered by one green triangle?

6. What fractional part of figure 5 is covered by one green triangle?

7. Cover figure 6 and figure 7 with blue blocks.

8. What fractional part of figure 6 is covered by one blue block?

9. What fractional part of figure 7 is covered by one blue block?

10. What fractional part of figure 8 is covered by one red block?

Place one blue block on figure 2. *Two thirds* of figure 2 is covered by the blue block.

Place one red block on figure 3. *Three fourths* of figure 3 is covered by the red block.

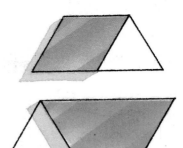

11. What fractional part of figure 3 is covered by one blue block?

12. What fractional part of figure 4 is covered by one red block?

13. What fractional part of figure 5 is covered by two red blocks?

SUMMING IT UP

Use crayons to color these fractional parts.
Use your recording sheet.

14. one half of figure 1

15. two thirds of figure 2

16. three fourths of figure 3

17. two sixths of figure 4

18. five eighths of figure 5

19. two halves of figure 6

20. two thirds of figure 7

21. zero halves of figure 8

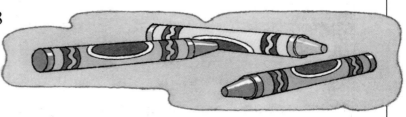

 MATH LOG

In your own words, tell what you know about fractions.

WRITING FRACTIONS

Jason is using Fraction Bars. This bar has four equal parts. One part is shaded. Jason wants to write a fraction for the shaded part of the bar.

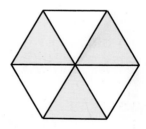

One fourth of the bar is shaded. He can write the fraction like this.

number of shaded parts $\longrightarrow$ 1 $\leftarrow$ **numerator**

number of equal parts $\longrightarrow$ 4 $\leftarrow$ **denominator**

One fourth, or $\frac{1}{4}$, of the Fraction Bar is shaded.

 Think

- What fraction names the part of the bar that is not shaded?

- If the whole bar were shaded, what fraction would name the shaded part?

Other Examples

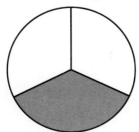

$\frac{1}{3}$

one third
is shaded

$\frac{2}{2}$

two halves
is shaded

$\frac{3}{6}$

three sixths
is unshaded

GUIDED PRACTICE

Write a fraction for the shaded part.

1.   2.    3.    4.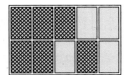

5. Write a fraction for the unshaded part in exercise 4.

INDEPENDENT PRACTICE

Write a fraction for the shaded part of the figure.
Then write a fraction for the unshaded part.

6.    7. 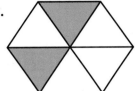   8.   9.

Match the picture with a fraction below.
Write *a, b, c,* or *d.*

10.    11.    12. 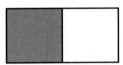   13.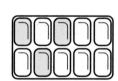

| a. $\frac{2}{4}$ | b. $\frac{3}{4}$ | c. $\frac{3}{10}$ | d. $\frac{1}{3}$ |

CHALLENGE • Geometry

Draw a rectangle like the one at the right. Shade $\frac{2}{6}$ of it.

Draw more rectangles like the one at the right. Find as many ways as you can to shade $\frac{2}{6}$.

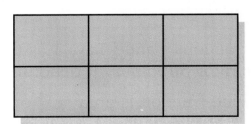

247

COMPARING FRACTIONS

You will need: Fraction Bars

▶ Use Fraction Bars to compare $\frac{1}{4}$ and $\frac{2}{4}$.

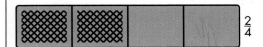

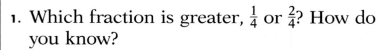

The fractions $\frac{1}{4}$ and $\frac{2}{4}$ have the same denominator but different numerators.

1. Which fraction is greater, $\frac{1}{4}$ or $\frac{2}{4}$? How do you know?

Use Fraction Bars to compare each pair of fractions. Write > or <.

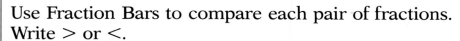

2. $\frac{3}{6}$ ⬤ $\frac{5}{6}$ 3. $\frac{3}{4}$ ⬤ $\frac{2}{4}$ 4. $\frac{1}{3}$ ⬤ $\frac{2}{3}$ 5. $\frac{1}{2}$ ⬤ $\frac{2}{2}$

6. In exercises 2–5, each pair of fractions has the same denominator. What do you notice about the size of the numerator and the size of the fraction?

▶ Now look at the Fraction Bars below.

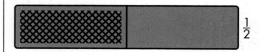

The fractions $\frac{1}{2}$ and $\frac{1}{6}$ have 1 as the numerator but different denominators.

7. Which fraction is greater, $\frac{1}{2}$ or $\frac{1}{6}$? How do you know?

Use Fraction Bars to compare each pair of fractions.
Write > or <.

8. $\frac{1}{2}$ ⬤ $\frac{1}{3}$ **9.** $\frac{1}{6}$ ⬤ $\frac{1}{4}$ **10.** $\frac{1}{3}$ ⬤ $\frac{1}{4}$ **11.** $\frac{1}{2}$ ⬤ $\frac{1}{6}$

12. In exercises 8–11, all the fractions have the same numerator, 1. What do you notice about the size of the denominator and the size of the fraction?

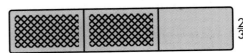

$\frac{2}{3}$

▶ The fractions $\frac{2}{3}$ and $\frac{3}{4}$ have different numerators and denominators.

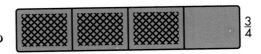

$\frac{3}{4}$

13. Which fraction is greater, $\frac{2}{3}$ or $\frac{3}{4}$? How do you know?

Use Fraction Bars to compare each pair of fractions.
Write >, <, or = .

14. $\frac{1}{4}$ ⬤ $\frac{2}{3}$ **15.** $\frac{3}{6}$ ⬤ $\frac{1}{2}$ **16.** $\frac{4}{6}$ ⬤ $\frac{2}{4}$ **17.** $\frac{1}{3}$ ⬤ $\frac{2}{6}$

18. How did you use fraction bars to compare the fractions in exercises 15 and 17?

SUMMING IT UP

19. When you compare fractions with the same denominator, how can you tell which fraction is greater without using Fraction Bars?

20. When you compare fractions with numerators of 1, how can you tell which fraction is greater without using Fraction Bars?

PROJECT • Ordering Fractions

Use your recording sheet. Put these fractions in order from least to greatest. Then write them on the number line. You may use Fraction Bars to help you.

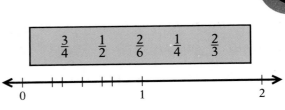

EQUIVALENT FRACTIONS

Groups: small groups

You will need: Fraction Bars

▶ Take a $\frac{1}{2}$ Fraction Bar.

1. How many parts are shaded?

Find a fourths bar that has the same amount shaded. Line up the fourths bar below the $\frac{1}{2}$ bar to check.

2. How many parts are shaded on the fourths bar?

3. What fraction does the bar show?

Now find a sixths bar that has the same amount shaded as the $\frac{1}{2}$ bar.

4. How many parts are shaded on the sixths bar?

5. What fraction does this bar show?

Fractions with the same amount shaded show **equivalent fractions.**

> **Equivalent** means "equal to."

Find other Fraction Bars that have the same amount shaded as the $\frac{1}{2}$ bar.

6. What other fractions are equivalent to $\frac{1}{2}$?

▶ Take a $\frac{3}{4}$ bar. Find an eighths bar that has the same amount shaded.

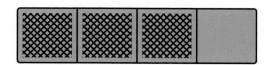

7. What fraction does it show?

8. Copy and complete. $\frac{3}{4} = \frac{}{8}$

▶ Take a $\frac{2}{3}$ bar. Find another Fraction Bar that has the same amount shaded.

9. Which fraction is equivalent to $\frac{2}{3}$?

SUMMING IT UP

10. In your own words, tell what equivalent fractions are.

11. How do you know when two fractions are equivalent?

PROJECT • Game

Play this game with a partner or small group. You will need a set of Fraction Bars.

a. Place all the Fraction Bars face down.

b. Take turns picking 2 bars. If the bars show equivalent fractions, keep them and take another turn. If not, put the bars back and let the next player go.

c. Keep playing until all the Fraction Bars are matched. The player with the most bars wins.

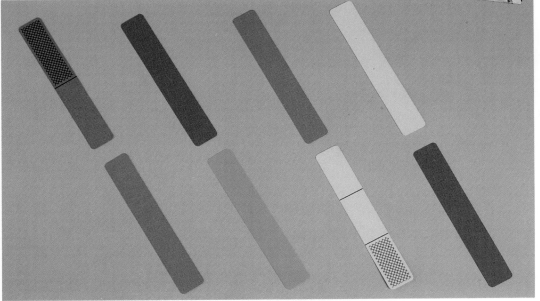

251

MENTAL MATH OR CALCULATOR

The calculator is a great tool to help you compute, but sometimes it is faster and easier to compute mentally.

Before you solve a problem, think about whether you can use a calculator or mental math.

Here are some questions to ask yourself:

- Can I quickly compute in my head?
- Will entering the problem into a calculator take too much time?

INDEPENDENT PRACTICE

Write the answer. Write whether you used a calculator or mental math.

1. $\begin{array}{r} 5 \\ \times\ 3 \\ \hline \end{array}$

2. $\begin{array}{r} 38 \\ \times\ 4 \\ \hline \end{array}$

3. $\begin{array}{r} 800 \\ -\ 300 \\ \hline \end{array}$

4. $\begin{array}{r} \$35.89 \\ +\ 63.42 \\ \hline \end{array}$

5. $80 \div 2$

6. $4000 + 2000$

7. $345 \div 5$

8. $350 - 100$

Problem Solving Use a calculator or mental math.

9. Janet wants to buy a bicycle that costs $100. She has saved $40 so far. How much more money does she need to save?

10. Phil has 129 stamps in his collection. Joy has 94 stamps in her collection. How many more stamps does Phil have than Joy?

11. Write a word problem of your own that would be easier to solve using mental math. Then write a problem that would be easier to solve using a calculator. Give your problems to a friend to solve.

SECTION REVIEW

for pages 244–252

Write the fraction for the shaded part.

1.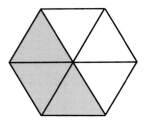

2.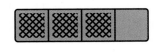

3.

4.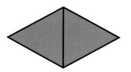

5.

6.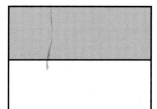

7.

8.

9.

Use Fraction Bars to compare each pair of fractions.
Write > or <.

10. $\frac{1}{2}$ ● $\frac{1}{3}$

11. $\frac{4}{6}$ ● $\frac{5}{6}$

12. $\frac{3}{4}$ ● $\frac{2}{3}$

13. $\frac{1}{2}$ ● $\frac{2}{3}$

14. $\frac{3}{4}$ ● $\frac{4}{4}$

15. $\frac{1}{6}$ ● $\frac{1}{8}$

Write a fraction that is equivalent to each fraction
below. Use Fraction Bars.

16. $\frac{2}{3}$

17. $\frac{1}{2}$

18. $\frac{3}{4}$

19. $\frac{2}{4}$

20. $\frac{4}{4}$

21. $\frac{1}{3}$

ESTIMATING FRACTIONS

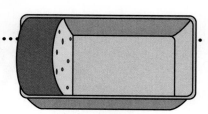

About how much of this loaf of banana bread is left?

Three useful fractions to use when estimating are $\frac{1}{4}$, $\frac{1}{2}$, and $\frac{3}{4}$.

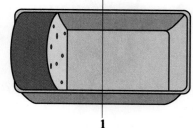

Imagine a whole loaf of banana bread cut into 2 equal parts, or halves.

Much less than $\frac{1}{2}$ of the bread is left.

About $\frac{1}{4}$ of the banana bread is left.

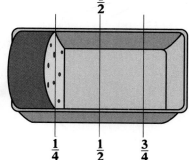

$\frac{1}{4}$ $\frac{1}{2}$ $\frac{3}{4}$

Think

• What fraction names about how much of the pan is empty?

Other Examples

About $\frac{1}{2}$ of the wall is painted.

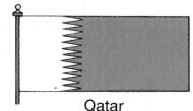

Qatar

About $\frac{1}{4}$ of the flag is white.

About $\frac{3}{4}$ of the cracker is left.

GUIDED PRACTICE

Estimate. Is more than or less than half of the wall painted? Write *more than* or *less than*.

1.

2.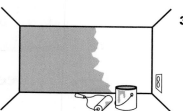

3.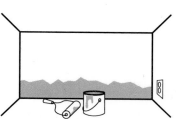

Estimate. About what fraction of the flag is red?
Write $\frac{1}{4}$, $\frac{1}{2}$, or $\frac{3}{4}$.

4.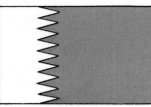

Bahrain

5.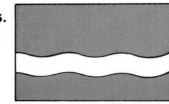

Seychelles

6.

Togo

7. Which flag has the most red?

INDEPENDENT PRACTICE

Estimate. About what fraction of the pizza is left?
Write $\frac{1}{4}$, $\frac{1}{2}$, or $\frac{3}{4}$.

8.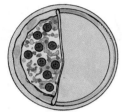

9.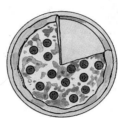

10.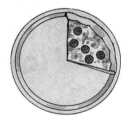

Estimate. About how full is the glass? Write $\frac{1}{4}$, $\frac{1}{2}$, or $\frac{3}{4}$.

11.

12.

13.

CHALLENGE • Estimation

Choose the correct estimate. Write *a* or *b*.

About how much of the circle is orange?

a. between $\frac{1}{4}$ and $\frac{1}{2}$

b. between $\frac{1}{2}$ and $\frac{3}{4}$

About how much of the strip is shaded?

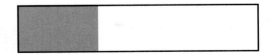

a. between $\frac{1}{4}$ and $\frac{1}{2}$

b. between $\frac{1}{2}$ and $\frac{3}{4}$

ADDING AND SUBTRACTING FRACTIONS

You can add and subtract fractions that have the same denominators.

Groups: small groups

You will need: Fraction Bars

▶ Follow these steps to add two fractions.

a. Show a $\frac{2}{6}$ Fraction Bar.

b. Then show a $\frac{3}{6}$ Fraction Bar.

c. Join the shaded parts as shown.

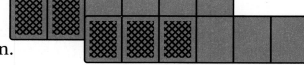

1. How many shaded sixths do you have now?

2. Do you have more than or less than a whole? Do you have more than or less than a half?

Use Fraction Bars to add. Record the sum.

3. $\frac{2}{4} + \frac{1}{4}$ 4. $\frac{1}{6} + \frac{1}{6}$ 5. $\frac{2}{3} + \frac{1}{3}$ 6. $\frac{1}{6} + \frac{2}{6}$

7. Write whether each sum above is more than, less than, or equal to a half.

8. Is any sum equal to a whole? If so, which one?

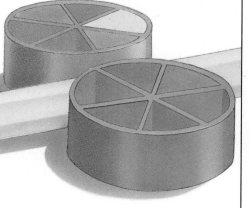

▶ Follow these steps to subtract fractions.

a. Show a $\frac{3}{4}$ fraction bar.

b. Put a $\frac{2}{4}$ Fraction Bar below it.

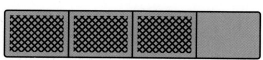

9. What is the difference between the shaded parts in the two bars? Is the difference more than or less than a half?

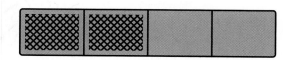

256

Use Fraction Bars to subtract. Record the difference.

10. $\frac{2}{3} - \frac{1}{3}$ **11.** $\frac{5}{6} - \frac{1}{6}$ **12.** $\frac{2}{2} - \frac{1}{2}$ **13.** $\frac{3}{4} - \frac{2}{4}$

14. Write whether each difference above is more than, less than, or equal to a half.

SUMMING IT UP

15. Use Fraction Bars to add two fractions. Write a number sentence to show the sum.

16. Now use Fraction Bars to subtract two fractions. Write a number sentence to show the difference.

17. How is adding and subtracting fractions that have the same denominator like adding and subtracting whole numbers?

18. How do you think you can add and subtract fractions that have the same denominator without using Fraction Bars?

CHALLENGE • Problem Solving

Follow these steps to make a new word. Each word is a whole. Each letter is a part.

a. Add the first $\frac{1}{2}$ of *blew* to the last $\frac{3}{5}$ of *track*.

b. Add the first $\frac{3}{4}$ of *salt* to the last $\frac{2}{3}$ of *lad*.

Make up a problem like the one above. Give it to a friend to solve.

If you get stuck, remember.... Tips for Problem Solving on pages 426–427

Mr. Decker has bought a hobby store. He needs to decide where in the store to put all the items.

He uses squared paper to make a plan. The plan is like a map of the store. Each square on the map stands for a large floor tile.

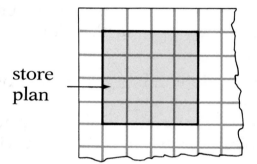

store plan →

Help Mr. Decker decide where to put the items in his store. Work in groups to solve each problem. Use squared paper and three different colored crayons.

1. How many floor tiles are in Mr. Decker's store?

2. Mr. Decker will have a Models section in his store. The Models section will be in $\frac{1}{4}$ of the store. How many floor tiles will the section cover?

3. Copy Mr. Decker's plan onto your squared paper. Color in where Mr. Decker can put the Models section.

4. Mr. Decker will put a Crafts section in $\frac{1}{2}$ of the store. How many floor tiles will the Crafts section cover?

5. Using a different color crayon, color in where the Crafts section of the store can be.

6. Mr. Decker wants to use the rest of the store for a Paint section. How many tiles will the Paint section cover? What fraction of the store will that be?

7. Using another crayon, color in where the Paint section can go in the store.

8. Which covers more tiles, the Paint and Models sections together or the Crafts section?

9. Draw a door, some windows, a desk, and shelves.
   a. In which section did you put the door?
   b. Which section has the most windows?

10. Compare your plan with other students' plans. How are they alike? How are they different?

CHALLENGE • Problem Solving

Mr. Decker opens a bigger hobby shop. Copy the plan. Color in the 3 sections. The Models section should be $\frac{1}{4}$ of the store, the Crafts section $\frac{1}{2}$, and the Paint section $\frac{1}{4}$.

MIXED NUMBERS

The picture graph shows the number of pies sold each day during a school bake sale.

Each ◯ stands for 1 pie.

On Thursday, 4 pies were sold. Each ◗ stands for $\frac{1}{2}$ pie.

On Monday, $3\frac{1}{2}$ pies were sold.

Numbers that have a whole number part and a fraction part are called **mixed numbers.**

For example, $3\frac{1}{2}$ is a mixed number.

Number of Pies	
Monday	◯◯◯ ◗
Tuesday	◯◯ ◗
Wednesday	◯
Thursday	◯◯◯◯
Friday	◯◯◯◯◯

◯ = 1 pie   ◗ = 1/2 pie

Think

- What are some ways you use mixed numbers?

- What other mixed number is shown on the picture graph?

Other Examples

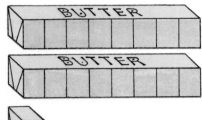

$2\frac{1}{8}$ sticks of butter

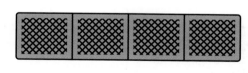
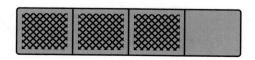

$1\frac{3}{4}$ parts shaded

GUIDED PRACTICE

Write a mixed number for the shaded part.

1.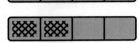

2.

3.

4. Which picture shows a mixed number that is closest to 6? How do you know?

INDEPENDENT PRACTICE

Write a mixed number for the shaded part.

5.

6.

7.

8.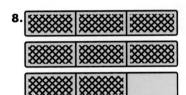

9.

10.

Problem Solving

11. José will be 9 years old in $\frac{1}{2}$ year. Write a mixed number for his age now.

12. Use the trail mix recipe on page 423 in the Data Book. Write the mixed numbers you see.

Maintain • **Mixed Practice**

Write the missing factor.

1. $2 \times \blacksquare = 18$
2. $\blacksquare \times 7 = 21$
3. $5 \times \blacksquare = 40$
4. $\blacksquare \times 4 = 24$

Write the quotient.

5. $3\overline{)18}$
6. $6\overline{)30}$
7. $7\overline{)49}$
8. $6\overline{)54}$
9. $8\overline{)72}$
10. $9\overline{)72}$

FRACTIONS AND TIME

Fractions may help you tell time.

From 10:00 to 10:15, $\frac{1}{4}$ of an hour has passed. One **quarter** is another name for $\frac{1}{4}$. You can say "ten-fifteen" or "quarter past ten."

From 10:00 to 10:30, $\frac{1}{2}$ of an hour has passed. You can say "ten-thirty" or "half past ten."

From 10:00 to 10:45, $\frac{3}{4}$ of an hour has passed. In $\frac{1}{4}$ hour, or one-quarter hour, it will be 11:00. You can say "ten-forty-five" or "quarter to eleven."

Think

• There are 60 minutes in one hour. How would you decide how many minutes are in $\frac{1}{2}$ an hour?

GUIDED PRACTICE

Write the time in words. Use *quarter past*, *half past*, or *quarter to*.

1.

2.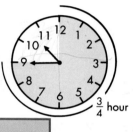

3.

4. What fraction of an hour has passed from 2:30 to 2:45? How do you know?

INDEPENDENT PRACTICE

Write the time. Use *quarter past, half past,* or *quarter to.*

5.   **6.**   **7.**

8. 5 : 30   **9.** 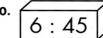 8 : 15   **10.** 6 : 45

Write the fraction of an hour that has passed.
Write $\frac{1}{4}$, $\frac{1}{2}$, or $\frac{3}{4}$.

11.    **12.**    **13.** 11:00 to 11:15

Rewrite the time. Use *quarter past, half past,* or
quarter to.

14. nine-fifteen   **15.** six forty-five   **16.** thirty minutes
past four

Problem Solving Draw a clock if you need help.

17. Tina spent $\frac{1}{2}$ hour on her
homework. Amy did her
homework from 6:45 to 7:00.
Who spent more time on
homework?

18. Matt washed the dishes from
7:00 to 7:15. For what
fraction of an hour did he
wash dishes?

Maintain • **Geometry**

Write whether each figure shows a slide or a flip.

1.   **2.** 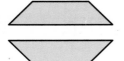   **3.**   **4.**

USING MATH SENSE

Mrs. Atwood is painting some rooms in her house. Solve each problem.

1. Mrs. Atwood painted this morning from 9:30 to 11:15. How many hours is that?

2. Mrs. Atwood has just painted $\frac{1}{4}$ of a door. What fraction of the door still needs to be painted?

3. The large can of paint at the left is $\frac{1}{2}$ full. The small can is $\frac{3}{4}$ full. Which can has more paint? How do you know?

4. Mark goes to the store to buy a paint brush for Mrs. Atwood. The store clerk says the brush costs a dollar and a half. Mark has a one-dollar bill and 2 quarters. Does he have enough money to buy the brush? How do you know?

5. Mrs. Atwood opens a fresh gallon of paint to start a wall in the living room. After she paints $\frac{1}{2}$ of the wall, she has about $\frac{3}{4}$ of the gallon left. Is there enough paint left in the can to finish the wall? How do you know?

6. Mrs. Atwood's neighbors are painting, too. Which neighbors have painted about $\frac{2}{3}$ of the side of their house?

the Bailys

the Cobbs

the Dodds

SECTION REVIEW
for pages 254–264

Estimate. Is more than or less than half the wall painted? Write *more than* or *less than*.

1. 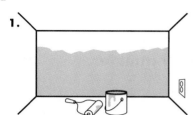   **2.** 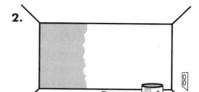   **3.**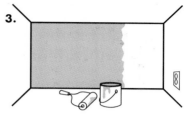

Estimate. About what fraction of the pizza is left? Write $\frac{1}{4}$, $\frac{1}{2}$, or $\frac{3}{4}$.

4.    **5.**    **6.**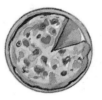

Write the answer. Use Fraction Bars if you like.

7. $\frac{1}{3} + \frac{1}{3}$ **8.** $\frac{2}{4} + \frac{1}{4}$ **9.** $\frac{5}{6} - \frac{1}{6}$ **10.** $\frac{2}{2} - \frac{1}{2}$

Write a mixed number for the shaded part.

11.    **12.** 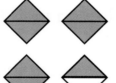   **13.**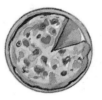

Write the time. Use *quarter past, half past,* or *quarter to.*

14.   **15.**    **16.**

CHAPTER REVIEW

Language Connection

Look at the recipe for meat loaf. It has fractions. If you look carefully, you will notice the recipe shows an example of each: **numerator, denominator, equivalent fractions, mixed number,** and **quarter.**

Write your own recipe. Use fractions in it.

MEATLOAF

1½ pound hamburger
½ onion
1 egg
⅓ cup bread crumbs
2 quarter-teaspoons salt (½ tsp in all)
¼ teaspoon pepper

Test ●●●●●●●

Write a fraction for the shaded part of the figure.

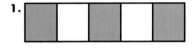

Write a mixed number for the shaded part.

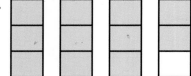

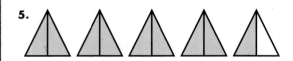

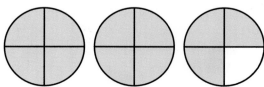

Write the time. Use *quarter past, half past,* or *quarter to.*

9.

10.

11.

12.

PROBLEM SOLVING

Solve each problem.

13. Sandy wants to buy a bookcase that costs $62. She has saved $38 so far. How much more money does she need to save?

14. Tony has 211 paper clips. Liz has 94 paper clips. How many more paper clips does Tony have than Liz?

15. On Tuesday, Mr. Diaz baked bread from 4:00 P.M. to 7:30 P.M. For how many hours did he bake bread?

16. Paul rode his bike 8 miles on Saturday and $4\frac{1}{2}$ miles on Sunday. How many miles did he ride?

CUMULATIVE REVIEW

Write a related division sentence.

17. $6 \times 3 = 18$

18. $4 \times 8 = 32$

19. $9 \times 6 = 54$

Write *slide, flip,* or *half turn* for the set of figures.

Is the angle greater than, less than, or equal to a square corner? Write $>$, $<$, or $=$.

20.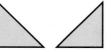

21.

22.

23.

EXCURSION

USING TECHNOLOGY

LOGO

You will need: Logo software, a computer, and squared paper.

You can make the turtle move without drawing its steps.

Logo Command	What You Can Type	What the Turtle Will Do
PENUP	PU	move without drawing
PENDOWN	PD	draw as it moves

Read the procedure below. Look at what the turtle drew. The dotted lines show when the turtle lifted its pen.

TO SQUARES

REPEAT 4 [FD 80 RT 90]
PU FD 20 RT 90 FD 20 PD
REPEAT 4 [FD 40 LT 90]

END

Sometimes a procedure does not work. A mistake in a procedure is called a **bug.**

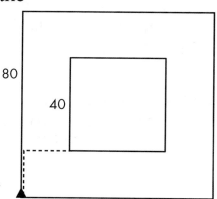

80

40

Start

1. Mike wants the turtle to draw a square.

   TO SQUARE
   REPEAT 3 [FD 30 RT 90]
   END

   The procedure has a bug in it. Type in the right procedure. Tell the turtle to DRAW SQUARE.

2. Jared wrote the procedure below to make the turtle draw the pattern at the right.

TO PATTERN

REPEAT 4 [FD 60 LT 90]
RT 90 FD 30 LT 45
REPEAT 4 [FD 60 RT 90]

END

Do you think Jared's procedure will work?

3. Type in the procedure. Tell the turtle to DRAW PATTERN. Did the turtle draw the correct pattern?

4. Find the bugs in Jared's procedure. Write the correct procedure. Type it in. Then tell the turtle to DRAW PATTERN again.

5. Write a procedure that tells the turtle how to draw this door. Type in your procedure. Tell the turtle to DRAW DOOR.

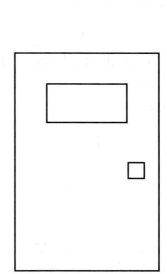

MEASUREMENT AND TIME

Someone Slow

I know someone who is so slow
It takes him all day and all night to go
From Sunday to Monday, and all week long
To get back to Sunday. He never goes wrong.
And he never stops. But oh, my dear,
From birthday to birthday it takes him all year!
And that's much too slow, as I know you know.
One day I tried to tell him so.
But all he would say was "tick" and "tock."
—Poor old slow GRANDFATHER CLOCK.

by John Ciardi

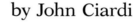

INCH

In the United States we usually use the **customary** system of measurement. The **inch (in.)** is a customary unit for measuring length.

The pictures show some objects that are about an inch long.

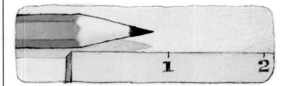

sharpened part of a pencil

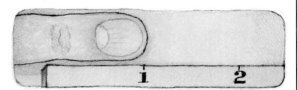

thumb from the knuckle to the tip

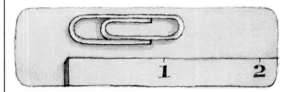

small paper clip

distance across a quarter

Think

• How could you use small paper clips to measure the length of your desk?

GUIDED PRACTICE

About how long is each object? Write the length in inches.

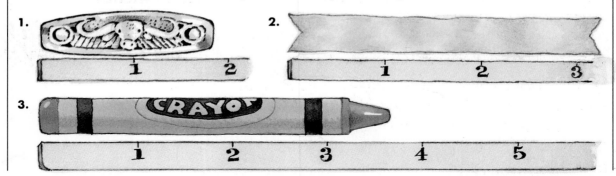

1.

2.

3.

Use a ruler to measure the length of each ribbon.
Write the length in inches.

4.

5.

6.

7. Without using a ruler, draw a line
   segment about 3 inches long. Then
   measure it. How close were you?

INDEPENDENT PRACTICE

Use a ruler to measure the length of each. Write
the length in inches.

8.

9.

10.

Use a ruler to draw the line segment.

11. 7 inches   12. 12 inches   13. 14 inches

PROJECT • Estimation

Work with a partner. Find three objects that
you think are between 5 inches and 8 inches
long. Measure each object and record its
length. Which ones were between 5 inches
and 8 inches long?

INCH AND HALF INCH

▶ Some rulers, like the one below, are marked at the **half inch.** The piece of string is about $3\frac{1}{2}$ inches long.

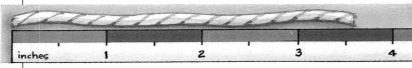

Think

• Suppose you measure the string above with a ruler marked only in inches. Would you say that it is 3 inches long or 4 inches long? Explain.

The length of the piece of string is a little more than $3\frac{1}{2}$ inches. It is $3\frac{1}{2}$ inches long to the **nearest half inch.** It is 4 inches long to the **nearest inch**.

▶ This piece of string is 2 inches to the nearest inch and 2 inches to the nearest half inch.

Inch marks are also half-inch marks.

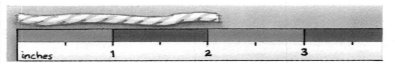

GUIDED PRACTICE

Write the length of each ribbon to the nearest inch. Then write the length to the nearest half inch.

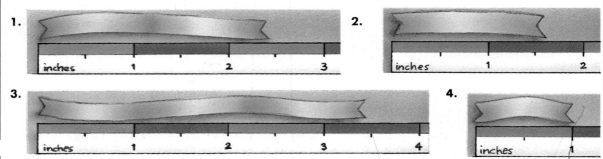

1.

2.

3.

4.

Measure the string to the nearest inch. Then measure to the nearest half inch. Write the lengths.

5.

6.

7. What do you notice about your answers to exercise 6? Explain.

....

INDEPENDENT PRACTICE

Measure each to the nearest inch. Then measure to the nearest half inch. Write the lengths.

8.   **9.**

10. length of your shoe   **11.** height of a wastebasket

Use a ruler to draw the line segment.

12. 5 inches   **13.** $7\frac{1}{2}$ inches   **14.** 3 inches   **15.** $13\frac{1}{2}$ inches

....

PROJECT • Measurement

Work with a partner. Make a chart like the one shown. Fill it in with your own measurements. Measure to the nearest half inch.

1. width of your shoulders

2. length of your upper arm (from shoulder to elbow)

3. length of your thumb

4. length of your ring finger

5. distance around your wrist (HINT: Use a piece of string.)

Save your completed chart.

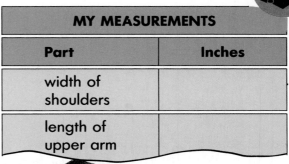

MY MEASUREMENTS	
Part	**Inches**
width of shoulders	
length of upper arm	

PERIMETER

Anita and Mark are making a valentine for their teacher. They want to put a lace border around it. About how much lace do they need?

To decide, they must measure around the card. The distance around something is called the **perimeter.**

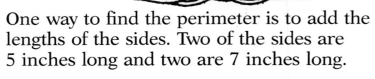

One way to find the perimeter is to add the lengths of the sides. Two of the sides are 5 inches long and two are 7 inches long.

5 in. + 5 in. + 7 in. + 7 in. = 24 in.

They will need about 24 inches of lace.

Think

• Do you think they should get exactly 24 inches of lace? Explain.

Other Examples

How much lace is needed for each card?

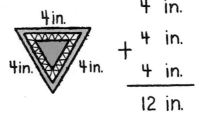

$$\begin{array}{r} 4 \ \text{in.} \\ 4 \ \text{in.} \\ + \ 4 \ \text{in.} \\ \hline 12 \ \text{in.} \end{array}$$

This card needs a little more than 12 inches of lace.

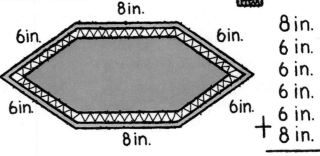

$$\begin{array}{r} 8 \ \text{in.} \\ 6 \ \text{in.} \\ 6 \ \text{in.} \\ 6 \ \text{in.} \\ 6 \ \text{in.} \\ + \ 8 \ \text{in.} \\ \hline 40 \ \text{in.} \end{array}$$

This card needs a little more than 40 inches of lace.

GUIDED PRACTICE

Write the perimeter.

1.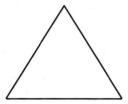
12 in.
4 in.
6 in.

2.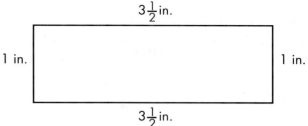
$3\frac{1}{2}$ in.
1 in.
1 in.
$3\frac{1}{2}$ in.

Measure each side to the nearest half inch. Write the perimeter.

3.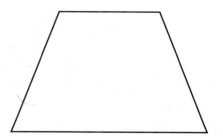

4.

5. Suppose you know the length of one side of a square. Can you find its perimeter? Explain.

INDEPENDENT PRACTICE

Write the perimeter.

6.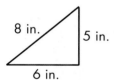
8 in.
5 in.
6 in.

7.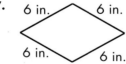
6 in. 6 in.
6 in. 6 in.

8.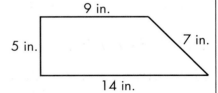
9 in.
5 in.
7 in.
14 in.

CHALLENGE • Estimation

Estimate which figure in each pair has the greater perimeter. Write *a* or *b*. Compare your results with a classmate's.

1. a.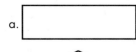

b.

2. a.

b.

3. a.

b.

FOOT, YARD, AND MILE

The **foot (ft)**, the **yard (yd)**, and the **mile (mi)** are other customary units for measuring length.

| 1 ft = 12 in. |
| 1 yd = 3 ft, or 36 in. |
| 1 mi = 5280 ft |

▶ One foot:

as long as a 12-inch ruler.

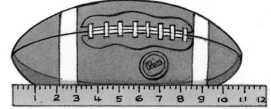

about as long as a football.

▶ One yard:

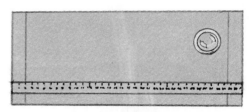

about as long as a baseball bat.

about as wide as a door.

▶ A mile is 5280 feet. It takes about 20 minutes to walk 1 mile.

Think

• Which is longer, a rope that is 3 feet long or a rope that is 3 yards long? Explain.

• How many inches are in half a foot? How do you know?

▶ David is 4 feet tall. Sarah is 45 inches tall. Who is taller?

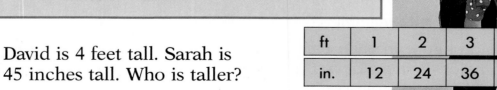

ft	1	2	3	4	5
in.	12	24	36	48	60

To compare 4 feet and 45 inches, you need to write them in the same unit of measure. You can see from the table that 4 feet is the same as 48 inches. Since 48 is greater than 45, David is taller.

Which unit would you use to measure each?
Write *foot, yard,* or *mile.*

1. length of your desk

2. distance to the North Pole

3. length of a football field

4. height of your school

Complete each sentence. Write *feet, yards,* or *miles.*

5. The desk is 4 ▨ long.

6. Julio lives 2 ▨ from school.

Complete. Write <, >, or =. You can use the table on page 278.

7. 12 in. ● 12 ft

8. $5\frac{1}{2}$ ft ● $5\frac{1}{2}$ yd

9. 36 in. ● 3 ft

10. In exercise 9, could you just compare the numbers 36 and 3 to get your answer? Explain.

INDEPENDENT PRACTICE

Complete each sentence. Write *feet, yards,* or *miles.*

11. Hugh's bus ride to school is 8 ▨ long.

12. A dog leash is about 4 ▨ long.

13. Marty's kitten is about 1 ▨ long.

14. You can walk 3 ▨ in about an hour.

Complete. Write <, >, or =. You can use the table on page 278.

15. 12 mi ● 12 yd

16. $7\frac{1}{2}$ ft ● $7\frac{1}{2}$ yd

17. 6 ft ● 2 yd

18. 29 in. ● 3 ft

19. 1 mi ● 2000 ft

20. 40 in. ● 1 yd

MATH LOG

What pattern do you see when writing feet as inches?

CUP, PINT, QUART, AND GALLON

When you measure the amount of liquid that a container holds, you measure its **capacity.**

| 1 pt = 2 c |
| 1 qt = 2 pt, or 4 c |
| 1 gal = 4 qt |

Cup (c), pint (pt), quart (qt), and **gallon (gal)** are customary units for measuring liquid capacity.

The tables below show how the customary units of capacity are related.

Table 1

qt		1		2		3
pt	1	2	3	4	5	6
c	2	4	6	8	10	12

Table 2

gal	1	2	3	4
qt	4	8	12	16

Think

- If Table 2 went to 5 gallons, how many quarts would be listed?

- How many cups are in half a pint?

GUIDED PRACTICE

Complete. Write <, >, or = . Use the tables if you like.

1. 4 cups ● 4 pints
2. 1 quart ● 1 pint
3. 2 gallons ● 8 quarts
4. 8 c ● 2 pt
5. 6 pt ● 3 qt
6. 1 gal ● 4 qt

7. Suppose you pour 12 cups of juice into pint containers. Would you use more pints than cups or fewer pints than cups? Explain.

INDEPENDENT PRACTICE

Complete. Write <, >, or =. You can use the tables on page 280.

8. 2 qt ⬤ 2 pt   **9.** 6 qt ⬤ 6 gal   **10.** 6 c ⬤ 4 pt   **11.** 8 c ⬤ 2 qt

Does the object hold more than or less than one quart? Write *more than* or *less than*.

12. bottle cap   **13.** mug   **14.** large bucket

15. bathtub   **16.** kitchen sink   **17.** baby bottle

Choose the better unit of measure. Write *a* or *b*.

18. water in a fish tank
   a. cup   **b.** gallon

19. glass of milk
   a. cup   **b.** quart

20. gasoline in a car
   a. pint   **b.** gallon

21. pitchers of juice
   a. quart   **b.** cup

Problem Solving

22. Adam is making 4 banana milk shakes. He needs 2 cups of milk for each shake. How many quarts of milk does he need?

23. Sonia needs to fill her 5-gallon fish tank with water. The jar she has holds only 1 quart. How many times will she need to fill the jar?

Maintain • **Mixed Practice**

Write the answer.

1. 136
      + 249

2. 493
      + 307

3. 903
      − 426

4. $8.50
      − 0.50

5. 39
        64
      + 54

OUNCE AND POUND

▶ The **ounce (oz)** and the **pound (lb)** are customary units for measuring weight.

▶ This table shows how pounds and ounces are related.

lb	1	2	3	4	5
oz	16	32	48	64	80

Six pencils weigh about 1 ounce.

A stapler weighs about 1 pound.

Think

- Is an 18-ounce bag of nuts heavier than a 2-pound bunch of grapes? Explain.

INDEPENDENT PRACTICE

Which unit would you use? Write *ounce* or *pound*.

1. large dog
2. 10 paper clips
3. box of crayons
4. full suitcase
5. apple
6. bag of apples

Complete. Write < or >. You can use the table.

7. 5 lb ● 5 oz
8. 10 oz ● 1 lb
9. 6 lb ● 150 oz

PROJECT • Estimation

Work in a group. You will need a scale.

a. Choose 5 objects. Put them in order from lightest to heaviest.
b. Estimate whether each object is less than 1 pound, about 1 pound, or more than 1 pound. Record your estimates.
c. Weigh the objects. Record the weights. How close were your estimates?

SECTION REVIEW
for pages 272–282

Which unit would you use to measure each?
Write *a, b,* or *c.*

1. length of your desk
   a. foot **b.** quart **c.** pound

2. amount of milk in a glass
   a. foot **b.** pound **c.** cup

3. distance between 2 cities
   a. inch **b.** mile **c.** gallon

4. weight of a seashell
   a. pint **b.** gallon **c.** ounce

Choose the better unit of measure. Write *a* or *b.*

5. length of a room
   a. foot **b.** mile

6. capacity of a bathtub
   a. gallon **b.** pint

7. weight of a big dog
   a. ounce **b.** pound

8. distance to the South Pole
   a. mile **b.** yard

Draw the line segment. Use a ruler.
9. 5 inches   10. $8\frac{1}{2}$ inches   11. $1\frac{1}{2}$ inches

Complete. Write <, >, or =.

12. 5 ft ⬤ 5 yd   13. 24 in. ⬤ 2 ft   14. 2 qt ⬤ 2 gal

15. 3 ft ⬤ 1 yd   16. 10 lb ⬤ 10 oz   17. 10 ft ⬤ 1 mi

Write the perimeter of the figure.

18.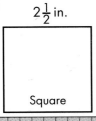
4 in. $6\frac{1}{2}$ in.
7 in.

19.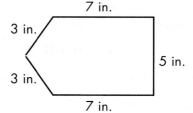
7 in.
3 in.
3 in.
5 in.
7 in.

20.
$2\frac{1}{2}$ in.
Square

21.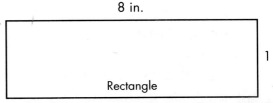
8 in.
1 in.
Rectangle

283

CENTIMETER

1 dm = 10 cm

The **metric** system is another measurement system. It is used in many countries. The **centimeter (cm)** is a metric unit for measuring length.

Some objects that measure about 1 centimeter:

a ones block.

the width of a large paper clip.

There are 10 centimeters in 1 **decimeter (dm).**
A decimeter is as long as a tens block.

The worm is nearer to 9 centimeters long than to 8 centimeters. The worm is 9 centimeters long **to the nearest centimeter.**

Think

- Is 1 centimeter longer than or shorter than 1 inch? How do you know?

GUIDED PRACTICE

Measure to the nearest centimeter. Write the length.

1.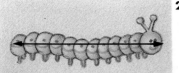

2.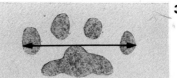

3.

4. length of your little finger

5. perimeter of a box of crayons

Use a centimeter ruler. Draw the line segment.

6. 10 cm

7. 24 cm

8. 1 dm

9. What do you notice about the line segments in exercises 6 and 8?

....

INDEPENDENT PRACTICE

Measure to the nearest centimeter. Write the length.

10.

11.

12. length of your desk

13. length of a pencil

Estimate the length in centimeters. Then measure to the nearest centimeter. Write the length.

14.

15.

....

PROJECT • Measurement

Work with a partner.

a. Use the chart you made for the Project on page 275. Add a centimeter column to it.

b. Take your measurements again. This time measure to the nearest centimeter.

METER AND KILOMETER

The **meter (m)** and **kilometer (km)** are metric units of length. They are used to measure longer lengths.

1 m = 100 cm
1 km = 1000 m

▶ A meter:

• 100 centimeters.

• the length of 10 tens blocks.

Some objects that measure about a meter:

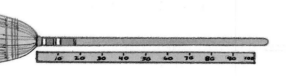

a broom handle.

the height of a chalkboard.

▶ A kilometer is used to measure longer distances. It takes about 15 minutes to walk 1 kilometer.

Think

Knoxville   12
12 mi or 19 km

• Which is longer, a mile or a kilometer? How do you know?

• How many centimeters are in half a meter?

• How many meters are in half a kilometer?

GUIDED PRACTICE

Complete. Write <, >, or =. You can use the table.

1. 10 m ● 10 km
2. 100 cm ● 1 m
3. 2500 m ● 2 km

Which unit would you use to measure each?
Write *meter* or *kilometer*.

4. distance between cities

5. length of your classroom

6. How did you get your answer to exercise 3?
Explain.

INDEPENDENT PRACTICE

Choose the better estimate. Write *a* or *b*.

7. length of a ball field

   a. 100 m   **b.** 100 km

8. length of a skateboard

   a. 75 cm   **b.** 75 m

9. depth of a swimming pool

   a. 3 cm   **b.** 3 m

10. length of a table

   a. 1 m   **b.** 1 km

Complete. Write < or >. You can use the table on
page 286.

11. 2000 m ⬤ 20 km   **12.** 3 km ⬤ 300 m   **13.** 10 m ⬤ 1 km

PROJECT • Meter

Work with a partner. You will need a tens block,
a long piece of string, and scissors.

a. Use the tens block to measure the length
of 10 tens blocks on your string. Cut the
string to measure 1 meter.

b. Find 3 objects that you think are 1 meter
long. Measure each object with your meter
string. Write whether each object is longer
than 1 meter, shorter than 1 meter, or
about as long as 1 meter.

c. Estimate the perimeter of the chalkboard
in meters. Write your estimate. Then use
your meter string to measure. Was your
estimate close?

If you get stuck, remember....
Tips for Problem Solving
on pages 426–427

Solve each problem.

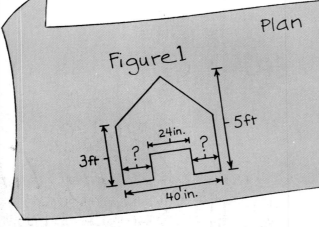

Plan

Figure 1

24 in.

? — ? —

3 ft

5 ft

40 in.

Figure 2

3 ft

4 ft

A lot of building is going on in Dogtown. Mr. Ruff is putting up a new house.

1. Look at Figure 1 in the Plan. How tall will Mr. Ruff's new house be?

2. The doorway will be in the center of the front of the house. How far will the edges of the doorway be from the sides of the house?

3. For 2 sides of the house, Mr. Ruff needs 2 pieces of wood like the one shown in Figure 2. He has a sheet of wood that is 8 feet long and 4 feet wide.

   a. Does Mr. Ruff have enough wood to build 2 sides of the house? How can you tell?

   b. What is the size of the wood that will be left over?

4. Draw a picture of the piece of wood Mr. Ruff needs for the back of his house. Label it. Show how wide it should be and how tall it should be.

5. The roof of Mr. Ruff's house will be made of 2 pieces of wood with the same shape. Draw the shape of each piece.

6. Mr. Ruff decided to put 8 windows in his house. He can paint 3 windows every 2 hours. He starts painting at 9:00 A.M. Will he finish by noon? How do you know?

7. Design your own model dog house. Draw the pieces on paper or cardboard. Cut them out. Paste or tape them together. What size is the window? What size is the door?

MILLILITER AND LITER

A **milliliter (mL)** and a **liter(L)** are metric units of capacity.

> 1 mL = about 5 drops of liquid
> 1 L = 1000 mL

> A hollow ones block would hold 1 mL of water.

1 liter

1 milliliter

The table shows how the units are related.

L	1	2	3	4	5
mL	1000	2000	3000	4000	5000

Think

• How many milliliters are in half a liter? How do you know?

GUIDED PRACTICE

Which unit would you use to measure the capacity?
Write *liter* or *milliliter*.

1.

2.

3.

Complete. Write <, >, or = . You can use the table.

4. 50 mL ⬤ 5 L

5. 2000 mL ⬤ 2 L

6. 1 L ⬤ 500 mL

7. Does each container in exercises 1–3 hold more than or less than a liter? Write *more than* or *less than*.

INDEPENDENT PRACTICE

Does the object hold more than or less than a liter?
Write *more than* or *less than*.

8. swimming pool

9. drinking glass

10. kitchen sink

11. can of soup

Complete. Write < or >. You can use the table on page 290.

12. 1200 mL ⬤ 2 L

13. 6 L ⬤ 600 mL

14. 500 mL ⬤ 5 L

Problem Solving

15. In science class, Emily needs 2 liters of water. The only container she has holds 500 milliliters. How can she use the container to measure 2 liters?

16. Tomas puts 3 teaspoons of honey on his cereal. A teaspoon holds about 5 milliliters. About how many milliliters of honey does Tomas eat?

PROJECT • Measurement

Work with a group. You will need water and a liter measure.

a. Find two containers that you think will hold about one liter each.

b. Now find two containers that you think will hold about one-half liter each.

c. Then use a liter measure and water to find the capacity of each container. How close were your predictions?

d. Compare your results with another group's results.

GRAM AND KILOGRAM

In the metric system, the **gram (g)** and the **kilogram (kg)** are used to weigh things.

$$1 \text{ kg} = 1000 \text{ g}$$

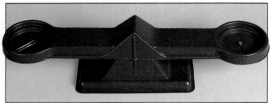

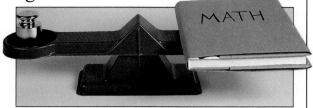

A large paper clip weighs about 1 gram.

Your math book weighs about 1 kilogram.

kg	1	2	3	4	5
g	1000	2000	3000	4000	5000

INDEPENDENT PRACTICE

Which unit would you use? Write *gram* or *kilogram*.

1. truck
2. large dog
3. slice of cheese
4. pencil
5. yourself
6. feather

Complete. Write <, >, or = . You can use the table.

7. 3000 g ● 3 kg
8. 2 kg ● 200 g
9. 5000 g ● 50 kg

PROJECT • Estimation

Work with a small group. You will need a balance.

a. Choose five objects.
b. Put them in order from heaviest to lightest.
c. Estimate whether each weighs less than 1 kilogram, about 1 kilogram, or more than 1 kilogram. Record your estimates.
d. Weigh the objects. Record the results.

How close were your estimates?

292

USING STRATEGIES

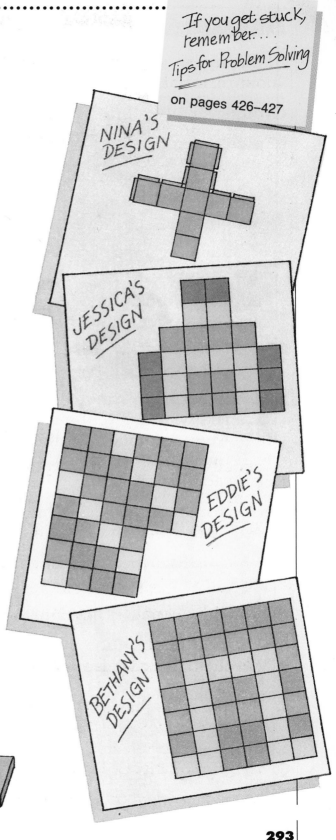

If you get stuck, remember....

Tips for Problem Solving

on pages 426–427

NINA'S DESIGN

JESSICA'S DESIGN

EDDIE'S DESIGN

BETHANY'S DESIGN

Solve each problem. You will need squared paper or dot paper.

1. Ms. Johnson's art class is making designs with tiles and sticks. The sticks are used for borders. The sticks are the same length as one side of a tile. How many more sticks does Nina need to finish the border for her design?

2. Jessica has a package of 15 sticks. How many more sticks will she need for the border of her design?

3. Look at Eddie's and Bethany's designs. Which design will need more sticks for its border?

4. Look at all 4 designs on this page. Which ones use more tiles than sticks?

5. Use squared paper or dot paper to draw your own tile design. Your design should need more sticks than tiles. Shade your tiles any color you wish. How many tiles does your design have? How many sticks do you need for the border?

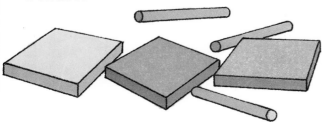

MEASUREMENT LAB

In this lesson you will discover some things about materials that you use every day.

Groups: small groups

You will need:

- 4 empty and clean half-pint milk containers
- pan balance
- 1-ounce, 2-ounce, 4-ounce, 8-ounce, and 1-pound weights
- as many of these materials as you can get: water, sand or gravel, salt, sugar, rice, unpopped popcorn
- recording sheet

▶ In this experiment, you will fill the milk containers with different materials. Then you will put two containers on the balance to see which material is heavier. After this, you will weigh each material.

Before you begin, predict which material is heavier. Answer each question.

1. Which is heavier, a container of water or a container of salt?

2. Which is heavier, a container of salt or a container of sugar?

3. Which is heavier, water or sand?

4. Which is heavier, sugar or unpopped popcorn?

5. Which is heavier, dry sand or wet sand?

Make as many other comparisons as you like.

Now see if your predictions were correct.

6. Fill the containers and, two at a time, put them on the balance. (Be sure to fill only to the fold line.)

7. Continue comparing the weights of the materials. How close were your predictions?

▶ Weigh each material.

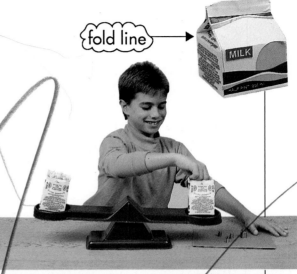

{fold line} →

8. Place a filled container on one side of the balance.

9. On the other side of the balance, place an empty container. Put the ounce and pound weights in this container to weigh the material.

10. Record the weight on your recording sheet. List only the materials you use.

Continue weighing each material and recording its weight.

....
SUMMING IT UP

11. When you are finished, make a list of all the materials you weighed. List the materials in order from heaviest to lightest.

WHAT DO THEY WEIGH?

Material	Weight (pounds and ounces)
water	
salt	
sugar	
sand	
unpopped popcorn	
dry sand	
wet sand	

TEMPERATURE

Temperature is a measure of how hot or cold something is. Temperature is measured in degrees.

The customary unit for measuring temperature is the **degree Fahrenheit (°F).** The metric unit is the **degree Celsius (°C).**

Ben's thermometer shows both scales. Look at his thermometer. It shows that the temperature is about 70°F, or about 20°C.

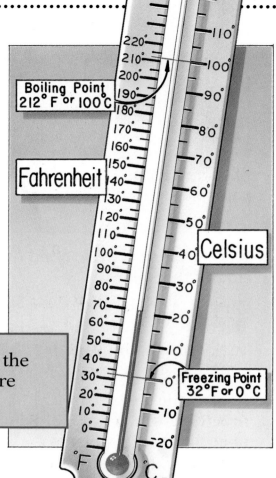

Think

- What happens to the red liquid in the thermometer when the temperature gets cooler?

GUIDED PRACTICE

Write the temperature each thermometer shows.

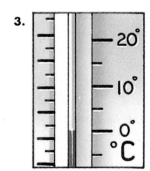

Use Ben's thermometer to answer the questions.

5. At what Celsius temperature does water boil?

6. Which is warmer, 20°C or 20°F?

7. How did you get your answer for exercise 6?

INDEPENDENT PRACTICE

Write the temperature each thermometer shows.

8. 9. 10. 11.

Use Ben's thermometer on page 296 to answer the questions.

12. At what Fahrenheit temperature does water freeze?

13. Which is cooler, 30°F or 30°C?

Problem Solving You can use the thermometer on page 296.

14. At 8:00 A.M., it was 60°F. By noon, it was 10° warmer. What was the temperature at noon?

15. At 6:30 P.M., it was 65°F. At 10 P.M., it was 15° cooler. What was the temperature at 10 P.M.?

16. Sally is going on a trip. It is 28°F where she is going. Is she more likely to go to the beach or downhill skiing?

17. An ice-skating party has been canceled because of the weather. It is 10°C outdoors. Is it too cold or too warm?

Maintain • **Fractions**

Write a fraction for the shaded part. Then write a fraction for the unshaded part.

1.   2. 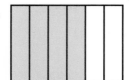 3.   4.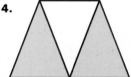

TIME

▶ You can use **seconds (s), minutes (min), hours (h),** and **days (d)** to measure time.

1 min = 60 s
1 h = 60 min
1 d = 24 h

- It takes about a second to open a door.
- It takes about a minute to write your name and address.
- Baseball practice may take about an hour.

▶ Look at the clock. What time is it?

The short hand is between 1 and 2. So it is after one o'clock.

The long hand shows how many minutes have passed since one o'clock.

To find how many minutes, skip-count by 5's from the 12 to the 5. Then count on by 1's until you reach the long hand.

The time is 27 minutes past one o'clock, or 1:27.

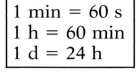

Think

• There are 24 hours in a day. How can you use a clock that has only 12 numbers to tell time?

▶ You know that the hours from midnight to noon are labeled *A.M.* These hours are in the *morning*.

The hours from noon to midnight are labeled *P.M.* These hours are in the *afternoon, evening,* or *night*.

GUIDED PRACTICE

Write the time shown on the clock.

1.

2.

3.

4. Write what you might be doing if the times in exercises 1–3 were A.M.

....

INDEPENDENT PRACTICE

Write the time shown on the clock.

5.

6.

7.

How much time would you spend on each activity? Choose the better estimate. Write *a* or *b*.

8. playing a soccer game
  a. 1 hour **b.** 1 minute

9. eating lunch
  a. 30 minutes **b.** 30 seconds

10. unlocking a door
  a. 5 seconds **b.** 1 hour

11. walking a mile
  a. 5 minutes **b.** 25 minutes

....

PROJECT • A.M. and P.M.

Make lists of what you do in a day.

a. Use 2 sheets of paper. Label one *A.M.* and the other, *P.M.*

b. Think of all the things you do in a day. Think of when you do them. Write the activities down on either the A.M. or P.M. list.

c. Share your list with a friend. How are they the same? How are they different?

ELAPSED TIME

Carmen gets on the school bus at Pine Road. Peter gets on the bus at Lee Street. For how long does Carmen ride the bus before Peter gets on?

Skip-count by 5's to find how many minutes Carmen rides the bus before Peter gets on.

Carmen rides for 15 minutes before Peter gets on.

For how long does Carmen ride the bus to school?

School Bus Pick-up Schedule	
Pine Road	7:50 A.M.
Lake Road	7:55 A.M.
Lee Street	8:05 A.M.
Whitney's Store	8:13 A.M.
School	8:28 A.M.

7:50 A.M.   8:05 A.M.

Think

• How can you estimate how long it takes Carmen to ride to school?

Skip-count by 5's and count on by 1's to find how many minutes Carmen is on the school bus.

From 7:50 to 8:25 is 35 minutes.
From 8:25 to 8:28 is 3 minutes.
So, from 7:50 to 8:28 is 38 minutes.

Carmen's bus ride takes 38 minutes.

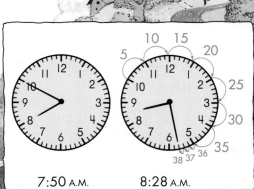

7:50 A.M.   8:28 A.M.

GUIDED PRACTICE

Use the bus schedule on page 300. Write *true* or *false*.

1. Carmen gets on the bus before Peter.

2. Carmen gets on the bus at the first stop.

3. Peter gets on at the last stop.

4. Carmen rides for one hour.

Write how much time has passed.

5.

6.

7. What time will it be 15 minutes from now? Write the time.

INDEPENDENT PRACTICE

Write how much time has passed.

8.

9.

Problem Solving Use the bus schedule on page 300.

10. Peter saves a seat on the bus for Jesse. At which stop does Jesse get on the bus?

11. It takes Peter 45 minutes to get ready for school and walk to the bus stop. If he wakes up at 7:15 A.M., will he be on time for the bus?

MATH LOG

What time do you get up in the morning? What time do you arrive at school? About how much time passes in between?

CALENDAR

Maya and her family are going on vacation in July. They will leave on July 4 and return 18 days later.

On what date will they return? What day of the week is that?

			JULY			
Sunday	Monday	Tuesday	Wednesday	Thursday	Friday	Saturday
	1	2	3	4	5	6
7	8	9	10	11	12	13
14	15	16	17	18	19	20
21	22	23	24	25	26	27
28	29	30	31			

Think

- If Maya were going to be away for 2 weeks, on what day of the week would she return?

Find July 4 on the calendar. Count on 18 days. July 22 is 18 days after July 4. It falls on a Monday.

Maya and her family will return on Monday, July 22.

INDEPENDENT PRACTICE

Write *true* or *false*. Use the calendar to help you.

1. There are 7 days in a week.

2. Maya will be gone more than 3 weeks.

3. Maya will be gone 3 Fridays.

4. There are exactly 4 weeks in every month.

302

PROJECT • Current Calendar

Work with a group. You will need blank calendar sheets and a calculator.

▶ Use the information on page 424 of the Data Book to help you make a calendar for this year. Mark any holidays that you know. Mark your birthday. Then use the calendar to answer the questions.

1. Which months have 30 days?

2. Which months have 31 days?

3. Does any month have fewer than 30 days? Which one? How many days does it have?

▶ Choose any Friday on your calendar.

4. What day of the week is 7 days later?

5. What day of the week is 6 days later?

6. Is this true for any Friday in the year? How can you tell?

7. Use your calculator to find out how many days are in this year.

Decide with your group how to decorate your calendar. You may want to use a theme, such as sports, seasons, or animals. When you are finished, share your group's calendar with the class.

PROBLEM SOLVING
USING STRATEGIES

Solve each problem.

1. On June 2, Greta reads an ad for a camping trip. In how many weeks does the trip start?

2. Greta looks in her drawer to see how much spending money she has. She has two $20 bills. How much more money does she need to go on the trip?

3. Greta is able to save enough money for the camping trip. She brings a book to read during the bus ride there. About how long does she have to read during the ride?

4. About how long will the hike to the campsite take on Saturday?

5. Greta and the other campers hike about 2 miles every hour. About how far is the campsite from where the hike begins?

6. On Sunday, the group must allow 6 hours for the hike back to the bus. What is the latest time that the group can leave the campsite?

Hike and camp in
Vermont

This 2-day hike (June 23-24) includes overnight tent camping, picnic meals, cookout supper.

Price: $75.00 per person

Schedule
Saturday, June 23
Bus leaves
Bus arrives at hike's starting place 9:30 P.M.
Picnic lunch 11:45 A.M.
Hike begins Noon-1:00 P.M.
Reach campsite 1:00 P.M.
Cookout 6:00 P.M.
7:00 - 8:30 P.M.

Sunday, June 24
Picnic breakfast
Nature talk 7:30 A.M.
Bus leaves for home 8:00 A.M.
3:00 P.M.

SECTION REVIEW
for pages 284–304

Which unit would you use to measure each?
Write *a*, *b*, or *c*.

1. your height
   a. gram
   b. centimeter
   c. liter

2. your weight
   a. meter
   b. milliliter
   c. kilogram

Choose the better unit to measure. Write *a* or *b*.

3. height of a tree
   a. meter   b. centimeter

4. capacity of a paper cup
   a. liter   b. milliliter

5. distance of a highway
   a. kilometer   b. meter

6. weight of a bear
   a. gram   b. kilogram

Complete. Write <, >, or = .

7. 10 cm ● 10 m

8. 6 L ● 6000 mL

9. 25 g ● 25 kg

10. 100 cm ● 1 m

11. 4 kg ● 4 g

12. 20 cm ● 2 m

Write the time.

13.

14.

15.

Write how much time has passed.

16.

17.

18.

19.

305

CHAPTER REVIEW

Language Connection

Write the vocabulary words below under the correct heading: *Length, Weight, Capacity, Temperature,* and *Time.* Underline those that are part of the customary system of measurement. Circle those that are part of the metric system.

> inch, gallon, degree Fahrenheit, kilogram, ounce, centimeter, degree Celsius, second, pound, decimeter, meter, minute, perimeter, foot, kilometer, hour, cup, yard, milliliter, day, pint, mile, liter, quart, gram

Test ●●●●●●

Write the measure to the nearest inch, half inch, or centimeter.

1.

2.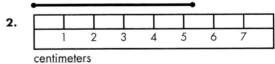

3.

4.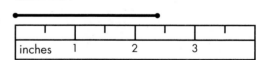

Write the perimeter.

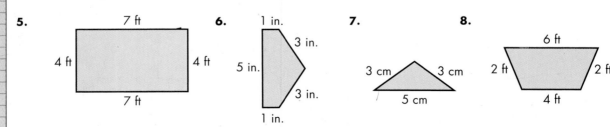

5. 7 ft, 4 ft, 4 ft, 7 ft

6. 1 in., 3 in., 5 in., 3 in., 1 in.

7. 3 cm, 3 cm, 5 cm

8. 6 ft, 2 ft, 2 ft, 4 ft

Write the time shown on the clock.

9.  **10.**  **11.**  **12.**

Choose the better unit to measure. Write *a* or *b*.

13. distance from city to city

    a. yards   **b.** miles

14. weight of a lion

    a. pounds   **b.** ounces

Complete. Write <, >, or = .

15. 2 ft ● 2 in.   **16.** 1 pt ● 1 gal   **17.** 3 lb ● 8 oz   **18.** 3 ft ● 1 yd

PROBLEM SOLVING

19. Mrs. Stinson runs 3 miles every day. How many miles does she run in a week?

20. Ben's dog Max weighs 45 pounds. Last month he weighed 39 pounds. How much weight did Max gain?

CUMULATIVE REVIEW

Is the angle greater than, less than, or equal to a square corner? Write >, <, or = .

21.   **22.**   **23.**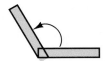

Write a fraction for the shaded part of the figure.

24. 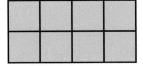   **25.**    **26.**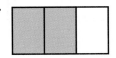

EXCURSION

USING DATA

TIME ZONES

Greg lives in Maine. Lance lives in Utah.
Greg wants to call Lance when it is 2:00 P.M.
in Utah. He needs to know what time in
Maine he should call Lance. He looks at a
map of the United States time zones for help.

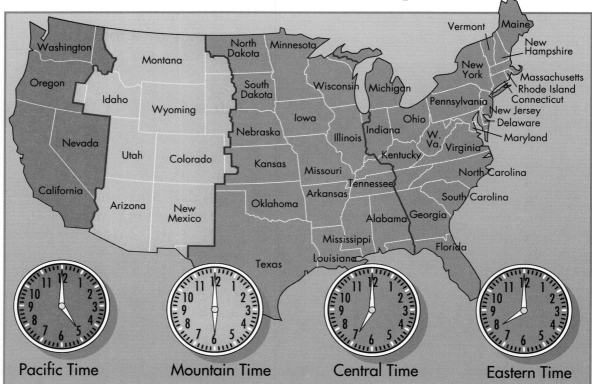

Utah is in the Mountain time zone. Maine is
in the Eastern time zone.

The map shows that when it is 6:00 in Utah,
it is 8:00 in Maine. It is 2 hours later in
Maine. So when it is 2:00 in Utah, it is 4:00
in Maine.

Greg's clock should show 4:00 P.M. when he
calls Lance.

Use the map on page 308 to solve each problem.

1. Jed lives in Massachusetts. In which time zone does he live?

2. When it is 2:00 P.M. in Colorado, what time is it in Florida?

3. In New York, it is 4:00. How many hours earlier is it in Oregon?

4. In Texas, Paula calls Dana at 5:00. Dana lives in Iowa. What time is it in Iowa?

5. Steve's family drives from Georgia to Arkansas. How many time zones do they drive in?

6. Marco lives in Wisconsin. At 1:00, he calls his uncle in Wyoming. What time is it in Wyoming when Marco calls?

7. What is the time in Iowa when it is 3:00 in Montana?

8. It is 6:00 in Florida. What time is it in Kansas?

9. Hannah flies from New York to California and back. She does not change the time on her watch. Is her watch showing the correct time back in New York? Explain.

10. Leah gets off a plane in Arizona. The airport's clock shows 2:00. Leah's watch shows 1:00. Did Leah come from Mississippi or California?

11. Copy and complete the table.

Pacific Time	Mountain Time	Central Time	Eastern Time
	2:00		4:00
7:00	8:00		
3:00			
		2:00	

CHAPTER 10

DECIMALS

Science

Decimals and Temperature What happens when you tell your parents that you are not feeling well? They may ask some questions and feel your forehead. If you feel warm, they take your temperature. They may use one of the three thermometers shown below.

The middle thermometer is like the one found in most homes. You read it just as you read a number line. The bottom one is digital. You read it like a clock or a calculator. The top one is sort of unusual. It is a strip made of plastic. Part of the strip changes color when placed on your forehead. The strip does not show a number, but it does show if you have a fever.

Normal body temperature for humans is about 98.6°F. Yours may be slightly higher or lower. But if your temperature is over 100°F, your parents may want to talk with a doctor.

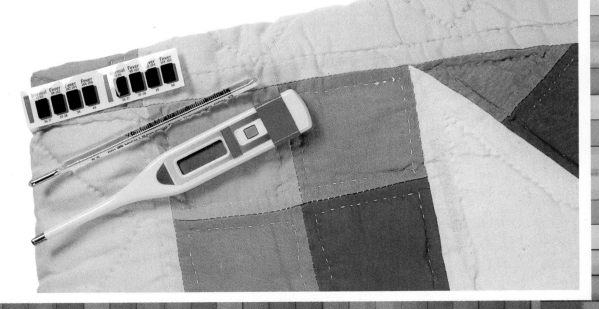

EXPLORING TENTHS

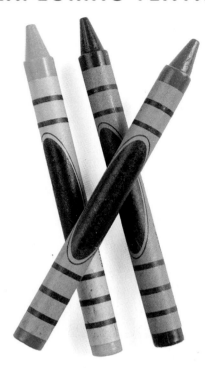

In this lesson you will use squares and discover some things about **tenths.**

Groups: partners

You will need:

- recording sheet
- crayons

Look at the square at the top of your recording sheet.

1. How many sections does it have?

2. Are the sections all the same size?

3. Write the fraction that names 1 section.

Shade 2 of the sections.

4. Write a fraction for the part you shaded.

5. How did you decide what number to use for the denominator?

6. How did you decide what number to use for the numerator?

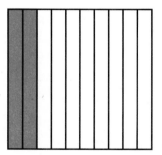

Now use three more squares.

Shade 4 sections of the first square.

7. Write a fraction for the part you shaded.

Shade 7 sections of the second square.

8. Write a fraction for the part you shaded.

Shade 5 sections of the third square.

9. Write a fraction for the part you shaded.

You do not always need to use fractions to write numbers in tenths. Numbers like $\frac{3}{10}$ and $\frac{8}{10}$ can be written as **decimals.**

 Fraction: $\frac{3}{10}$
Decimal: 0.3
You read both as "three tenths."

 Fraction: $\frac{8}{10}$
Decimal: 0.8
You read both as "eight tenths."

Look at the squares you shaded in exercises 7–9.

10. Write the decimal that names each.

Look at each square below. Write a fraction and a decimal that name the shaded part.

11.

12.

13.

Use your recording sheet. Shade a square to show the fraction or decimal.

14. two tenths

15. 0.9

16. five tenths

17. 0.4

18. eight tenths

19. $\frac{10}{10}$

20. Look at the square you shaded for exercise 19. Write a whole number for it.

SUMMING IT UP

21. What fraction does each section of a square stand for?

22. What decimal does each section of a square stand for?

23. What fraction does the whole square stand for?

24. What whole number does the whole square stand for?

DECIMALS GREATER THAN 1

In this lesson you will learn about decimals greater than 1.

Groups: partners

You will need:
- recording sheet
- crayons
- calculator

1. Look at Figure 1 on your recording sheet. Write a mixed number for the shaded parts.

Another way to write the mixed number $1\frac{3}{10}$ is 1.3.

> Remember: A mixed number has a whole number part and a fraction part.

$1\frac{3}{10}$
1.3
Read: "one and three tenths."

Here is another example.

$2\frac{1}{10}$
2.1
Read: "two and one tenth."

Look at the squares below. Write a decimal for the shaded part.

2.   3.

4.

Write the decimal.

5. one and three tenths

6. six and two tenths

7. four and seven tenths

8. nine tenths

9. $6\frac{5}{10}$

10. $\frac{4}{10}$

11. $5\frac{2}{10}$

12. $3\frac{3}{10}$

You can use a calculator to learn about decimals.

13. Press these keys on your calculator: $\boxed{3}\boxed{.}\boxed{1}$
Write what is shown on the display.

14. Shade Figure 2 to show 3.1.

On some calculators you can count by tenths.

15. Count 10 tenths. Press: $\boxed{0}\boxed{.}\boxed{1}\boxed{+}\boxed{=}$
Keep pressing $\boxed{=}$ until you have counted 10 tenths.
What number comes after 0.9?

16. Count on by tenths. Press: $\boxed{1}\boxed{+}\boxed{0}\boxed{.}\boxed{1}\boxed{=}\boxed{=}\boxed{=}\boxed{=}$
Write the number that is displayed each time you
press $\boxed{=}$.

17. Write the missing numbers. 1.5, 1.6, ▨, 1.8, ▨, 2.0

18. Count back by tenths. Press: $\boxed{1}\boxed{-}\boxed{0}\boxed{.}\boxed{1}\boxed{=}\boxed{=}\boxed{=}\boxed{=}$
Write the number that is displayed each time you
press $\boxed{=}$.

19. Write the missing numbers. 2.4, 2.3, ▨, 2.1, ▨, 1.9

SUMMING IT UP

Use a calculator.

20. Start with 4.5. Count on 0.1. What
decimal do you get? Shade Figure 3 to
match the decimal.

21. Start with 3.7. Count back 0.1. What
decimal do you get? Shade Figure 4 to
match the decimal.

315

TENTHS

Every morning Steve rides the bus to school.
He walks four tenths of a mile to the bus stop.

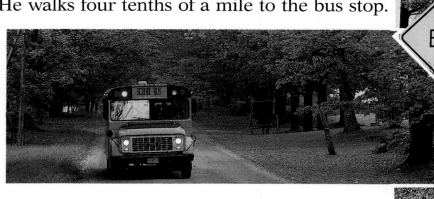

You can write four tenths as a fraction.
You write: $\frac{4}{10}$.

You also can write it as a decimal.
You write: 0.4.

This tenths square is shaded to show $\frac{4}{10}$, or 0.4.

A decimal can be written in a place-value
chart.

Think

- Why do you write a zero to the left of
  the decimal point?

- How many more tenths would have to
  be shaded to show 1, or 1.0?

Ones	Tenths
0	4

0.4

The decimal point
separates the ones
place from the
tenths place.

The tenths squares below show $1\frac{7}{10}$, or 1.7.
The place-value chart shows the same number.

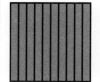 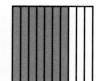

Ones	Tenths
1	7

You read both $1\frac{7}{10}$ and 1.7 as "one and seven
tenths."

Write the decimal.

1.

2.

3.

Ones	Tenths
0	7

4.

Ones	Tenths
1	0

5.

Ones	Tenths
7	5

6. $\frac{6}{10}$

7. 4 and 8 tenths

8. two and one tenth

9. What is the word name for the decimal in exercise 2?

Write the decimal.

10.

11.

12.

Ones	Tenths
0	8

13.

Ones	Tenths
0	1

14.

Ones	Tenths
9	2

15. $\frac{3}{10}$

16. $5\frac{2}{10}$

17. 3 tenths

18. 10 tenths

19. four tenths

20. two and five tenths

21. six and zero tenths

 MATH LOG

How are decimals and fractions alike?
How are they different?

MAKE A LIST

Sometimes making a list can help you solve a problem.

One time we made a list to set up puppet shows.

PUPPET SHOW TODAY

OUR PROBLEM

The stars of the puppet shows were a lion, a bear, and a zebra. We wanted each show to be different. We planned to start some shows with the lion, some with the bear, and others with the zebra. We wanted to know how many different shows we could have.

OUR SOLUTION

We decided to make a list.

First, we listed all the shows that could begin with the bear:

Then we listed all the shows that could begin with the lion:

Last, we listed all the shows that could begin with the zebra:

Then we counted all the shows we had listed. Because the list was organized, we knew that we did not leave out any shows.

We could have 6 different shows.

bear, lion, zebra
bear, zebra, lion

lion, bear, zebra
lion, zebra, bear

zebra, bear, lion
zebra, lion, bear

GUIDED PRACTICE

Solve this problem. Copy and complete the list to help you.

1. Donna needs to do her chores. She has to walk the dog, sweep the steps, and water the plants. In how many different orders can she do her chores?

dog, steps, plants
dog, plants, steps
steps

APPLICATION

Work with a group. Copy and complete the list to solve each problem.

2. Randy bought a truck-making kit. There are 2 colors for front pieces and 3 colors for back pieces. How many different ways can he put a truck together?

red front with red back
red front with blue back
red front with green back
blue front with red back
blue front with

3. A penny, a nickel, and a dime are in a jar. Rita picks 2 of the coins. What are the different amounts of money she might get?

$1¢ + 5¢ = 6¢$
$1¢ +$

4. Look at the rectangle below. How many different ways can you shade 2 of the 4 squares?

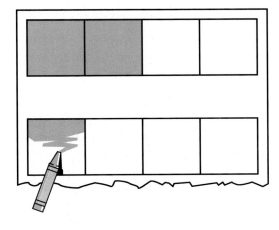

COMPARING DECIMALS

Katie's mother is buying potatoes. One bag is marked 0.9 kilogram. Another is marked 0.5 kilogram. Which bag is heavier?

One way to compare 0.9 and 0.5 is to use tenths squares:

You can see that 0.9 is greater that 0.5. So the bag marked 0.9 kilogram is heavier.

0.9   0.5

Another way to compare decimals is to use a number line:

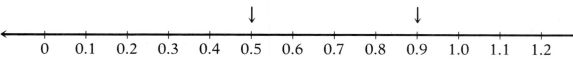

0   0.1   0.2   0.3   0.4   0.5   0.6   0.7   0.8   0.9   1.0   1.1   1.2

Since 0.5 is to the left of 0.9, then 0.5 < 0.9 and 0.9 > 0.5.

Suppose Katie's mother sees bags marked 2.3 kilograms and 2.8 kilograms. Which is heavier?

You can see that the numbers in the ones place are the same. So compare the numbers in the tenths place.

You know that 0.3 < 0.8, so you know that 2.3 < 2.8.

Think

- If you compare 2.4 and 3.6, do you need to compare the tenths? Why or why not?

GUIDED PRACTICE

Complete. Write <, >, or = . Use tenths squares or
a number line if it helps.

1. 0.7 ● 0.5

2. 0.9 ● 1.3

3. 3.4 ● 2.4

4. 2.5 ● 2.2

5. 3.8 ● 4.2

6. 2.0 ● 2

7. For exercise 3, which digits did you look
at to decide which decimal was greater?

....

INDEPENDENT PRACTICE

Complete. Write <, >, or = . Use tenths squares or
a number line if it helps.

8. 0.6 ● 0.2

9. 8.1 ● 8.4

10. 5.9 ● 6.0

11. 3.8 ● 3.5

12. 4 ● 4.0

13. 1.7 ● 2.3

Problem Solving Use the picture to solve each problem.

14. The goldfish tank holds 1 liter of water
when full. Choose the best estimate for
the amount of water in it now.
a. 0.7 L   b. 0.3 L   c. 1.3 L

15. Do you need more than or less than
0.5 liter of water to fill the tank to the top?

Maintain ● **Measurement**

Which unit would you use to measure each?
Write *a* or *b*.

1. your weight
   a. foot   b. pound

2. length of a room
   a. foot   b. kilometer

3. height of a tree
   a. meter   b. centimeter

4. capacity of a glass
   a. gram   b. cup

ORDERING DECIMALS

The table lists the top five finishers in the Harwood School mini-marathon. The marathon lasts for 15 minutes and tests who can run the farthest in that time.

List the finishers in order.

You can use a number line to help you.

MINI-MARATHON DISTANCES	
Name	**Miles**
Dan	1.5
Diane	2.0
Gail	1.8
Mary	1.5
Norm	1.4

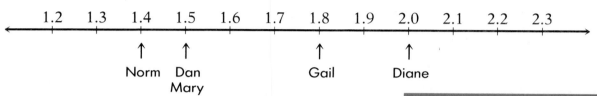

So, Diane came in first, Gail came in second, Dan and Mary tied for third, and Norm came in fourth.

Think

- The fifth-place finisher was Todd, who ran 1.2 miles. How much farther did Norm run than Todd?

Marcia won the 50-yard dash in a time of 7.8 seconds. Is her score closer to 8 seconds or to 7 seconds?

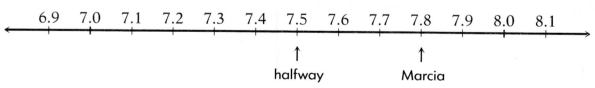

Marcia's time is more than halfway between 7.0 and 8.0 seconds. So, her time is closer to 8 seconds.

GUIDED PRACTICE

Write the decimals the arrows are pointing to.

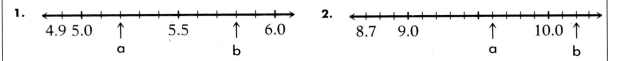

1.
4.9 5.0 ↑ 5.5 ↑ 6.0
      a   b

2.
8.7 9.0 ↑ 10.0 ↑
      a   b

Write the decimals from least to greatest. Draw a number line if it helps.

3. 2.7, 2.5, 3.0   **4.** 0.3, 1.0, 0.5   **5.** 21.3, 12.3, 13.2

6. Look at your answer for exercise 3. Write a decimal that comes between 2.5 and 2.7.

INDEPENDENT PRACTICE

Write the decimals from least to greatest. Draw a number line if it helps.

7. 0.9, 0.5, 1.5   **8.** 17.0, 18.1, 17.9   **9.** 4.3, 3.4, 3.3

Problem Solving

Tom, Mike, Wayne, and Ralph run the relay race. Here are their relay times in seconds: Tom—16.8, Mike—17.1, Wayne—15.5, and Ralph—17.3.

10. Who ran the fastest?

11. Which relay time is between 16.0 and 17.0 seconds?

Use the picture to answer each question.

12. About how far is the man from home?

13. About how far is the dog from home?

14. About how far is the tree from the store?

0 miles   0.5 mile   1.0 mile

USING STRATEGIES

At the Rainbow County Fair, the most popular game is Test Your Strength. A player hits the metal block with the big hammer to make the green ball rise. The higher the score, the bigger the prize.

TEST YOUR STRENGTH WIN A PRIZE

Muscle Monster	1·0
Power-house	0·8
Big Hitter	0·6
Mighty Mite	0·4
Beginner	0·2
	0

HOW STRONG ARE YOU?

RATING	PRIZE
Muscle Monster	Model Space Rocket
Power House	Stuffed Bear
Big Hitter	Kite
Mighty Mite	Key Chain
Beginner	No Prize

Solve each problem.

1. Ben scores 0.3. Is this enough to be a Mighty Mite?

2. On Pablo's first try, he scores 0.7. Is this enough to win the model space rocket?

3. Jean wins a stuffed bear. Which of these scores could she have made?
   a. 0.3   b. 0.5   c. 0.7

4. What is the lowest score that Van can make and still win a prize?

5. Donna sends the ball halfway to the top. Which prize does she win?

6. Hal sends the ball $\frac{1}{4}$ of the way to the top. Which prize does he win?

7. It costs 25¢ for two tries with the hammer. Richie spends 75¢. How many times does he test his strength?

SECTION REVIEW
for pages 312–324

Write the decimal.

1.

2.

3.

Ones	Tenths
7	3

4.

Ones	Tenths
1	4

5. $6\frac{2}{10}$

6. 9 and 1 tenth

7. four tenths

Write the next decimal. You may use tenths squares.

8. 0.2, 0.3, 0.4, ▨

9. 3.7, 3.8, 3.9, ▨

10. 10.8, 10.9, 11.0, ▨

Complete. Write <, >, or = . You may use tenths squares or a number line.

11. 0.8 ⬤ 0.7

12. 0.9 ⬤ 1.0

13. 5.2 ⬤ 4.2

14. 1.3 ⬤ 2.4

15. 10.0 ⬤ 10

16. 6.1 ⬤ 6.3

Write the decimals from least to greatest.

17. 3.8, 4.0, 3.3

18. 0.7, 0.4, 0.1

19. 9.9, 10.3, 10.1

20. 2.0, 1.9, 2.1

21. 0.9, 0.6, 1.6

22. 22.2, 2.2, 2.8

Solve each problem.

23. It is 3 kilometers around the park. Beth ran around the park twice. Jane ran 5.5 kilometers. Who ran farther?

24. Carl measures how far he can jump. He jumps 1.3 meters, 1.5 meters, and 1.2 meters. Which was his longest jump?

ADDING AND SUBTRACTING DECIMALS

You can use tenths squares to add and subtract decimals.

Groups: partners

You will need: tenths squares

Take the tenths square with 3 tenths sections shaded.

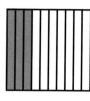

1. Write the decimal for the shaded part.

Take the tenths square with 4 tenths shaded.

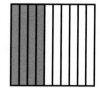

2. Write the decimal for the shaded part.

Line up the tenths squares, as shown.

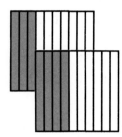

3. What is the total number of shaded tenths?

4. Copy and complete the number sentence to show the total number of shaded tenths.
0.3 + 0.4 = ▨

Now take your tenths squares that have 10 tenths shaded and 5 tenths shaded.

5. Write a decimal to show the shaded part.

Take your tenths square that has 7 tenths shaded.

6. Write a decimal to show the shaded part.

Line up the tenths squares, as shown.

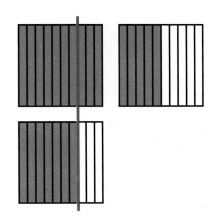

7. What is the difference between the number of shaded tenths?

8. Copy and complete the number sentence to show the difference.

$1.5 - 0.7 = \blacksquare$

....

SUMMING IT UP

9. Look at the number sentences at the right. How is adding and subtracting decimals like adding and subtracting whole numbers?

$$0.2 + 0.3 = 0.5$$
$$2 + 3 = 5$$

$$1.7 - 0.8 = 0.9$$
$$17 - 8 = 9$$

10. Write an addition sentence to show the total number of shaded tenths.

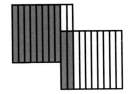

11. Write a subtraction sentence to show the difference in shaded tenths.

....

CHALLENGE • Number Sense

Use the decimals in the box to answer the questions.

6.2	7.1	0.9
1.3	2.1	3.8

1. Who am I?
   I am less than 3.2.
   I am greater than 1.0.
   I have a 1 in the tenths place.

2. Who are we?
   We are greater than 2.
   If you add us together, our sum is 10.

ADDING AND SUBTRACTING DECIMALS

Jason is making a model of a zoo. One piece of wood is 1.5 meters long. The other is 0.7 meter long. How long are the two pieces together?

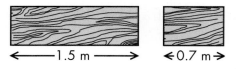

←——1.5 m——→   ←0.7 m→

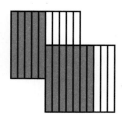

You can use tenths squares to add the lengths.

Here is another way.

● Line up the places.	● Add the tenths. Regroup if you need to.	● Add the ones. Write the decimal point in the answer.
$\begin{array}{r} 1.5 \text{ m} \\ + 0.7 \text{ m} \\ \hline \end{array}$	$\begin{array}{r} ^{1} \\ 1.5 \text{ m} \\ + 0.7 \text{ m} \\ \hline 2 \end{array}$	$\begin{array}{r} ^{1} \\ 1.5 \text{ m} \\ + 0.7 \text{ m} \\ \hline 2.2 \text{ m} \end{array}$

The two pieces together are 2.2 meters long.

Think

• Why is it important to line up the decimals by place value?

This piece of board is 4.2 centimeters long. Jason wants a piece 3.5 centimeters long. How much should he cut off?

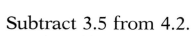

←——— 4.2 cm ———→

←——— 3.5 cm ———→

Subtract 3.5 from 4.2.

● Line up the places.	● Subtract the tenths. Regroup if you need to.	● Subtract the ones. Write the decimal point.
$\begin{array}{r} 4.2 \text{ cm} \\ - 3.5 \text{ cm} \\ \hline \end{array}$	$\begin{array}{r} ^{3\ 12} \\ \not{4}.\not{2} \text{ cm} \\ - 3.5 \text{ cm} \\ \hline 7 \end{array}$	$\begin{array}{r} ^{3\ 12} \\ \not{4}.\not{2} \text{ cm} \\ - 3.5 \text{ cm} \\ \hline 0.7 \text{ cm} \end{array}$

So, he should cut off 0.7 centimeter.

Write the answer. You may use tenths squares.

1.	2.	3.	4.	5.
1.9	5.5 km	3.9	0.9	16.8
+ 0.4	+ 6.7 km	− 2.4	− 0.7	− 5.9

6. 0.7 + 0   **7.** 2.6 − 1.8   **8.** 2.3 + 1.4   **9.** 0.9 − 0

10. What rules about zero helped you answer exercises 6 and 9?

Write the answer. You may use tenths squares.

11.	12.	13.	14.	15.
0.4	1.6 cm	6.7	2.7	7.0 m
+ 0.5	+ 0.5 cm	+ 4.8	− 1.4	− 1.4 m

16. 1.9 − 0.6   **17.** 4.5 + 2.8   **18.** 13.0 + 0.6   **19.** 7.9 − 3.9

Problem Solving

20. One baby elephant stands 0.9 meter tall. Another baby elephant is 1.1 meters tall. Which elephant is taller? How much taller?

21. The body and head of a pygmy shrew is 1.7 inches long. Its tail is 1.2 inches long. How long is the shrew from the tip of its nose to the end of its tail?

Maintain • **Using Data**

During the summer, Fred's family drives across Oklahoma. Fred makes a tally of the first 100 license plates he sees. How many license plates from each state does he see?

LICENSE PLATES		
State	Tally	Number
Oklahoma	ℍℍ ℍℍ ℍℍ ℍℍ ℍℍ ℍℍ |||	
Texas	ℍℍ ℍℍ ℍℍ ℍℍ ℍℍ ||	
Kansas	ℍℍ ℍℍ ℍℍ ℍℍ		
Arkansas	ℍℍ ℍℍ ℍℍ ||||	

PROMBLEM SOLVING STRATEGY

PROBLEM SOLVING STRATEGY

MAKE A LIST

When you make a list, use a pattern. That will help you to avoid leaving anything out. It will also help you to avoid listing the same thing twice.

Julie and Kim own a frozen yogurt stand. They have 2 flavors of yogurt and 3 kinds of toppings. They want to know how many different kinds of sundaes they can sell.

Julie and Kim each start making a list to solve the problem.

Look at the two lists they started.

Kim & Julie's Frozen Yogurt

Flavors:
  Vanilla
  Strawberry

Toppings:
  Fresh Fruit
  Mixed Nuts
  Coconut

Kim's List
Flavor Topping
Vanilla with Fresh Fruit
Strawberry with Mixed Nuts
Vanilla with Coconut
Vanilla with

Julie's List
Flavor   Topping
Vanilla with Fresh Fruit
Vanilla with Mixed Nuts
Vanilla with Coconut
Strawberry with

Think

• Which list has a pattern? What is the pattern?

• Which list would you choose to solve the problem? Why?

Use the list you chose to solve the problem.

GUIDED PRACTICE

Read the problem. Choose the list you think will be more helpful. Copy and complete that list to solve the problem.

1. Joe, Ken, and Lisa sit in the back seat of their parents' car. Each time they go for a ride, the 3 children want to sit in different orders. How many rides can they go on before they have to sit in the same order again?

List A
Joe, Ken, Lisa
Lisa, Joe, Ken
Ken,

List B
Joe, Ken, Lisa
Joe, Lisa, Ken
Ken,

....

APPLICATION

Work in groups to solve each problem. Make a list when it helps you.

2. John has homework in reading, math, and social studies. In how many different orders could he do his homework?

Sandwiches **Drinks**

Tuna   Milk
Cheese   Lemonade
Turkey
Peanut Butter

3. Each child at Adam's party can choose a sandwich and a drink. There are 7 children at the party. Can they each have a different lunch? How many different lunches can there be?

4. How many different paths can Steve take from his house to school that are less than 2 miles?

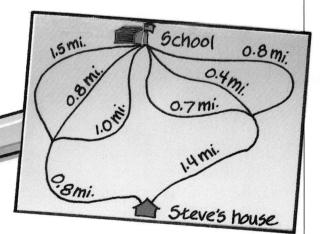

331

USING STRATEGIES

If you get stuck, remember...
Tips for Problem Solving
on pages 426–427

Solve each problem. Remember, some problems may not have enough information.

1. Kyle lives 1.5 miles from the library. He leaves the library and walks 0.5 mile toward home. Is he more than halfway home?

2. Yoko is 10 years old. Her father was born in 1950. How old is Yoko's father?

3. Lee has a dollar bill, some quarters, a dime, and 3 pennies. Does he have enough money to buy 2 packages of stickers?

4. A shelf in Jill's room is 36 inches long. Jill wants to put 9 toy cars on the shelf end to end. Each car has 4 wheels. Will all the cars fit on the shelf?

5. Carla has 7 nickels in her bank. Every day she puts in 1 nickel and then takes out 2 nickels. When will her bank be empty?

6. Jesse wants to pack 2 kinds of fruit for lunch. He has a banana, an apple, an orange, and a pear.
   a. What are all the possible combinations of fruit he can pack?
   b. How many combinations are there?
   c. How many combinations have an orange?

7. John is at home. He must go to the bank, the library, and the store in any order. Then he must go back home.
   a. Draw the shortest route he can take.
   b. How long is the route you chose?

STICKERS 79¢

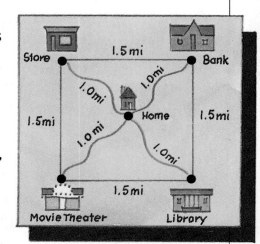

SECTION REVIEW

for pages 326–332

Write the letter of the correct answer.

1. 4.5 + 0.8
   a. 53
   b. 4.13
   c. 5.3
   d. 0.53

2. 5.6 + 3.4
   a. 0.9
   b. 8.10
   c. 90
   d. 9.0

3. 6.5 + 0.4
   a. 10.5
   b. 6.9
   c. 0.69
   d. 69

4. 8.0 − 0.1
   a. 0.79
   b. 8.1
   c. 7
   d. 7.9

5. 9.1 − 7.4
   a. 1.7
   b. 17
   c. 2.3
   d. 0.17

6. 8.4 − 0.7
   a. 1.4
   b. 7.7
   c. 0.77
   d. 8.3

Write the sum or difference.

7. 0.4
  + 0.4

8. 1.2
  + 0.5

9. 4.9 cm
  + 0.6 cm

10. 5.5
   + 1.8

11. 12.4
   + 9.1

12. 0.9
   − 0.8

13. 2.7 m
   − 1.3 m

14. 5.1
   − 2.7

15. 12.4
   − 8.6

16. 1.7
   − 0.9

Solve each problem.

17. Steve walks 0.4 mile to the bus stop. After school, he walks the same distance home. How far does he walk to and from the bus stop? Is it more than or less than 1 mile?

18. On Sports Day, Sue runs the 50-meter race in 7.9 seconds. Betsy runs the race in 8.3 seconds. Who runs faster? By how many seconds?

19. The body and neck of an adult giraffe is 3.2 meters long. The legs are 1.8 meters long. About how tall is the giraffe?

20. Julie lives 1.3 miles from Jean. Julie walks 0.7 mile toward Jean's house. Is she more than halfway there?

CHAPTER REVIEW

Test

Complete. Write <, >, or =.

1. 0.6 ● 0.2
2. 3.6 ● 3.9
3. 4.0 ● 4
4. 5.8 ● 6.1

5. 4.6 ● 4.9
6. 3.8 ● 3.3
7. 9.1 ● 8.9
8. 2 ● 2.0

Order the decimals from least to greatest.

9. 0.5, 1.2, 0.2
10. 6.3, 6.1, 6.6
11. 4.9, 3.9, 4.6

Order the decimals from greatest to least.

12. 0.3, 0.6, 0.2
13. 1.0, 1.9, 0.9
14. 5.4, 5.7, 4.5

Write the decimal.

15. $\frac{6}{10}$
16. 4 and 1 tenth
17. $3\frac{5}{10}$
18. 8 tenths

19. $7\frac{3}{10}$
20. 2 and 2 tenths
21. $\frac{9}{10}$
22. four tenths

Write the answer.

23.	24.	25.	26.
0.2	1.8	2.3	9.1
+ 0.6	− 0.7	+ 5.9	− 3.5

27. 6.9 + 4.3   **28.** 7.2 − 5.4   **29.** 1.4 + 3.7   **30.** 8.7 − 6.5

PROBLEM SOLVING

Solve each problem.

31. Tyrone ran 5.4 kilometers. Chris ran 6.7 kilometers. Who ran farther? How much farther?

32. Bobo the elephant has a tail that is 22.3 inches long. At birth, Bobo's tail was 10.1 inches long. How many inches did Bobo's tail grow?

33. Michael swims a lap in 30.6 seconds. Helen swims hers in 29.8 seconds. Keisha swims hers in 30.1 seconds. Who swims the fastest?

34. The head and body of one wild turkey is 0.8 meter long. Its tail is 0.3 meter long. How long is the turkey from head to tail?

CUMULATIVE REVIEW

Write the measure to the nearest inch or centimeter.

35.    **36.** 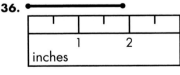   **37.**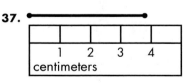

Write a mixed number for the shaded part.

38. 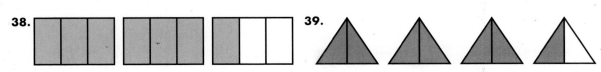   **39.**

335

EXCURSION

NUMBER SENSE

DETERMINING INEQUALITIES

Amy counts the number of games she played
in at soccer camp. This summer, her team
won 4 games and lost 2 games. Last summer,
her team won 3 games and lost 5 games.
Is it true or false that Amy played in more
games this summer?

You can solve the problem in three steps.

STEP 1   Find the number of games
Amy played in this summer.

4 games won + 2 games lost = 6 games total

STEP 2   Find the number of games
Amy played in last summer.

3 games won + 5 games lost = 8 games total

STEP 3   Compare the sums. $6 < 8$

It is false that Amy played in more games
this summer.

Other Examples

True or false?

$5 - 1 > 6 - 3$ $54 \div 9 > 7 \times 6$ $5.3 + 2.1 = 9.5 - 2.1$

$4 > 3$ $6 > 42$ $7.4 = 7.4$

    true   false   true

Write *true* or *false*.

1. $6 + 3 > 5 + 2$

2. $6.9 - 1.7 < 8.5 - 5.4$

3. $2 \times 8 = 4 \times 5$

4. $9 \times 9 > 6 \times 7$

5. $42 + 25 > 77 - 17$

6. $24 \div 3 > 36 \div 9$

7. $3.2 + 2.0 < 8.5 - 2.5$

8. $7 \times 5 < 81 \div 9$

Complete. Write $<$, $>$, or $=$.

9. $7.9 - 3.0$ ● $2.7 + 3.0$

10. 3×2 ● $48 \div 8$

11. 5×3 ● 2×3

12. $26 + 60$ ● $51 + 49$

13. $54 \div 9$ ● $64 \div 8$

14. $8.4 - 3.2$ ● $7.4 - 4.2$

Write the letter of the answer that will make the sentence true.

15. $18 +$ ▨ $= 36 + 27$

a. 15

16. $7.6 - 2.4 =$ ▨ $- 0.1$

b. 5.9

17. $16 + 27 = 28 +$ ▨

c. 45

18. $2.2 + 1.8 =$ ▨ $- 1.9$

d. 5.3

Use the table to solve each problem.

19. Which team played the most games? How many games did they play?

20. How many more games did the Stallions play than the Power Kickers?

21. Which team played the fewest games? How many games did they play?

Camp Soccer Teams		
Team	Won	Lost
Power Kickers	ⵧ	IIII
Netters	IIII	II
Aces	II	III
Stallions	ⵧ III	II

337

MULTIPLYING
BY 1-DIGIT NUMBERS

Science

Multiplication in Nature Like most birds, ducks lay several eggs at one time. Mallard ducks lay between 8 and 10 eggs. The eggs hatch in about 21 days.

As you can see, the duck shown below hatched at least 8 eggs. Suppose she hatches the same number of eggs each year. How many ducklings would she produce in two years? In five years?

Different animals produce different numbers of young. Choose 3 or 4 animals from the list. Then find out how many young are produced by each animal. Share your findings with the class.

Barn owl
Bobcat
Coyote
Fruit bat
Garter snake
Humpback whale
Mountain goat
Polar bear
Raccoon
Virginia opossum

EXPLORING MULTIPLICATION

Mr. Chan's class is packing greeting cards they made to raise money. Each box holds 36 cards. Troy has 7 empty boxes. How many cards will he need to fill his boxes?

You could add:

$$36 + 36 + 36 + 36 + 36 + 36 + 36.$$

That is a lot to add! Try another way.

Groups: small groups

You will need: place-value blocks

Show 1 set of 36.

1. How many ones do you have? How many tens?

Show 6 more sets of 36.

2. How many sets of 36 do you have in all?

3. How many ones do you have? How do you write this number?

4. How many tens do you have? How do you write this number?

5. How many greeting cards will Troy need? How did you get your answer?

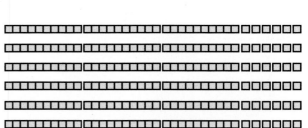

To show the total numbers of cards, you can write a multiplication sentence: $7 \times 36 = 252$.

Now show 3 sets of 28 with your blocks. Find the total number your blocks show. Use the method your group likes best.

6. Write a number sentence to show how you found the total.

Write a multiplication sentence for each.

7. 6 sets of 45

8. 5 sets of 31

....

SUMMING IT UP

Show 8 sets of 19 with your blocks.

9. Write an addition sentence to show the total.

10. Write a multiplication sentence to show the total.

11. How does knowing the number of addends help you to write a multiplication sentence?

12. What are three ways you can find the product of 5 × 95?

Maintain • Using Data

Write the answer. Use the table about birds on page 417 in the Data Book.

1. Write the names of the birds in order from the warmest body temperature to the coolest body temperature.

2. A person's normal body temperature is 98.6°F. How much warmer is an ostrich's temperature?

ESTIMATING PRODUCTS

The managers of the Hillside Ranch feed their horses 26 bales of hay each day. About how many bales of hay do the horses eat in a week?

There are 7 days in a week. To estimate 7 × 26, work with numbers you can multiply mentally.

I will use the 20 in 26.
7 x 20 = 140

26 is close to 30.
7 x 30 = 210

Both 140 and 210 are reasonable estimates. The horses will eat between 140 and 210 bales of hay each week.

Think

- Do you think the actual product of 7 × 26 is greater than or less than 140? Explain.

- Do you think the actual product of 7 × 26 is greater than or less than 210? Explain.

Other Examples

Estimate: 3 × 251

3 × **200** = 600   3 × **300** = 900

Both 600 and 900 are reasonable estimates.

Estimate: 5 × $4.65

5 × **$4** = $20   5 × **$5** = $25

Both $20 and $25 are reasonable estimates.

GUIDED PRACTICE

1. Which two numbers in the box have a product of:

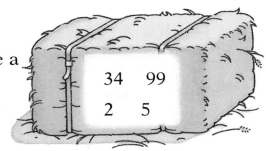

34 99

2 5

a. about 60?   **b.** about 150?

c. about 500?   **d.** about 200?

Estimate the product.

2. 42	3. 29	4. 337	5. $6.52
× 3	× 5	× 3	× 4

Problem Solving

6. Can you buy 3 horse brushes with $15 if each brush costs $4.78? Explain.

7. Is the actual product in exercise 3 less than or greater than 150? Explain.

INDEPENDENT PRACTICE

Estimate the product.

8. 28	9. $34	10. 438	11. $3.67
× 3	× 5	× 2	× 3

12. 9 × 42   **13.** 3 × 328   **14.** 3 × 98   **15.** 5 × $4.12

Problem Solving

16. Can you buy 3 mane-and-tail combs with $6? Why or why not?

17. Can you buy 4 currycombs with $10? Why or why not?

18. Can you buy 4 body brushes with $25? Why or why not?

Body Brush $5.68

Curry Comb $3.35

Mane and Tail Comb $2.19

MAKE A TABLE

Sometimes making a table can help you solve a problem.

One time we made a table to help plan the training camp for our track team.

OUR PROBLEM

There were going to be 6 runners at the training camp. We were in charge of supplies for the week. We had to buy 15 oranges for each runner. We needed to know how many oranges to buy.

OUR SOLUTION

We made a table and began to fill it in. For 1 runner, we would need 15 oranges.

runners	1
oranges	15

For 2 runners, we would need another 15 oranges. That would make 15 + 15, or 30 oranges in all.

runners	1	2
oranges	15	30

For 3 runners, we would need another 15 oranges. That would make 30 + 15, or 45 oranges in all.

runners	1	2	3
oranges	15	30	45

We kept filling in our table until we reached 6 runners.

runners	1	2	3	4	5	6
oranges	15	30	45	60	75	90

So, we needed to buy 90 oranges.

GUIDED PRACTICE

Copy and complete the table to solve the problem.

1. Camille wants to take a crafts class for $75. She already has $35. If she saves $8 each week, in which week will she have enough money saved?

Weeks	Money
now	$35
1	$43
2	

APPLICATION

Work in pairs. Copy and complete the table to solve each problem.

2. A basketball team is buying new team sweatshirts. Each shirt costs $18. How much will 7 of these shirts cost?

Shirts	1	2	3	4
Cost	$18	$36	$54	

3. Mr. Hanna is the guide for a canoe trip. He says the canoes can travel 13 miles each hour. How far can they travel in 5 hours?

Hours		1	2	
Miles		13		

4. The cook at Camp Oakwood needs to order at least 90 cans of beans. It is cheaper to buy by the carton. Each carton contains 24 cans. How many cartons will the cook have to order?

Cartons	Cans
1	24
2	

5. A carton of apple juice contains 12 cans. The cook needs a total of 75 cans. He has 27 already. How many cartons does he need to order?

Cartons	Cans
0	27
1	

MULTIPLYING WITH AN ARRAY

Pete and Kim need to multiply 18 by 6, but they do not have any place-value blocks. Pete starts to draw blocks to help him multiply.

Kim uses squared paper to show 6 × 18. The colored squares on her paper stand for place-value blocks. Kim has made a squared paper **array.**

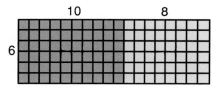

Think

- Which squares on the squared paper stand for the tens blocks? The ones blocks?

You can use an array to help you multiply 18 by 6.

First, write 6 × 18 as 18
                        × 6.

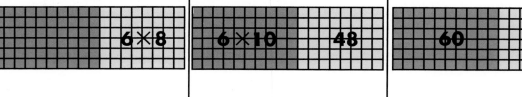

● Multiply the ones.	● Multiply the tens.	● Add.
18	18	18
× 6	× 6	× 6
48	48	48
	60	+ 60
		108

The product of 6 × 18 is 108.

346

GUIDED PRACTICE

Write the product. You can use the array.

1.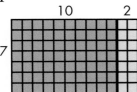
12
× 7

2. 4 × 24

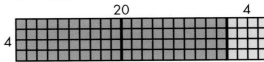

Use squared paper. Draw an array to show the multiplication. Then write the product.

3. 3 × 16

4. 5 × 25

5. 9 × 13

6. Would you draw an array to help you multiply: 3 × 50? Why or why not?

INDEPENDENT PRACTICE

Write the product. You can use the array.

7. 19
× 3

8. 23
× 5

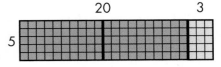

9. 6 × 12

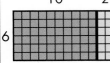

10. 8 × 24

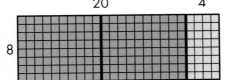

11. 9 × 26

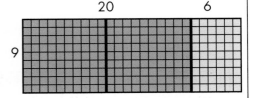

Write the product. Draw an array if you like.

12. 3 × 11

13. 5 × 12

14. 4 × 23

Problem Solving Use the bar graph on page 419 in the Data Book.

15. On Saturday, Lorraine and 2 friends go skiing at Killington. How much do their tickets cost?

16. Mr. and Mrs. Gomez want to ski one day at Mission Ridge. Will $40 be enough money for their tickets?

MULTIPLYING 2-DIGIT NUMBERS

▶ Mr. Ruiz is building a model train for his grandchild. The train will have 24 cars with 8 wheels on each car. How many wheels will he need for the train?

You can multiply: $\begin{array}{r} 24 \\ \times\ 8 \end{array}$.

An array may help you multiply. Here is a shorter way.

 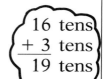

● Multiply the ones. Regroup if necessary.	● Multiply the tens.	● Add the regrouped tens.
$\begin{array}{r} ^3 \\ 24 \\ \times\ 8 \\ \hline 2 \end{array}$ $\left(\begin{array}{r} 4 \\ \times\ 8 \\ \hline 32 \end{array}\right)$	$\begin{array}{r} ^3 \\ 24 \\ \times\ 8 \\ \hline 2 \end{array}$ $\left(\begin{array}{r} 2\ \text{tens} \\ \times\ 8 \\ \hline 16\ \text{tens} \end{array}\right)$	$\begin{array}{r} ^3 \\ 24 \\ \times\ 8 \\ \hline 192 \end{array}$ $\left(\begin{array}{r} 16\ \text{tens} \\ +\ 3\ \text{tens} \\ \hline 19\ \text{tens} \end{array}\right)$

Mr. Ruiz needs 192 wheels for the train.

Think

• Why is there a 3 above the 2?

• How can you estimate to see if the product of 192 is reasonable?

▶ Mr. Ruiz buys 4 circus train kits with 7 cars in each kit. Each car has 8 wheels. How many wheels are in the 4 kits?

Multiply: $4 \times 7 \times 8$.
You can multiply in any order.

$4 \times 7 \times 8$	$7 \times 8 \times 4$	$4 \times 8 \times 7$
$\left(4 \times 7 = 28\right)$ $\begin{array}{r} ^6 \\ 28 \\ \times\ 8 \\ \hline 224 \end{array}$	$\left(7 \times 8 = 56\right)$ $\begin{array}{r} ^2 \\ 56 \\ \times\ 4 \\ \hline 224 \end{array}$	$\left(4 \times 8 = 32\right)$ $\begin{array}{r} ^1 \\ 32 \\ \times\ 7 \\ \hline 224 \end{array}$

There are 224 wheels.

GUIDED PRACTICE

Write the product.

1.	2.	3.	4.	5.
21	16	39	84	45
× 3	× 6	× 5	× 4	× 7

6. 3 × 29   7. 7 × 3 × 9   8. 2 × 8 × 5

9. How could you use mental math to do exercise 8?

INDEPENDENT PRACTICE

Write the product. Use mental math when you can.

10.	11.	12.	13.	14.
34	34	21	88	62
× 2	× 4	× 9	× 7	× 6

15. 3 × 25   16. 6 × 25   17. 8 × 13

18. 4 × 2 × 6   19. 5 × 2 × 7   20. 3 × 8 × 4

Problem Solving

21. A film about new toys is shown at a toy fair. The theater seats 75 people. The film is shown every hour. The first showing is at 10:00 A.M. and the last is at 3:00 P.M.
    a. How many shows are there in one day?
    b. How many people can see the film in one day?

22. Which is the better buy?

3 BOXES FOR $10

4 BOXES FOR $10

EXACT OR ESTIMATE

An estimate tells you about how much. Many times that is all you need to know. Other times you need an exact answer.

These questions may help you decide which answer you need.

- Is "about how much" all I need to know?

- Do I have paper and pencil or a calculator?

- Is it possible to get an exact answer?

- Am I just checking to see if an answer is reasonable?

Think

- Would you estimate or figure out the exact number of fish in a lake? Why?

....

INDEPENDENT PRACTICE

Solve each problem. Write whether you estimated or computed exactly.

1. Is $10 enough to buy both?

2. How much more does the larger watermelon weigh?

3. Is the answer reasonable?

4. About how many golf balls are in 4 boxes?

SECTION REVIEW

for pages 340–350

Write the letter of the correct answer.

1. 4×57
   a. 208
   b. 138
   c. 228
   d. 288

2. 6×56
   a. 486
   b. 236
   c. 306
   d. 336

3. 9×16
   a. 464
   b. 144
   c. 94
   d. 544

4. 4×43
   a. 162
   b. 202
   c. 172
   d. 82

5. 3×27
   a. 81
   b. 61
   c. 211
   d. 91

6. $2 \times 3 \times 8$
   a. 14
   b. 48
   c. 40
   d. 30

7. $5 \times 6 \times 3$
   a. 33
   b. 23
   c. 48
   d. 90

8. $8 \times 3 \times 4$
   a. 96
   b. 44
   c. 36
   d. 28

9. $7 \times 3 \times 7$
   a. 52
   b. 147
   c. 70
   d. 42

Solve each problem.

10. The Garden Club plants 4 rows of bulbs. They plant 18 bulbs in each row. It takes them 2 hours to finish. How many bulbs do they plant?

11. Mrs. Perez's class sets up 30 rows of 9 chairs for a class play. There will be 300 guests. How many more chairs do they need?

12. Caitlin earns $5 a week baby-sitting. Will she earn enough money in 12 weeks to buy a radio that costs $49.95?

13. There are 11 boys and 13 girls in Mrs. Perez's class. Each student will get 2 free tickets to the play. How many free tickets will the class get?

MULTIPLYING 3-DIGIT NUMBERS

Rob's father drives 375 miles 3 times a week to deliver fresh fruits and vegetables. How many miles does he drive each week to deliver the produce?

▶ You can multiply: 3 × 375.

Write 3 × 375 as
$$\begin{array}{r} 375 \\ \times\ \ 3 \end{array}$$

● **Multiply the ones.**

$$\begin{array}{r} 375 \\ \times\ 3 \\ \hline 15 \end{array}$$

● **Multiply the tens.**

$$\begin{array}{r} 375 \\ \times\ 3 \\ \hline 15 \\ 210 \end{array}$$

● **Multiply the hundreds.**

$$\begin{array}{r} 375 \\ \times\ 3 \\ \hline 15 \\ 210 \\ 900 \end{array}$$

● **Add.**

$$\begin{array}{r} 375 \\ \times\ 3 \\ \hline 15 \\ 210 \\ +\ 900 \\ \hline 1125 \end{array}$$

▶ A shorter way to do this is to regroup.

● **Multiply ones. Regroup?**

$$\begin{array}{r} {}^{1} \\ 375 \\ \times\ 3 \\ \hline 5 \end{array}$$

$$\begin{array}{r} 5 \\ \times\ 3 \\ \hline 15 \end{array}$$

● **Multiply tens. Add tens. Regroup?**

$$\begin{array}{r} {}^{2\,1} \\ 375 \\ \times\ 3 \\ \hline 25 \end{array}$$

7 tens	21 tens
× 3	+ 1 ten
21 tens	22 tens

● **Multiply hundreds. Add hundreds.**

$$\begin{array}{r} {}^{2\,1} \\ 375 \\ \times\ 3 \\ \hline 1125 \end{array}$$

$$\begin{array}{r} 3 \text{ hundreds} \\ \times\ 3 \\ \hline 9 \text{ hundreds} \end{array}$$

$$\begin{array}{r} 9 \text{ hundreds} \\ +\ 2 \text{ hundreds} \\ \hline 11 \text{ hundreds} \end{array}$$

Rob's father drives 1125 miles each week.

Think

≡ • Estimate. About how many miles would Rob's father drive if he made 5 deliveries a week?

Estimate the product. Write *a, b,* or *c.*

1. 5 × 102
   a. 50
   b. 500
   c. 5000

2. 2 × 29
   a. 60
   b. 600
   c. 6000

3. 4 × 518
   a. 20
   b. 200
   c. 2000

4. 2 × 197
   a. 40
   b. 400
   c. 4000

Write the product.

5.	6.	7.	8.	9.
423	303	421	263	409
× 2	× 3	× 4	× 6	× 2

10. 5 × 111   11. 4 × 434   12. 2 × 868

13. How could you use mental math to do exercise 10?

Estimate the product. Write *a, b,* or *c.*

14. 4 × 21
    a. 80
    b. 800
    c. 8000

15. 3 × 305
    a. 90
    b. 900
    c. 9000

16. 2 × 99
    a. 20
    b. 200
    c. 2000

17. 2 × 513
    a. 10
    b. 100
    c. 1000

Write the product.

18.	19.	20.	21.	22.
221	109	193	324	100
× 2	× 6	× 4	× 5	× 7

Problem Solving

23. Rob's father delivers peaches to 7 stores. Lilly's Market gets 50 pounds of peaches. The other stores get 100 pounds each. How many pounds of peaches does he deliver?

24. Rob's father delivers 8 crates of eggs to Lilly's Market. Each crate holds 120 eggs. How many eggs did he deliver to the market?

MAKE A TABLE

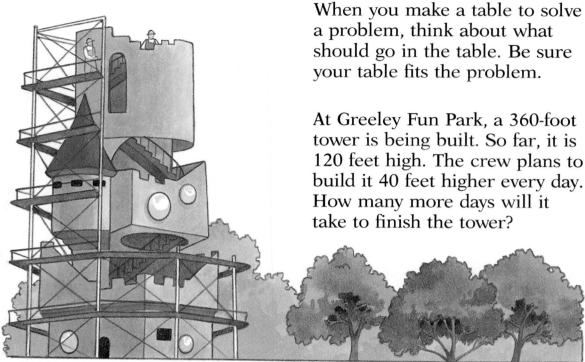

When you make a table to solve a problem, think about what should go in the table. Be sure your table fits the problem.

At Greeley Fun Park, a 360-foot tower is being built. So far, it is 120 feet high. The crew plans to build it 40 feet higher every day. How many more days will it take to finish the tower?

Look at the two tables below.

Table A

Days	Feet
now	120
1	160
2	200

Table B

Days	Feet
1	120
2	240
3	360

Think

- How are the two tables alike?

- How are they different?

- Which of the two tables would you choose to solve the problem? Why?

Copy and complete one of the tables to solve the problem.

Read the problem. Then copy and complete one of the tables to solve the problem.

1. Lilly buys a bottle of 50 vitamins. For about how many weeks will the vitamins last if she takes 1 vitamin each day?

Table A

weeks	1	2	3
vitamins used	7	14	

Table B

weeks	0	1	2	3
vitamins left	50	43	36	

····················

APPLICATION

Work in groups to solve each problem. You can make a table to help you.

2. Sue earns $5 each week walking dogs. She has $7 now. If she saves all her money, when will she be able to buy a new sweater that costs $22?

3. Theater tickets go on sale at 6:00 P.M. At 2:00 P.M., 15 people are in line waiting to buy tickets. Every 30 minutes, 5 more people get in line. At what time will there be 35 people in line?

4. Jerry has $85 to spend for meals on his vacation trip. If he spends $15 each day for meals, how much will he have left after 4 days?

5. Write a word problem that can be solved by using a table. Give your problem to a friend to solve.

USING MULTIPLICATION

The Tower Hotel will be serving breakfast, lunch, and dinner to each group on the convention list. How many meals must the manager order to serve all the members of the Cartoon Writers of America?

TOWER HOTEL CONVENTION LIST	
Name of Group	Number of Guests
Quiltmakers' Club	729
Cartoon Writers of America	609
Jugglers of the World	107
Nautilus Society	452

 Think

• Will your answer be more than or less than 1800? How can you tell?

You can multiply to find the answer. Multiply 609 by 3.

$$\begin{array}{r} \overset{2}{609} \\ \times\ \ 3 \\ \hline 1827 \end{array}$$

The manager must order 1827 meals for the Cartoon Writers of America.

WELCOME
Cartoon Writers
Of America

GUIDED PRACTICE

Solve each problem.

1. How many meals must the manager order to serve 3 meals to the Quiltmakers Club?

2. How many guests are on the hotel's convention list?

3. The breakfast tables seat 4 people each. Does the Nautilus Society need more than or less than 100 tables?

4. The Jugglers of the World want to go to the circus. Tickets cost $5 each. How much will it cost the group to go to the circus?

PROJECT • Application

The Nautilus Society is at the Tower Hotel to honor the French writer Jules Verne. Verne lived in the 1800's and wrote the book *Twenty Thousand Leagues Under the Sea* about a submarine called *Nautilus*.

The manager wants to serve submarine sandwiches to the Nautilus Society. Help her out by writing a recipe for a submarine sandwich. She has already chosen salami.

▶ Choose at least 4 other ingredients from the list. Write the number of slices for each ingredient you choose.

▶ Make a chart like the one shown. Write how many slices of each ingredient are needed to serve the Nautilus Society.

NAUTILUS SOCIETY		
Number of Sandwiches: 452		
Ingredient	**Slices for 1 sandwich**	**Total number of slices**
Salami	2	904

▶ Write a different submarine sandwich recipe for another group at the Tower Hotel. Use the information on page 356 to find the total number of slices of each ingredient needed for the group. Give your sub a name.

Share your recipe with the rest of the class.

The Nautilus Sub
(Served on an Italian Roll)

 2 slices of salami
___ slices of cheese
___ leaves of lettuce
___ slices of onion
___ slices of turkey
___ slices of tomato
___ slices of ham
___ slices of green pepper
___ slices of roast beef

MULTIPLYING MONEY

Willy's Starshop has its grand opening today. All space toys are on sale. In the first hour, 6 mini-robots are sold. How much money does Willy collect?

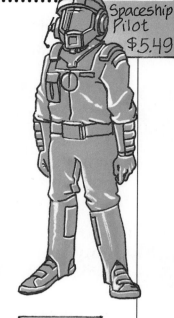

Spaceship Pilot $5.49

Jet Parachute $8.49

Starship $9.98

Crown $7.99

Think

• Does Willy collect more than $30? How do you know?

• Does Willy collect less than $36? How do you know?

Helmet $6.98

Mini-Robot $5.95

You can multiply: 6 × $5.95.

● Multiply as you would with whole numbers.	● Write the dollar sign ($) and decimal point (.) in the product.
^{5 3} $5.95 × 6 ——— 3570	^{5 3} $5.95 × 6 ——— $35.70

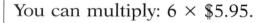

Willy collects $35.70.

Other Examples

⁴ $7.06 × 8 ——— $56.48	³ $2.60 × 5 ——— $13.00	$0.09 × 6 ——— $0.54

GUIDED PRACTICE

Write the product.

1.	$0.27	2.	$1.70	3.	$3.12	4.	$2.75	5.	$6.45
	× 3		× 3		× 4		× 2		× 7

6. 9 × $0.80   7. 5 × $2.00   8. 6 × $4.12

9. Is $10.00 enough to buy 2 mini-robots? How do you know?

10. How could you use mental math to do exercise 7?

....

INDEPENDENT PRACTICE

Write the product. Use mental math when you can.

11.	$0.25	12.	$2.50	13.	$1.19	14.	$3.68	15.	$2.75
	× 8		× 8		× 5		× 3		× 3

16. 7 × $1.00   17. 6 × $3.01   18. 4 × $8.90

Problem Solving Use the prices shown on page 358.

19. Mr. Lee has $20.00. Can he buy 3 spaceship pilots for his children?

20. Which costs more, 4 mini-robots or 3 jet parachutes?

....

 • **Mixed Practice**

Write the decimal.

1.   2. $3\frac{2}{10}$ 3. four and five tenths

Copy and complete. Write < or >.

4. 0.3 ● 0.1   5. 1.2 ● 1.9   6. 5.0 ● 4.9   7. 12.5 ● 21.2

Pizzas come and go quickly at Pappy's Pizza Palace. Help Pappy and his customers by solving these problems. Work in groups.

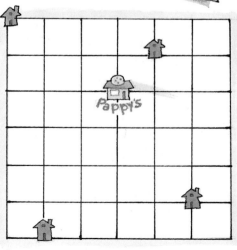

1. Jake is planning a pizza party for 15 people. At Pappy's, each pizza is cut into 8 slices. Jake figures that each person will eat 3 slices.

   a. How many pizzas should Jake order?

   b. How many slices will be left if each person does eat 3 slices?

2. Carmen is having a pizza party on Tuesday. She sees the sign about free pizzas. Carmen needs 16 pizzas. How many of the 16 pizzas will be free?

3. It takes 7 minutes for a pizza to bake. Pappy has 3 ovens. Each oven can bake 4 pizzas at the same time. How long will it take to bake the 16 pizzas for Carmen's party?

4. Luke delivers pizzas on his bicycle. The map shows the 4 houses that are to get pizzas. The lines stand for roads. Copy the map. Draw the shortest route Luke can take. He must start and end at Pappy's and go to all 4 houses. (Be sure Luke stays on the roads.)

SECTION REVIEW

for pages 352–360

Write the letter of the correct answer.

1. 4×576
   a. 202, 824
   b. 3264
   c. 2304
   d. 2484

2. 2×856
   a. 1802
   b. 1822
   c. 161, 012
   d. 1712

3. 9×206
   a. 1804
   b. 1854
   c. 2254
   d. 1944

4. 6×453
   a. 243, 018
   b. 2808
   c. 2718
   d. 4268

5. 5×288
   a. 1440
   b. 4000
   c. 104, 040
   d. 1800

6. 6×703
   a. 4278
   b. 4268
   c. 4218
   d. 4208

7. 3×406
   a. 1238
   b. 1208
   c. 1248
   d. 1218

8. 7×703
   a. 4901
   b. 4921
   c. 5041
   d. 4991

9. 5×372
   a. 1860
   b. 1550
   c. 3500
   d. 1950

Solve each problem.

10. Red, white, and blue balloons are sold at the Fourth of July parade. One balloon costs $1.50. How much would 8 balloons cost?

11. At the parade, small flags cost $2.50.
    a. Could you buy 5 small flags for $12?
    b. How much would 5 small flags cost?

12. Casey gets 75¢ every time he walks his neighbor's dog, Lucky. He walks Lucky 9 times. How much money does he earn?

13. In exactly 3 weeks, Keith will be 9 years old. How many days is it until Keith's birthday?

CHAPTER REVIEW

Language Connection

Some words, such as *array,* have many different meanings. Read this dictionary entry. What meaning do you already know? How is that meaning like any other meanings you see? What do the meanings have in common? Write one or two sentences telling two details you learned about the word *array.*

array *noun* 1. a regular arrangement 2. a group of people in regular order, such as soldiers 3. beautiful or expensive clothing 4. a display or group that affects someone strongly 5. a group arranged in rows and columns

Test ●●●●●●●

Write the product.

1. 23 × 5	**2.** 128 × 3	**3.** $2.64 × 4	**4.** 92 × 2
5. 306 × 3	**6.** $0.49 × 7	**7.** 86 × 9	**8.** 235 × 4
9. $1.78 × 2	**10.** 55 × 8	**11.** 402 × 3	**12.** $0.83 × 5

13. 143 × 8　　　**14.** $5.37 × 4　　　**15.** 381 × 6　　　**16.** $4.15 × 2

17. 29 × 7　　　**18.** 12 × 3　　　**19.** 56 × 2　　　**20.** 31 × 8

21. 1 × 3 × 2　　　**22.** 4 × 5 × 3　　　**23.** 6 × 8 × 2　　　**24.** 3 × 4 × 7

PROBLEM SOLVING

Solve each problem.

25. At the carnival, lemonade costs $0.60 for a small glass and $0.80 for a large glass. How much will 8 small glasses of lemonade cost?

26. Mr. Sanchez buys 4 stuffed animals that cost $1.75 each. If he pays with a $10 bill, how much change will he get?

27. The carnival begins on Monday. It ends later that week on Friday. The carnival is open 11 hours each day. For how many hours is the carnival open?

28. The carnival sells 225 boxes of popcorn on the first day. If the same number of boxes are sold on the other 4 days, will more than 1000 boxes be sold in all?

CUMULATIVE REVIEW

Write the decimal.

29. $\frac{7}{10}$　　**30.** $5\frac{6}{10}$　　**31.** 3 tenths　　**32.** 6 and 1 tenth

Write the decimals from least to greatest.

33. 4.8, 4.7, 5.5　　**34.** 1.1, 0.9, 1.3　　**35.** 6.5, 6.2, 5.6

Write the answer.

36.　4.4
　　+ 2.5

37.　6.2
　　− 3.6

38.　9.4
　　− 8.5

39.　1.8
　　+ 3.4

40. 9.6 − 4.6　　**41.** 3.2 + 0.4　　**42.** 5.5 − 3.2　　**43.** 6.4 + 2.6

Write the perimeter.

44.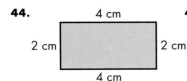

45.

46.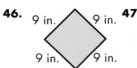

47.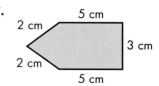

EXCURSION

ESTIMATION

MULTIPLICATION TARGETS

Play Multiplication Targets. It can help you keep your estimation skills sharp.

You need to get as close as you can to the target number without going over it.

Follow these steps.

A

3	6
	8

B

99	58
46	65

Target Number 550

a. Estimate. Choose one factor from box A and one factor from box B that will give a product of about 550. Write the factors on a sheet of paper.

> I will choose 8 and 65. Their product will be at least 480.

b. Use a calculator to multiply.

 8 × 6 5 =

c. Is the product close to, but not greater than, the target number?

> 520 is close to 550, but less than 550.
>
> Maybe I should have chosen 6 and 99. Their product would be about 540.

Suppose you think that another pair of factors would have a product even closer to the target number.

d. Write these factors on a sheet of paper and multiply.

 6 × 9 9 =

Remember: If you are not sure that the factors you chose gave the product closest to the target number, try again.

> 594 is greater than 550. So, 8 × 65 is the closer product.

Choose the factors that give a product that is closest to, but not greater than, the target number. Use a calculator to find the exact answer.

1.

A	B
2 7 4	23 61 43 36

Target Number  180

2.

A	B
5 9 2	71 86 12 94

Target Number  360

3.

A	B
8 3 6	85 21 13 52

Target Number  160

4.

A	B
4 2 6	203 622 875 518

Target Number  3500

5.

A	B
9 5 3	615 225 109 820

Target Number  1000

6.

A	B
8 7 3	165 202 817 463

Target Number  3600

CHAPTER 12

DIVIDING BY 1-DIGIT NUMBERS

Operation Sense

Planning a Field Trip

Ms. Buckley planned a field trip to the science museum. She and some other adults took the entire third grade—112 students. Use this information to answer these questions.

- School rules say there must be 1 adult for every 8 students. How many adults went on the trip?
- Each bus seats up to 65 people. Were 2 buses enough?
- The trip cost $2 for each student. Ms. Buckley collected $206. How many students still need to pay?

COOPERATIVE LEARNING

EXPLORING DIVISION

You can use counters to explore division.

Groups: small groups

You will need:
- 40 counters
- recording sheet

Separate the 40 counters into 3 equal sets. If you have any left over, put them aside.

1. How many counters are there in each of the 3 equal sets?

2. Were you able to separate the 40 counters exactly into 3 equal sets? Why or why not?

Use your recording sheet. Complete the first row of the table.

Now separate the counters into 4 equal sets.

3. How many counters are there in each of the 4 equal sets?

4. Write a division sentence to show what you did.

Record the results in the table.

Use counters to help you complete the table for:
- 5 equal sets.
- 6 equal sets.
- 7 equal sets.
- 8 equal sets.
- 9 equal sets.

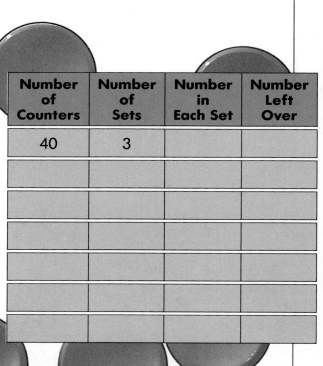

Number of Counters	Number of Sets	Number in Each Set	Number Left Over
40	3		

SUMMING IT UP

Look at your recording sheet.

5. Which numbers divide 40 exactly? What division sentences show this?

6. Which numbers do not divide 40 exactly?

7. For each row, compare the number left over with the number of sets. What do you notice about their sizes?

8. Suppose you separated some counters into 9 equal sets. What is the greatest number of counters that could be left over? How do you know?

9. How can you use multiplication or division facts to decide which numbers will divide 35 exactly?

Decide which exercises will have a number left over. Use multiplication and division facts. Write *yes* or *no*.

10. $34 \div 8$ 11. $85 \div 9$ 12. $63 \div 7$ 13. $57 \div 6$

14. $42 \div 6$ 15. $26 \div 8$ 16. $78 \div 8$ 17. $18 \div 3$

18. Write the multiplication or division facts you used to answer exercises 10–17.

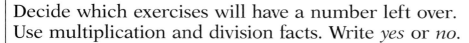

PROJECT • Number Sense

Write 3 division exercises that divide exactly. Write 3 that do not divide exactly. Mix up the order. Then trade papers with a classmate.

Decide which exercises do not divide exactly. Check with your classmate to see if you are right. Discuss how you got your answers.

FRACTIONAL PARTS OF A SET

Rob wants to give $\frac{2}{3}$ of his Frisbees to his younger sister. If he does this, how many will he give her?

To find two thirds of a set, you divide the set into 3 equal parts.

$$6 \div 3 = 2$$

One third of 6 is 2.

So, two thirds of 6 is 2×2, or 4.

Rob gives his sister 4 Frisbees.

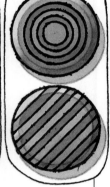

Think

- Would it have been possible for Rob to give his sister $\frac{1}{4}$ of his Frisbees? Explain.

Other Examples

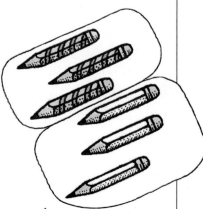

$\frac{3}{4}$ white

$\frac{1}{4}$ black

$\frac{3}{5}$ red

$\frac{2}{5}$ blue

$\frac{1}{2}$ white

$\frac{1}{2}$ striped

GUIDED PRACTICE

Write a fraction for the shaded part of each set.

1.  **2.** 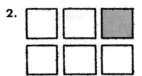 **3.**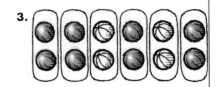

4. Which picture shows $\frac{2}{3}$ shaded?

a.  **b.** 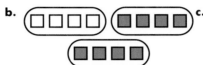 **c.**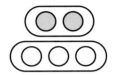

5. What is $\frac{4}{6}$ of 12? (Hint: Look at exercise 3.)

....
INDEPENDENT PRACTICE

Write a fraction for the shaded part of each set.

6. 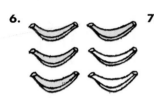 **7.** 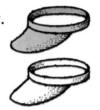 **8.** 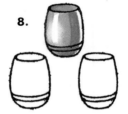 **9.**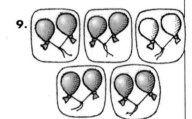

10. Write a fraction for the unshaded part of each set in exercises 6–9.

Problem Solving Use objects or pictures if you like.

11. Beth has 16 marbles. She gives $\frac{1}{2}$ of them to Bryan. How many marbles does she give to Bryan?

12. Todd has 12 eggs. He uses $\frac{1}{3}$ of them to make a cake. How many eggs are left?

13. Sarah has a basket of fruit. She has 4 red apples, 2 green apples, and 3 ripe bananas.
  a. What fractional part of the set is apples?
  b. What fractional part of the set is green?
  c. What fractional part of the set is fruit?

DIVISION WITH REMAINDERS

Kate separates the 26 Eagle Day campers into volleyball teams of 6 campers. The remaining campers keep score. How many teams are there? How many campers keep score?

You can use counters to divide 26 by 6.

Here is another way.

26 ÷ 6 = ▨ asks the same question as 6 × ▨ = 26.

You know 6 × 4 = 24 and 6 × 5 = 30.

No whole number times 6 equals 26. So, the quotient is between 4 and 5.

Divide: 26 ÷ 6.

$$\begin{array}{r} 4 \text{ R2} \\ 6\overline{)26} \\ -\underline{24} \leftarrow 6 \times 4 \\ 2 \end{array}$$

The number left over is called the remainder.

Check your answer by multiplying and adding.

$$\begin{array}{r} 4 \\ \times 6 \\ \hline 24 \end{array} \qquad \begin{array}{r} 24 \\ + 2 \\ \hline 26 \end{array}$$

The quotient with remainder is 4 R2. There are 4 teams, with 6 campers on each team. Two campers keep score.

Think

• When you check division by multiplying, what do you do with the remainder?

Write the quotient and the remainder. Use counters
if it helps.

1. 5)23   2. 6)9   3. 4)20   4. 7)69   5. 2)19

6. 14 ÷ 3   7. 26 ÷ 8   8. 59 ÷ 7   9. 19 ÷ 4   10. 27 ÷ 9

11. Which exercises had no remainders?
    Write a division or multiplication fact for
    each of these exercises.

INDEPENDENT PRACTICE

Write the quotient and the remainder.

12. 2)15   13. 4)30   14. 5)17   15. 8)23   16. 3)29

17. 24 ÷ 5   18. 74 ÷ 9   19. 66 ÷ 8   20. 25 ÷ 3   21. 45 ÷ 6

Divide only the exercises with a remainder.
Write the quotient and the remainder.

22. 7 ÷ 1   23. 13 ÷ 2   24. 24 ÷ 3   25. 19 ÷ 4

26. 9 ÷ 2   27. 49 ÷ 7   28. 39 ÷ 6   29. 40 ÷ 5

Problem Solving

30. Kate is setting up 2 softball
    teams of 9 players each.
    There are 15 players. How
    many more players are
    needed to make the teams
    complete?

31. The pool is open from 10 A.M.
    to 6 P.M. There are 4 swim
    teams that want to practice.
    Only 1 team can practice at a
    time. How long can each
    team practice?

MATH LOG

How can knowing multiplication and
division facts help you divide?

INTERPRETING REMAINDERS

When you divide and have a remainder, you need to decide what to do with the remainder. There are three ways to interpret remainders.

▶ You can *use the remainder.*

Mrs. Perez takes 5 children to the boat show. The film in her camera is enough for 36 pictures. How many pictures can each child take? How many are left for Mrs. Perez?

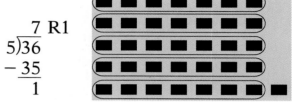

$$\begin{array}{r} 7 \text{ R1} \\ 5)\overline{36} \\ -35 \\ \hline 1 \end{array}$$

Each child can take 7 pictures. There is 1 picture left for Mrs. Perez.

▶ You can *drop the remainder.*

At a folk-dance festival, 51 people want to square dance. Each square needs 8 dancers. How many squares can be formed?

$$\begin{array}{r} 6 \text{ R3} \\ 8)\overline{51} \\ -48 \\ \hline 3 \end{array}$$

Only 6 squares can be formed. The 3 people left cannot form a square.

▶ You can *include the remainder in the answer by writing the next whole number.*

There are 17 children going to the carnival. Each car can take 5 children. How many cars are needed to carry all the children?

$$\begin{array}{r} 3 \text{ R2} \\ 5)\overline{17} \\ -15 \\ \hline 2 \end{array}$$

To carry all the children, 4 cars are needed. Only 3 of the cars will be full.

Think

• How can you decide what to do with a remainder?

GUIDED PRACTICE

Read the problem. Decide what you will do with the remainder. Then solve the problem.

1. Each picnic table at the folk-dance festival can seat 8 people. How many tables are needed for 43 people?

2. There are 25 cans of juice for 9 people. If the cans are divided equally, how many cans will each person get?

3. What did you do with the remainders in exercises 1 and 2? Explain.

INDEPENDENT PRACTICE

Solve each problem. You can draw pictures or use models.

4. The troika is danced in groups of 3. There are 28 people who sign up for a troika lesson. How many complete groups will there be?

5. There are 49 people signed up for Irish step dancing. They want to form equal groups. Should they perform in groups of 5, 6, or 7? Why?

6. The African harvest dancers have 17 baskets. Each of the 4 groups must have 5 baskets. How many more baskets are needed?

7. The next dance will be held 17 days after Tuesday. On what day of the week will the dance be?

Solve each problem. Use the table about vehicles on page 418 in the Data Book.

8. A group of 26 people need a ride to the airport. How many minivans are needed?

9. There are 5 station wagons full of students. All the students need to board the school bus. Will they all fit?

MATH LOG

Write your own division word problem for $20 \div 6$.

USING STRATEGIES

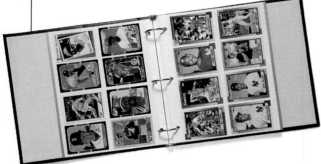

Bill and his friends collect baseball cards. They each buy a new album for their cards. Each album page can hold 8 cards. Each album has 24 pages.

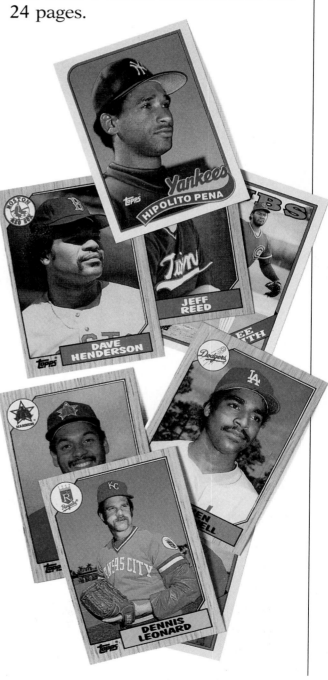

Solve each problem.

1. Bill has 50 cards to put in his album.
   a. How many pages will he need?
   b. How many cards will be on the last page he uses?
   c. How many empty spaces will there be on the last page he uses?

2. Jack has 200 cards to put in his album.
   a. Will they all fit?
   b. Tell how many extra spaces there will be or how many extra cards there will be.

3. Lisa has already put cards in her album. She has only 3 empty pages and 1 page that is half filled.
   a. How many cards are in Lisa's album?
   b. She puts 16 more cards in her album. How many cards will be on the last page she uses?

SECTION REVIEW
for pages 368–376

Write the letter of the correct answer.

1. $9\overline{)74}$
   a. 8
   b. 9
   c. 8 R2
   d. 82

2. $7\overline{)53}$
   a. 7 R4
   b. 8
   c. 74
   d. 7

3. $8\overline{)67}$
   a. 83
   b. 9
   c. 8
   d. 8 R3

4. $28 \div 3$
   a. 10
   b. 8 R4
   c. 9 R1
   d. 25

5. $6\overline{)48}$
   a. 7
   b. 8
   c. 8 R1
   d. 7 R2

6. $56 \div 6$
   a. 9 R2
   b. 8 R8
   c. 50
   d. 11

7. $43 \div 5$
   a. 39
   b. 9 R7
   c. 11
   d. 8 R3

8. $37 \div 8$
   a. 3 R13
   b. 4 R5
   c. 9
   d. 29

9. $7\overline{)65}$
   a. 9 R2
   b. 10
   c. 92
   d. 9

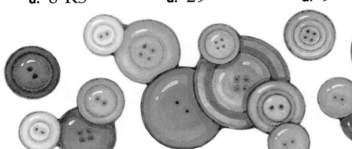

Solve each problem.

10. Amy has 60 buttons. She sews the same number of buttons on 7 dresses. She uses as many buttons as she can. How many buttons are on each dress?

11. There are 60 children going on a trip to Echo Lake. Each van can hold 7 children. How many vans are needed?

ESTIMATING QUOTIENTS

▶ Estimation can help you to divide.

Divide: $75 \div 6 = \blacksquare$.

It asks the same question as $6 \times \blacksquare = 75$.

● **First, decide how many digits are in the quotient.**

$6 \times 1 = 6$
$6 \times 10 = 60$

> 75 is between 60 and 600.

$6 \times 100 = 600$

The quotient is between 10 and 100. It has 2 digits.

● **To get an estimate, use multiples of 10.**

$6 \times 10 = 60$

> 75 is between 60 and 120.

$6 \times 20 = 120$

So, the quotient is between 10 and 20 because 75 is between 60 and 120.

▶ You can estimate with larger dividends.

Divide: $115 \div 4 = \blacksquare$.

It asks the same question as $4 \times \blacksquare = 115$.

● **How many digits?**

$4 \times 1 = 4$
$4 \times 10 = 40$

> 115 is between 40 and 400.

$4 \times 100 = 400$

The quotient is between 10 and 100. It has 2 digits.

● **To get an estimate, use multiples of 10.**

$4 \times 10 = 40$
$4 \times 20 = 80$

> 115 is between 80 and 120.

$4 \times 30 = 120$

So, the quotient is between 20 and 30 because 115 is between 80 and 120.

Think

• Will the quotient of $115 \div 4$ be closer to 20 or to 30? How do you know?

Look at the blue numbers in the number sentences.
Write the two numbers the quotient is between.

1. 4)83   4 × 10 = 40
             4 × 20 = 80
             4 × 30 = 120

2. 5)367   5 × 50 = 250
            5 × 60 = 300
            5 × 70 = 420

Write the letter of the better estimate.

3. 98 ÷ 3   Estimate between: **a.** 30 and 40   **b.** 20 and 30

4. 372 ÷ 4 Estimate between: **a.** 80 and 90   **b.** 90 and 100

5. For exercise 1, will the quotient be closer
   to 20 or to 30? Explain.

Look at the blue numbers. Write the two numbers
the quotient is between.

6. 2)68   2 × 20 = 40
            2 × 30 = 60
            2 × 40 = 80

7. 7)432   7 × 60 = 420
            7 × 70 = 490
            7 × 80 = 560

Write the letter of the better estimate.

8. 93 ÷ 3   Estimate between: **a.** 20 and 30   **b.** 30 and 40

9. 257 ÷ 4 Estimate between: **a.** 50 and 60   **b.** 60 and 70

10. 626 ÷ 8 Estimate between: **a.** 70 and 80   **b.** 80 and 90

·······································

Maintain • Elapsed Time
Write how much time has passed.

1.    2.   3.

TWO-DIGIT QUOTIENTS

Carla makes toy animals with spools and pipe cleaners. She has 75 spools. If she uses 6 spools to make a giraffe, how many giraffes can she make?

NUMBER OF SPOOLS TO MAKE ANIMALS	
Animal	**Spools**
Lion	5
Giraffe	6
Elephant	9

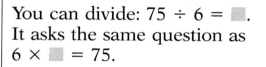

You can divide: $75 \div 6 = $ ■.
It asks the same question as
$6 \times$ ■ $= 75$.

To get an estimate, use multiples of 10.
$6 \times 10 = 60$
$6 \times 20 = 120$ ⟵ 75
So, the quotient is between 10 and 20.

● **Write the tens. Multiply. Subtract.**

$$
\begin{array}{r}
10 \\
6\overline{)75} \\
-60 \\
\hline
15
\end{array}
$$
⟵ 6×10

● **Write the ones. Multiply. Subtract.**

$$
\begin{array}{r}
2 \\
10 \\
6\overline{)75} \\
-60 \\
\hline
15 \\
-12 \\
\hline
3
\end{array}
$$
⟵ 6×10
⟵ 6×2

● **Add to find the quotient. Is there a remainder?**

$$
\begin{array}{r}
2 \\
10 \\
6\overline{)75} \\
-60 \\
\hline
15 \\
-12 \\
\hline
3
\end{array}
$$
$10 + 2 = 12$
⟵ 6×10
⟵ 6×2

The quotient with the remainder is 12 R3.
Carla can make 12 giraffes.

Check by multiplying and adding.

$$
\begin{array}{rr}
12 & 72 \\
\times\ 6 & +\ 3 \\
\hline
72 & 75
\end{array}
$$

Think

• How can you tell if the remainder is correct?

GUIDED PRACTICE

Write the quotient and remainder. Check your answer.

1. $9\overline{)69}$ 2. $4\overline{)56}$ 3. $5\overline{)68}$ 4. $2\overline{)19}$ 5. $8\overline{)89}$

6. $47 \div 3$ 7. $45 \div 9$ 8. $84 \div 7$ 9. $86 \div 6$

Estimate which quotient is greater. Write *a* or *b*.

10. a. $3\overline{)47}$ b. $3\overline{)57}$ 11. a. $5\overline{)23}$ b. $7\overline{)23}$

12. How did you decide which quotients were greater in exercises 10 and 11?

....

INDEPENDENT PRACTICE

Write the quotient and remainder. Check your answer.

13. $8\overline{)48}$ 14. $7\overline{)91}$ 15. $5\overline{)96}$ 16. $6\overline{)83}$ 17. $3\overline{)64}$

18. $81 \div 9$ 19. $47 \div 4$ 20. $75 \div 3$ 21. $88 \div 5$

Estimate which quotient is greater. Write *a* or *b*.

22. a. $7\overline{)93}$ b. $8\overline{)93}$ 23. a. $4\overline{)62}$ b. $4\overline{)72}$

Problem Solving Use the table on page 380.

24. How many lions can Carla make with 65 spools? Will she have any left over?

25. What is the greatest number of elephants that Carla can make with 49 spools?

26. Suppose you have 43 spools, and you want to use them all. What animals would you make? How many of each?

....

Maintain • **Multiplication**

Write the product.

1. 3×15 2. 5×78 3. $3 \times \$5.99$ 4. 7×408

DIVIDING LARGER NUMBERS

There are 114 people signed up for a hot-air balloon ride. Only 4 passengers can ride at one time. How many trips are needed for all the passengers?

You can divide 114 by 4.

Think

- Will the answer be the number of groups or the number in each group?

$114 \div 4 = \blacksquare$ asks the same question as $4 \times \blacksquare = 114$.

To get an estimate, use multiples of 10.

$4 \times 20 = 80$
$\longleftarrow 114$
$4 \times 30 = 120$

So, the quotient is between 20 and 30.

● Write the tens. Multiply. Subtract.	● Write the ones. Multiply. Subtract.	● Add to find the quotient. Is there a remainder?

● Write the tens. Multiply. Subtract.

$$\begin{array}{r} 20 \\ 4\overline{)114} \\ -80 \\ \hline 34 \end{array} \longleftarrow 4 \times 20$$

● Write the ones. Multiply. Subtract.

$$\begin{array}{r} 8 \\ 20 \\ 4\overline{)114} \\ -80 \\ \hline 34 \\ -32 \\ \hline 2 \end{array} \begin{array}{l} \\ \\ \\ \longleftarrow 4 \times 20 \\ \\ \longleftarrow 4 \times 8 \end{array}$$

● Add to find the quotient. Is there a remainder?

$$\begin{array}{r} 8 \\ 20 \\ 4\overline{)114} \\ -80 \\ \hline 34 \\ -32 \\ \hline 2 \end{array} \begin{array}{l} 20 + 8 = 28 \\ \\ \\ \longleftarrow 4 \times 20 \\ \\ \longleftarrow 4 \times 8 \end{array}$$

The quotient with the remainder is 28 R2. For all the passengers, 29 trips are needed.

Check by multiplying and adding.

$$\begin{array}{r} 28 \\ \times\ 4 \\ \hline 112 \end{array} \qquad \begin{array}{r} 112 \\ +\ 2 \\ \hline 114 \end{array}$$

GUIDED PRACTICE

Divide. Check your answer.

1. $3\overline{)126}$ 2. $5\overline{)456}$ 3. $7\overline{)542}$ 4. $4\overline{)352}$ 5. $6\overline{)316}$

6. $158 \div 2$ 7. $207 \div 5$ 8. $873 \div 9$ 9. $340 \div 8$

10. What would you do if your remainder were larger than your divisor?

INDEPENDENT PRACTICE

Divide. Check your answer.

11. $8\overline{)368}$ 12. $5\overline{)283}$ 13. $3\overline{)257}$ 14. $4\overline{)264}$ 15. $7\overline{)498}$

16. $358 \div 4$ 17. $729 \div 9$ 18. $648 \div 9$ 19. $473 \div 8$

Choose the best estimate. Write *a, b,* or *c.*

20. $515 \div 6$ Between: a. 70 and 80   b. 80 and 90   c. 30 and 40

21. $113 \div 2$ Between: a. 60 and 70   b. 70 and 80   c. 50 and 60

Problem Solving Use the information on page 382 to help you.

22. One more person decides to take a balloon ride. So the total is 115 passengers. Now how many trips will be needed?

23. Still more people want rides. Now 36 trips are needed. How many people want rides?

....

CHALLENGE • Logical Reasoning

Find the mystery numbers.

1. The quotient of two numbers is 6. Their difference is 20. What are the two numbers?

2. The quotient of two numbers is 9. Their difference is 56. What are the two numbers?

PROBLEM SOLVING
USING MATH SENSE

If you get stuck, remember....

Tips for Problem Solving

on pages 426–427

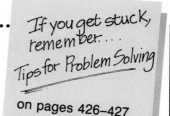

Solve each problem.

1. Each car on the Surfing Safari ride can hold 8 people. There are 52 people waiting in line. How many cars will be needed?

2. The owners of the Surfing Safari ride do not like to have empty seats on any cars. How many more people must come so there will be no empty seats?

3. Books at the Grove School book sale cost $3 each. How many books can Nathan buy with $25?

4. Mark has 4 stacks of nickels with 10 nickels in each stack. How much money does he have?

5. Which is worth more, a stack of dimes 5 inches high or a stack of nickels 5 inches high? How do you know?

6. Aaron has saved $5.00. He earns $3.00 every other week. Suppose Aaron saves all his money. How long will it take him to save enough to buy a baseball glove that costs $19.95?

7. Lois is making a necklace. She will use the pattern shown in the picture. The blue beads are 2 inches long and the green beads are 1 inch long. How many of each color does she need to make a necklace 25 inches long?

8. In how many different ways can 5 eggs be arranged in the box?

SECTION REVIEW

for pages 378–384

Write the letter of the correct answer.

1. $6\overline{)92}$
   a. 1 R2
   b. 20
   c. 15 R2
   d. 114 R2

2. $7\overline{)81}$
   a. 11 R4
   b. 20
   c. 110 R4
   d. 1 R1

3. $4\overline{)62}$
   a. 114 R2
   b. 20
   c. 1 R2
   d. 15 R2

4. $8\overline{)97}$
   a. 20
   b. 12 R1
   c. 1 R7
   d. 111 R1

5. $232 \div 6$
   a. 3 R5
   b. 30 R52
   c. 38 R4
   d. 37 R10

6. $356 \div 6$
   a. 59 R2
   b. 50 R56
   c. 58 R8
   d. 5 R5

7. $143 \div 4$
   a. 34 R7
   b. 30 R23
   c. 3 R2
   d. 35 R3

8. $337 \div 8$
   a. 40 R17
   b. 42 R1
   c. 4 R1
   d. 41 R9

9. $531 \div 9$
   a. 58 R9
   b. 61 R2
   c. 59
   d. 58

Solve each problem.

10. The Good Morning Bakery can fit 6 muffins in a box. How many boxes would they use for an order of 75 muffins?

11. The third-graders raised $310. They want to buy calculators that cost $7 each. How many can they buy?

CHAPTER REVIEW

Language Connection

Suppose you are making tables. By mistake, you buy nine legs. What do you do with the remainder? You could throw it out. Or you could make something else out of it. You could make one table with four legs and one with five legs. You also could make 3 three-legged tables.

Problems can have many solutions. Try to find several solutions to this problem.

You are making peach pies. You need five peaches for each pie. You have 53 peaches. What could you do with the leftover peaches?

Test •••••••

Write a fraction for the shaded part of the set.

1.  2.

Write a fraction for the unshaded part of the set.

3.

4.

Write the quotient.

5. $4\overline{)12}$

6. $3\overline{)10}$

7. $6\overline{)6}$

8. $2\overline{)9}$

9. $11 \div 3$

10. $15 \div 3$

11. $8 \div 2$

12. $9 \div 6$

13. $3\overline{)53}$

14. $7\overline{)84}$

15. $8\overline{)94}$

16. $6\overline{)75}$

Write the quotient.

17. $86 \div 4$ 18. $85 \div 5$ 19. $59 \div 4$ 20. $27 \div 2$

21. $3\overline{)253}$ 22. $7\overline{)515}$ 23. $4\overline{)348}$ 24. $6\overline{)426}$

25. $251 \div 9$ 26. $210 \div 8$ 27. $371 \div 5$ 28. $411 \div 7$

PROBLEM SOLVING

Solve each problem. Decide what to do with the remainder before you write the answer.

29. Each table in the art room can seat 4 students. How many tables are needed for 23 students?

30. Annie needs 9 wooden spools to make a toy elephant. How many elephants can Annie make with 146 spools?

31. Mr. Palmer bought a bag of 13 apples. He divided the apples equally among his 4 children and kept the remaining apple. How many apples did each child get?

32. There are 59 campers who want to play softball. They make 6 teams. Each team has 9 players. Extra players serve as substitutes. How many substitutes are there?

CUMULATIVE REVIEW

Complete. Write $<$, $>$, or $=$.

33. $0.6 \bullet 0.4$ 34. $5.0 \bullet 5$ 35. $7.9 \bullet 8.1$

Write the product.

36. $\begin{array}{r} 24 \\ \times\ 2 \\ \hline \end{array}$ 37. $\begin{array}{r} 17 \\ \times\ 6 \\ \hline \end{array}$ 38. $\begin{array}{r} 104 \\ \times\ 2 \\ \hline \end{array}$ 39. $\begin{array}{r} 212 \\ \times\ 3 \\ \hline \end{array}$

EXCURSION

PROBLEM SOLVING

DECISION MAKING

Pretend you are on vacation in Boston, Massachusetts. You want to visit the Museum of Science. Read the events and plans below. Then decide which plan you would rather use.

You may use a calculator to help figure out your costs.

Plan 1:
Spend 1 day at the museum.
See 3 events

Plan 2:
Spend 2 days at the museum.
Day 1 - See 2 events
Day 2 - See 2 events

Events

Exhibit Halls: Learn and play with science.
Open from 9:00 A.M. to 9:00 P.M.

Omni Theater: Exciting giant-screen movies.
Shows every hour.

Planetarium: View the stars, inside.
Shows at 1:30, 3:30, 4:30

Laser shows: Laser lights to rock music.
Shows at 5:30, 8:30, 10:00

To help you decide, think about the following:

- If you choose Plan 1, you can go somewhere else the next day.

- It costs $1.50 to take the bus to the museum and back.

- Do you want to go to all of the events at the museum?

- How much money will you need to visit the museum for 1 day? For 2 days?

- Will you want to buy something at the gift shop or museum restaurant?

- Is there anything else you need to think about to help you choose a plan?

Which plan did you choose? Explain why.

PROJECT • Problem Solving

Read the two plans below. Then decide which plan you would rather use.

To help you decide, make a list of the things you need to think about. You can use a calculator to help figure out your costs.

Which plan did you choose? Why?

Plan 1
A BASEBALL GAME
AT FENWAY PARK
Admission:.....................$10
Extra costs:
Food :..........................$5
Gifts from Fenway:.....$10
Time: 3 hours for game
or 5 hours for game
and batting pracitce
Batting practice starts
at 11:00 A.M.
Game starts at 1:00 P.M.
Free bat today!

Plan 2
VISIT THE
CHILDREN'S MUSEUM
and
THE BOSTON
TEA PARTY SHIP
(Two museums on the same block)

Children's Museum
Admission:
from 10:00 P.M. to 5:00 P.M..$5
from 5:00 P.M. to 9:00 P.M....$1
Magic Show.............................$1

Boston Tea Party Ship
Admission:.........................$3.75
Extra costs:
Food:............................$5
Gifts from museum shops:..$10
Magic show starts at
7:00 P.M. Show is 1 hour long.

More Practice

USE WITH PAGES 10–11.

Write the sum.

1. 8
    $+ 8$

2. 6
    $+ 5$

3. 8
    $+ 9$

4. 8
    $+ 7$

5. 7
    $+ 7$

6. 7
    $+ 6$

7. 7
    $+ 5$

8. 6
    $+ 8$

9. 7
    $+ 9$

10. 8
    $+ 4$

11. 10
    $+ 10$

12. 11
    $+ 12$

13. 9
    $+ 9$

14. 9
    $+ 10$

15. 5
    $+ 5$

16. 5
    $+ 6$

17. 7
    $+ 8$

18. 4
    $+ 4$

19. $4 + 5$

20. $6 + 6$

21. $9 + 8$

22. $10 + 10$

USE WITH PAGES 14–15.

Write the sum.

1. 7
    $+ 5$

2. 4
    $+ 8$

3. 6
    $+ 4$

4. 9
    $+ 5$

5. 8
    $+ 6$

6. 7
    $+ 8$

7. 6
    $+ 7$

8. 4
    $+ 6$

9. 9
    $+ 4$

10. 4
    $+ 7$

11. 8
    $+ 2$

12. 3
    $+ 15$

13. 9
    $+ 4$

14. 7
    $+ 7$

15. 5
    $+ 5$

16. 9
    $+ 3$

17. 6
    $+ 9$

18. 7
    $+ 3$

19. $8 + 3$

20. $7 + 4$

21. $7 + 9$

22. $3 + 6$

23. $4 + 5$

24. $9 + 2$

25. $5 + 7$

26. $6 + 5$

USE WITH PAGES 16–17.

Write the sum.

1.	2.	3.	4.	5.	6.
8 1 + 2	7 5 + 3	3 9 + 8	3 10 + 4	4 4 + 4	1 3 + 4

7.	8.	9.	10.	11.	12.
6 6 + 7	5 2 + 8	7 1 + 6	9 4 + 6	5 3 + 7	1 6 + 7

13.	14.	15.	16.	17.	18.
6 6 + 6	7 3 + 1	9 0 + 1	8 9 + 2	7 7 + 2	4 9 + 1

19. $10 + 2 + 1$ **20.** $4 + 2 + 6$ **21.** $8 + 9 + 3$

22. $5 + 6 + 5$ **23.** $5 + 4 + 10$ **24.** $6 + 6 + 2$

USE WITH PAGES 20–21.

Write the difference.

1.	2.	3.	4.	5.	6.
13 − 4	11 − 3	12 − 2	18 − 9	15 − 0	11 − 7

7.	8.	9.	10.	11.	12.
10 − 2	7 − 7	13 − 9	5 − 5	6 − 0	7 − 4

13.	14.	15.	16.	17.	18.
15 − 9	16 − 9	14 − 7	20 − 9	12 − 4	10 − 9

19. $10 − 8$ **20.** $9 − 9$ **21.** $14 − 2$ **22.** $15 − 6$

23. $12 − 3$ **24.** $13 − 3$ **25.** $14 − 5$ **26.** $15 − 7$

USE WITH PAGES 20–21.

Copy and complete the number sentence.

1. $8 + \blacksquare = 17$
2. $\blacksquare + 7 = 15$
3. $\blacksquare + 9 = 14$
4. $\blacksquare + 7 = 16$

5. $8 + \blacksquare = 16$
6. $6 + \blacksquare = 14$
7. $\blacksquare + 8 = 15$
8. $9 + \blacksquare = 18$

9. $5 + \blacksquare = 13$
10. $\blacksquare + 9 = 13$
11. $7 + \blacksquare = 13$
12. $10 + \blacksquare = 16$

USE WITH PAGES 28–29.

Write the number sentence that is missing from the fact family.

1. $4 + 5 = 9$
   $5 + 4 = 9$
   $9 - 4 = 5$

2. $15 - 8 = 7$
   $15 - 7 = 8$
   $7 + 8 = 15$

3. $6 + 6 = 12$

4. $5 + 8 = 13$
   $13 - 8 = 5$
   $8 + 5 = 13$

5. $0 + 9 = 9$
   $9 - 0 = 9$
   $9 - 9 = 0$

6. $10 - 5 = 5$

Write a family of facts for these numbers.

7. 5, 7, 12
8. 8, 8, 16
9. 8, 7, 15
10. 0, 4, 4
11. 13, 6, 7

USE WITH PAGES 42–43.

Write the number in standard form.

1. six hundred eighteen
2. $400 + 7$
3. two hundred thirty
4. $400 + 60 + 1$
5. one hundred sixty
6. nine hundred nine
7. 8 hundreds + 2 tens + 3 ones
8. 6 hundreds + 7 tens

Write the value of the blue digit.

9. 654 10. 137 11. 867 12. 520 13. 196

14. 602 15. 476 16. 398 17. 516 18. 753

USE WITH PAGES 46–47.

Write in standard form.

1. one thousand fifteen

2. five thousand six hundred eleven

3. nine thousand eight hundred

4. six thousand nine hundred forty

5. two thousand seven

6. eight thousand one hundred fifty-six

7. $9000 + 400 + 20$ 8. $4000 + 300 + 1$ 9. $8000 + 500 + 10 + 2$

Write the value of the blue digit.

10. 2431 11. 8056 12. 690 13. 2435 14. 6209

15. 129 16. 3790 17. 3014 18. 2641 19. 25

USE WITH PAGES 50–51.

Write the answer.

1. $\begin{array}{r} 60 \\ + 30 \\ \hline \end{array}$
2. $\begin{array}{r} 400 \\ + 600 \\ \hline \end{array}$
3. $\begin{array}{r} 30 \\ + 20 \\ \hline \end{array}$
4. $\begin{array}{r} 8000 \\ - 2000 \\ \hline \end{array}$
5. $\begin{array}{r} 15,000 \\ - 7,000 \\ \hline \end{array}$

6. $\begin{array}{r} 40 \\ + 90 \\ \hline \end{array}$
7. $\begin{array}{r} 5000 \\ + 5000 \\ \hline \end{array}$
8. $\begin{array}{r} 16,000 \\ - 8,000 \\ \hline \end{array}$
9. $\begin{array}{r} 700 \\ - 300 \\ \hline \end{array}$
10. $\begin{array}{r} 100 \\ - 80 \\ \hline \end{array}$

Write the answer.

11. 700	12. 1000	13. 600	14. 12,000	15. 1600
+ 400	+ 9000	− 300	− 5,000	− 900

USE WITH PAGES 54–55.

Copy and complete. Write < or >.

1. 98 ● 99
2. 634 ● 643
3. 2643 ● 2638
4. 3136 ● 7982
5. 7413 ● 7143
6. 3784 ● 3874

Order from least to greatest.

7. 96, 69, 71
8. 123, 119, 132
9. 471, 741, 417
10. 1312, 684, 1296
11. 752, 546, 2016
12. 1560, 1078, 643
13. 461, 68, 276
14. 2932, 2039, 2392
15. 8422, 5478, 634

USE WITH PAGES 60–61.

Write the amount. Use a dollar sign and decimal point.

1. two dollars and thirty-two cents
2. eighty-five cents
3. twelve dollars
4. eight dollars and ten cents
5. 5 dollars and 3 cents
6. 11 dollars and 15 cents
7. 75 cents
8. 1 dollars and 3 cents
9. two dimes
10. 6 nickels

USE WITH PAGES 80–81.

Write the sum.

1. 30
    + 36

2. 69
    + 18

3. 41
    + 89

4. $0.35
    + 0.71

5. 67
    + 92

6. 12
    + 19

7. 74
    + 88

8. $0.42
    + 0.56

9. 25 feet
    + 26 feet

10. 82
    + 91

11. 31 + 70

12. 26 + 53

13. 87 + 68

14. 95 + 78

15. 40 + 27

16. 42 + 62

17. 55 + 45

18. 95 + 77

USE WITH PAGES 82–83.

Write the answer.

1. 425
    + 528

2. 771
    + 269

3. $5.94
    + 3.32

4. 262
    + 35

5. 931
    + 78

6. 653
    + 29

7. 529
    + 274

8. $1.00
    + 8.47

9. 735
    + 628

10. $3.85
    + 0.15

11. 700 + 189

12. 674 + 35

13. 730 + 805

14. 459 + 786

15. $4.00 + $3.00

16. 139 + 47

17. 184 + 229

18. 500 + 25

USE WITH PAGES 86–87.

Write the sum.

1. 386
     52
    + 342

2. 57
    43
    + 80

3. 28
    35
    + 91

4. $1.93
     0.18
    + 3.22

5. 45
    10
    + 77

Write the sum.

6. 708 miles + 66 miles + 37 miles   7. 536 + 52 + 55

8. 460 + 50 + 64 + 30   9. $0.84 + $3.55 + $8.80 + $0.85

10. 633 + 418 + 185 + 876   11. 210 + 143 + 631 + 104

USE WITH PAGES 92–93.

Write the difference.

1. $\begin{array}{r} 81 \\ -\ 50 \\ \hline \end{array}$
2. $\begin{array}{r} 53 \\ -\ 29 \\ \hline \end{array}$
3. $\begin{array}{r} 94 \text{ yards} \\ -\ 58 \text{ yards} \\ \hline \end{array}$
4. $\begin{array}{r} \$0.81 \\ -\ 0.69 \\ \hline \end{array}$
5. $\begin{array}{r} 78 \\ -\ 12 \\ \hline \end{array}$

6. $\begin{array}{r} 91 \\ -\ 87 \\ \hline \end{array}$
7. $\begin{array}{r} \$0.61 \\ -\ 0.28 \\ \hline \end{array}$
8. $\begin{array}{r} 93 \\ -\ 46 \\ \hline \end{array}$
9. $\begin{array}{r} 66 \\ -\ 47 \\ \hline \end{array}$
10. $\begin{array}{r} \$0.95 \\ -\ 0.51 \\ \hline \end{array}$

11. $0.34 − $0.25   12. 72 − 7   13. 67 − 12

14. $0.75 − $0.25   15. 50 meters − 17 meters   16. 99 − 10

USE WITH PAGES 94–95.

Write the difference.

1. $\begin{array}{r} 359 \\ -\ 45 \\ \hline \end{array}$
2. $\begin{array}{r} \$7.17 \\ -\ 0.56 \\ \hline \end{array}$
3. $\begin{array}{r} 637 \\ -\ 44 \\ \hline \end{array}$
4. $\begin{array}{r} 347 \\ -\ 175 \\ \hline \end{array}$
5. $\begin{array}{r} 612 \\ -\ 467 \\ \hline \end{array}$

6. $\begin{array}{r} \$7.81 \\ -\ 6.92 \\ \hline \end{array}$
7. $\begin{array}{r} 854 \\ -\ 66 \\ \hline \end{array}$
8. $\begin{array}{r} 323 \\ -\ 277 \\ \hline \end{array}$
9. $\begin{array}{r} 495 \\ -\ 10 \\ \hline \end{array}$
10. $\begin{array}{r} \$4.69 \\ -\ 2.92 \\ \hline \end{array}$

11. 366 − 171   12. 523 − 235   13. 243 feet − 76 feet

14. 732 − 300   15. 279 − 79   16. 634 meters − 76 meters

USE WITH PAGES 100–101.

Write the difference.

1. $\begin{array}{r} 580 \\ -\ 163 \end{array}$

2. $\begin{array}{r} 550 \\ -\ 30 \end{array}$

3. $\begin{array}{r} 807 \\ -\ 22 \end{array}$

4. $\begin{array}{r} 304 \\ -\ 246 \end{array}$

5. $\begin{array}{r} \$9.00 \\ -\ 0.33 \end{array}$

6. $\begin{array}{r} 703 \\ -\ 57 \end{array}$

7. $\begin{array}{r} 508 \\ -\ 413 \end{array}$

8. $\begin{array}{r} 130 \\ -\ 77 \end{array}$

9. $\begin{array}{r} 902 \\ -\ 747 \end{array}$

10. $\begin{array}{r} 930 \\ -\ 56 \end{array}$

11. $800 - 592$

12. $790 - 482$

13. $600 \text{ feet } - 91 \text{ feet}$

14. $403 - 181$

15. $300 - 42$

16. $\$7.30 - \$1.45$

17. $670 - 70$

18. $500 - 200$

19. $\$8.05 - \$2.06$

USE WITH PAGES 118–119.

Use the pictograph to solve each problem.

Muffins Sold at the Lakeside School Bake Sale	
Banana Muffins	🧁🧁🧁
Blueberry Muffins	🧁🧁🧁🧁🧁🧁🧁
Bran Muffins	🧁🧁
Corn Muffins	🧁🧁🧁
Raisin Nut Muffins	🧁🧁🧁🧁🧁

🧁 = 5 muffins

1. How many kinds of muffins were sold at the bake sale?

2. How many corn muffins were sold?

3. Which muffins were the most popular?

4. How many muffins were sold in all?

397

USE WITH PAGES 120–121.

Use the bar graph to solve each problem.

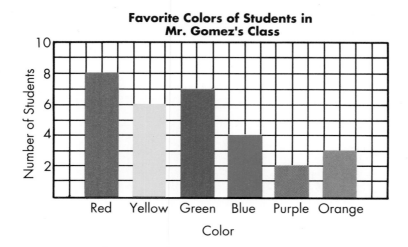

Favorite Colors of Students in Mr. Gomez's Class

1. How many students named green as their favorite color?

2. Which color was chosen most?

3. Which color was chosen least?

4. Which colors were chosen by more than four students?

5. How many more students chose red than chose orange?

USE WITH PAGES 122–123.

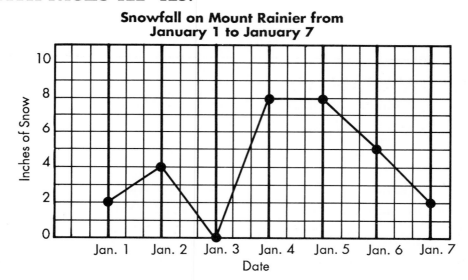

Snowfall on Mount Rainier from January 1 to January 7

Use the line graph to solve each problem.

1. Which day had the least amount of snowfall?

2. On which two days did the same amount of snow fall?

3. On which days did less than 5 inches of snow fall?

4. How many more inches of snow fell on January 6 than on January 2?

USE WITH PAGES 144–145.

Write the product.

1. 5×2
2. 2×3
3. 4×2
4. 1×2
5. 3×2
6. 2×1
7. 2×2
8. 2×5

USE WITH PAGES 150–151.

Write the quotient.

1. $6 \div 2$
2. $8 \div 2$
3. $10 \div 2$
4. $4 \div 2$

USE WITH PAGES 154–155.

Write the answer.

1. $\begin{array}{r} 3 \\ \times 2 \\ \hline \end{array}$
2. $\begin{array}{r} 5 \\ \times 3 \\ \hline \end{array}$
3. $\begin{array}{r} 3 \\ \times 1 \\ \hline \end{array}$
4. $\begin{array}{r} 4 \\ \times 3 \\ \hline \end{array}$

5. 3×5
6. 3×3
7. $15 \div 3$
8. $6 \div 3$
9. 3×4
10. $12 \div 3$
11. 2×3
12. $9 \div 3$

USE WITH PAGES 156–157.

Write the answer.

1. $\begin{array}{r} 3 \\ \times 4 \\ \hline \end{array}$
2. $\begin{array}{r} 1 \\ \times 4 \\ \hline \end{array}$
3. $\begin{array}{r} 4 \\ \times 5 \\ \hline \end{array}$
4. $\begin{array}{r} 4 \\ \times 2 \\ \hline \end{array}$
5. $\begin{array}{r} 4 \\ \times 4 \\ \hline \end{array}$

6. 2×4
7. $16 \div 4$
8. 4×5
9. $20 \div 4$
10. $12 \div 4$

11. $12 \div 3$
12. 5×4
13. $15 \div 3$
14. $8 \div 4$
15. 4×4

USE WITH PAGES 158–159.

Write the answer.

1. $\begin{array}{r} 5 \\ \times 3 \\ \hline \end{array}$
2. $\begin{array}{r} 4 \\ \times 5 \\ \hline \end{array}$
3. $\begin{array}{r} 1 \\ \times 5 \\ \hline \end{array}$
4. $\begin{array}{r} 5 \\ \times 2 \\ \hline \end{array}$
5. $\begin{array}{r} 5 \\ \times 5 \\ \hline \end{array}$

6. $15 \div 5$
7. 4×5
8. 5×1
9. $25 \div 5$

10. 5×5
11. 3×5
12. $20 \div 5$
13. $10 \div 5$

USE WITH PAGES 172–173.

Write the missing factor.

1. $3 \times \blacksquare = 15$
2. $\blacksquare \times 2 = 8$
3. $4 \times \blacksquare = 16$

4. $\blacksquare \times 4 = 12$
5. $\blacksquare \times 3 = 9$
6. $2 \times \blacksquare = 10$

7. $3 \times \blacksquare = 6$
8. $\blacksquare \times 5 = 25$
9. $\blacksquare \times 4 = 20$

10. $4 \times \blacksquare = 8$
11. $\blacksquare \times 2 = 4$
12. $\blacksquare \times 5 = 20$

Write a multiplication sentence that asks the same question.

13. $15 \div 3 = \blacksquare$
14. $20 \div 4 = \blacksquare$
15. $16 \div 4 = \blacksquare$

16. $6 \div 3 = \blacksquare$
17. $12 \div 2 = \blacksquare$
18. $9 \div 3 = \blacksquare$

Write a division sentence that asks the same question.

19. $4 \times \blacksquare = 20$ **20.** $4 \times \blacksquare = 16$ **21.** $\blacksquare \times 3 = 9$

22. $3 \times \blacksquare = 12$ **23.** $\blacksquare \times 2 = 6$ **24.** $\blacksquare \times 5 = 25$

USE WITH PAGES 180–181.

Write the answer.

1. $\begin{array}{r} 3 \\ \times\ 6 \\ \hline \end{array}$ **2.** $\begin{array}{r} 6 \\ \times\ 5 \\ \hline \end{array}$ **3.** $\begin{array}{r} 6 \\ \times\ 6 \\ \hline \end{array}$ **4.** $\begin{array}{r} 9 \\ \times\ 6 \\ \hline \end{array}$

5. $\begin{array}{r} 6 \\ \times\ 1 \\ \hline \end{array}$ **6.** $\begin{array}{r} 2 \\ \times\ 6 \\ \hline \end{array}$ **7.** $\begin{array}{r} 0 \\ \times\ 6 \\ \hline \end{array}$ **8.** $\begin{array}{r} 7 \\ \times\ 6 \\ \hline \end{array}$

9. $6 \div 6$ **10.** $48 \div 6$ **11.** $18 \div 6$ **12.** $30 \div 6$

13. 6×2 **14.** 6×8 **15.** 4×6 **16.** 6×7

17. $12 \div 6$ **18.** $24 \div 6$ **19.** $36 \div 6$ **20.** $42 \div 6$

USE WITH PAGES 182–183.

Write the answer.

1. $\begin{array}{r} 7 \\ \times\ 7 \\ \hline \end{array}$ **2.** $\begin{array}{r} 4 \\ \times\ 7 \\ \hline \end{array}$ **3.** $\begin{array}{r} 7 \\ \times\ 1 \\ \hline \end{array}$ **4.** $\begin{array}{r} 9 \\ \times\ 7 \\ \hline \end{array}$

5. $7\overline{)63}$ **6.** $7\overline{)56}$ **7.** $7\overline{)49}$ **8.** $7\overline{)7}$

9. 2×7 **10.** 7×8 **11.** 7×5 **12.** 3×7

13. $42 \div 7$ **14.** $14 \div 7$ **15.** $21 \div 7$ **16.** $28 \div 7$

17. 7×0 **18.** $35 \div 7$ **19.** 6×7 **20.** $7 \div 1$

USE WITH PAGES 186–187.

Write the answer.

1. $\begin{array}{r} 5 \\ \times\ 8 \\ \hline \end{array}$
2. $\begin{array}{r} 9 \\ \times\ 8 \\ \hline \end{array}$
3. $\begin{array}{r} 4 \\ \times\ 8 \\ \hline \end{array}$
4. $\begin{array}{r} 8 \\ \times\ 1 \\ \hline \end{array}$

5. $8\overline{)48}$
6. $8\overline{)64}$
7. $8\overline{)72}$
8. $8\overline{)8}$

9. 8×8
10. 8×2
11. 7×8
12. 3×8

13. $32 \div 8$
14. $56 \div 8$
15. $16 \div 8$
16. $24 \div 8$

17. $40 \div 8$
18. 8×6
19. $8 \div 8$
20. 8×0

USE WITH PAGES 188–189.

Write the answer.

1. $\begin{array}{r} 4 \\ \times\ 9 \\ \hline \end{array}$
2. $\begin{array}{r} 7 \\ \times\ 9 \\ \hline \end{array}$
3. $\begin{array}{r} 9 \\ \times\ 3 \\ \hline \end{array}$
4. $\begin{array}{r} 9 \\ \times\ 2 \\ \hline \end{array}$

5. $9\overline{)36}$
6. $9\overline{)9}$
7. $9\overline{)54}$
8. $9\overline{)63}$

9. 8×9
10. 9×0
11. 9×9
12. 5×9

13. $72 \div 9$
14. $45 \div 9$
15. $81 \div 9$
16. $27 \div 9$

17. $9 \div 1$
18. 9×6
19. $18 \div 9$
20. 9×1

USE WITH PAGES 212–213.

1. Write the letters of the angles in order from the smallest angle to the largest angle.

a.
b.
c.
d.

Tell whether each angle is less than a square corner,
greater than a square corner, or a square corner.

2. **3.**  **4.** **5.**

Look at the figures and answer each question.

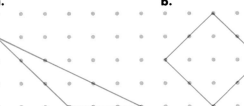 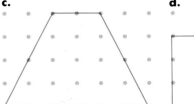 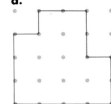

6. How many square corners
does each figure have?

7. Which figure has the most
corners of any kind?

8. Which figure has the largest
angle?

9. Which figure has the smallest
angle?

USE WITH PAGES 214–215.

Tell which pairs of figures are the same size
and shape.

1.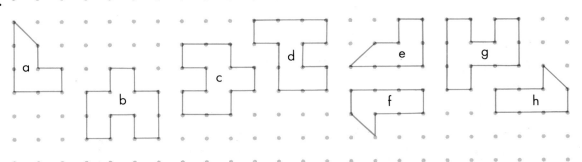

Copy each figure onto square dot paper. Next to each, draw another figure that is the same size and shape.

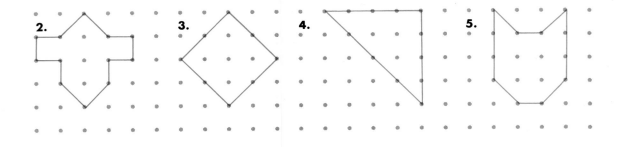

2.   3.   4.   5.

USE WITH PAGES 228–229.

Use the grid to solve each problem.
each problem.

1. Which square is the green house in?

2. What is in square A1?

3. Which house is in C2?

4. How many squares is the green house in?

Use the grid to solve each problem.
each problem.

5. Which circle is in D5?

6. Which shape is closest to the red circle? Which square is it in?

7. What is in G5?

8. Where is the purple square?

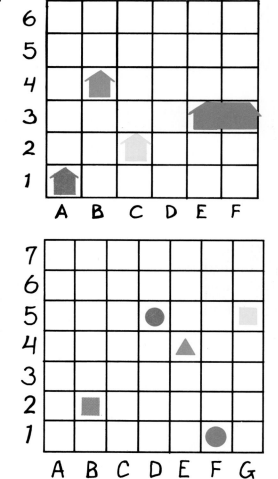

USE WITH PAGES 246–247.

Write a fraction for the shaded part of the figure.
Then write a fraction for the unshaded part.

1.

2.

3.

4.

5.

6.

7.

8.

USE WITH PAGES 260–261.

Write a mixed number for the shaded part.

1.   **2.**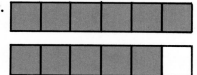

3.   **4.**

5. 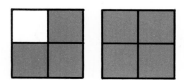   **6.**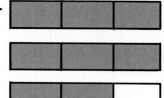

USE WITH PAGES 274–275.

Use a ruler to draw the line segment.

1. 2 inches

2. $5\frac{1}{2}$ inches

3. 6 inches

4. 1 inch

2. $3\frac{1}{2}$ inches

3. $9\frac{1}{2}$ inches

USE WITH PAGES 276–277.

Write the perimeter of the figure.

1.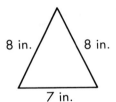

8 in.   8 in.   7 in.

2.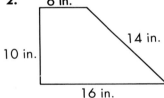

6 in.   14 in.   10 in.   16 in.

3.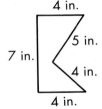

4 in.   5 in.   7 in.   4 in.   4 in.

USE WITH PAGES 278–279.

Choose the better estimate. Write *a* or *b*.

1. distance across Texas

   a. 771 yd   **b.** 771 mi

2. length of a book

   a. 9 in.   **b.** 9 yd

3. perimeter of a bedroom

   a. 44 in.   **b.** 44 ft

4. length of a soccer field

   a. 100 yd   **b.** 100 mi

5. length of a spoon

   a. 5 in.   **b.** 50 in.

6. height of a man

   a. 6 ft.   **b.** 2 ft.

USE WITH PAGES 280–281.

Does the object hold more than or less than a gallon? Write *more than* or *less than*.

1. spoon
2. washing machine
3. well
4. cereal bowl
5. juice glass
6. duck pond

USE WITH PAGES 286–287.

Choose the better estimate. Write *a* or *b*.

1. distance across town

   a. 15 km   b. 15 m

2. height of a glass

   a. 10 m   b. 10 cm

3. length of a boat

   a. 5 m   b. 5 km

4. length of a finger

   a. 7 cm   b. 7 m

5. height of a child

   a. 14 cm   b. 123 cm

6. length of a desk

   a. 14 cm   b. 1 m

USE WITH PAGES 290–291.

Does the object hold more than or less than a liter?
Write *more than* or *less than*.

1. paper cup
2. shoe
3. bathroom sink
4. wheelbarrow
5. straw
6. soap dish

USE WITH PAGES 298–299.

Write the time.

1.

2.

3.

4.

5.

6.

7.

8.

Write how much time has passed.

9.

10.

11.

12.

409

USE WITH PAGES 316–317.

Write the decimal.

1.

2.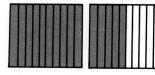

3.

4.

5.

Ones	Tenths
0	4

6.

Ones	Tenths
3	7

7. $\frac{1}{10}$

8. $2\frac{3}{10}$

9. $6\frac{2}{10}$

10. 5 and 7 tenths

11. 2 and 4 tenths

12. 1 and 9 tenths

USE WITH PAGES 320–321.

Write <, >, or =.

1. 0.4 ● 0.2

2. 3.6 ● 3.8

3. 4.5 ● 3.7

4. 8.7 ● 8.6

5. 1.3 ● 1.4

6. 2.0 ● 2

USE WITH PAGES 322–323.

Write the decimals from least to greatest.

1. 3.4, 3.1, 3.5

2. 0.6, 1.3, 0.3

3. 0.8, 0.5, 1.4

4. 0.7, 0.6, 0.4

5. 4.8, 3.7, 6.2

6. 12.4, 1.2, 2.4

USE WITH PAGES 328–329.

Write the sum.

1. $\begin{array}{r} 0.2 \\ + \ 0.6 \\ \hline \end{array}$
2. $\begin{array}{r} 1.0 \\ + \ 0.6 \\ \hline \end{array}$
3. $\begin{array}{r} 5.3 \\ + \ 2.1 \\ \hline \end{array}$
4. $\begin{array}{r} 4.8 \\ + \ 0.5 \\ \hline \end{array}$

5. 0.8 cm + 0.8 cm
6. 0.3 + 0.7
7. 2.1 + 0.7

USE WITH PAGES 328–329.

Write the difference.

1. $\begin{array}{r} 8.2 \\ - \ 1.0 \\ \hline \end{array}$
2. $\begin{array}{r} 0.9 \\ - \ 0.3 \\ \hline \end{array}$
3. $\begin{array}{r} 9.0 \text{ m} \\ - \ 0.5 \text{ m} \\ \hline \end{array}$
4. $\begin{array}{r} 4.2 \\ - \ 3.9 \\ \hline \end{array}$

5. 8.6 − 8.2
6. 0.7 − 0.6
7. 5.3 cm − 0.6 cm
8. 9.2 − 6.4

USE WITH PAGES 348–349.

Write the product.

1. $\begin{array}{r} 94 \\ \times \ 5 \\ \hline \end{array}$
2. $\begin{array}{r} 54 \\ \times \ 3 \\ \hline \end{array}$
3. $\begin{array}{r} 18 \\ \times \ 4 \\ \hline \end{array}$
4. $\begin{array}{r} 47 \\ \times \ 6 \\ \hline \end{array}$
5. $\begin{array}{r} 72 \\ \times \ 9 \\ \hline \end{array}$

6. $\begin{array}{r} 97 \\ \times \ 2 \\ \hline \end{array}$
7. $\begin{array}{r} 85 \\ \times \ 7 \\ \hline \end{array}$
8. $\begin{array}{r} 32 \\ \times \ 6 \\ \hline \end{array}$
9. $\begin{array}{r} 48 \\ \times \ 8 \\ \hline \end{array}$
10. $\begin{array}{r} 17 \\ \times \ 2 \\ \hline \end{array}$

11. 7×12
12. 3×72
13. 3×22
14. $(7 \times 2) \times 5$
15. $(6 \times 4) \times 9$
16. $(9 \times 5) \times 4$

USE WITH PAGES 352–353.

Write the product.

1. $\begin{array}{r} 322 \\ \times\ 4 \\ \hline \end{array}$

2. $\begin{array}{r} 408 \\ \times\ 2 \\ \hline \end{array}$

3. $\begin{array}{r} 701 \\ \times\ 5 \\ \hline \end{array}$

4. $\begin{array}{r} 316 \\ \times\ 3 \\ \hline \end{array}$

5. $\begin{array}{r} 475 \\ \times\ 4 \\ \hline \end{array}$

6. $\begin{array}{r} 601 \\ \times\ 8 \\ \hline \end{array}$

7. $\begin{array}{r} 129 \\ \times\ 8 \\ \hline \end{array}$

8. $\begin{array}{r} 454 \\ \times\ 2 \\ \hline \end{array}$

9. $\begin{array}{r} 924 \\ \times\ 5 \\ \hline \end{array}$

10. $\begin{array}{r} 117 \\ \times\ 7 \\ \hline \end{array}$

11. $\begin{array}{r} 785 \\ \times\ 4 \\ \hline \end{array}$

12. $\begin{array}{r} 434 \\ \times\ 8 \\ \hline \end{array}$

13. $\begin{array}{r} 897 \\ \times\ 9 \\ \hline \end{array}$

14. $\begin{array}{r} 452 \\ \times\ 1 \\ \hline \end{array}$

15. $\begin{array}{r} 889 \\ \times\ 6 \\ \hline \end{array}$

16. 2×942

17. 8×407

18. 4×227

19. 3×933

20. 9×109

21. 7×516

22. 5×706

23. 4×475

24. 9×967

USE WITH PAGES 358–359.

Write the product.

1. $\begin{array}{r} \$9.83 \\ \times\ 6 \\ \hline \end{array}$

2. $\begin{array}{r} \$0.06 \\ \times\ 7 \\ \hline \end{array}$

3. $\begin{array}{r} \$7.54 \\ \times\ 7 \\ \hline \end{array}$

4. $\begin{array}{r} \$0.22 \\ \times\ 4 \\ \hline \end{array}$

5. $\begin{array}{r} \$9.94 \\ \times\ 9 \\ \hline \end{array}$

6. $\begin{array}{r} \$3.66 \\ \times\ 6 \\ \hline \end{array}$

7. $\begin{array}{r} \$1.86 \\ \times\ 3 \\ \hline \end{array}$

8. $\begin{array}{r} \$9.83 \\ \times\ 8 \\ \hline \end{array}$

9. $\begin{array}{r} \$9.03 \\ \times\ 4 \\ \hline \end{array}$

10. $\begin{array}{r} \$0.17 \\ \times\ 3 \\ \hline \end{array}$

11. $\$6.33 \times 9$

12. $\$2.85 \times 6$

13. $\$7.26 \times 2$

14. $\$4.08 \times 9$

15. $\$1.44 \times 4$

16. $\$1.93 \times 7$

USE WITH PAGES 372–373.

Write the quotient and the remainder.

1. $4\overline{)25}$ 2. $6\overline{)35}$ 3. $7\overline{)34}$ 4. $4\overline{)19}$ 5. $2\overline{)15}$

6. $5\overline{)36}$ 7. $9\overline{)33}$ 8. $6\overline{)56}$ 9. $3\overline{)28}$ 10. $4\overline{)15}$

11. $3\overline{)14}$ 12. $6\overline{)56}$ 13. $8\overline{)21}$ 14. $7\overline{)69}$ 15. $4\overline{)37}$

16. $26 \div 5$ 17. $10 \div 6$ 18. $47 \div 7$ 19. $15 \div 7$ 20. $35 \div 6$

21. $53 \div 8$ 22. $27 \div 5$ 23. $15 \div 2$ 24. $52 \div 7$ 25. $17 \div 7$

26. $60 \div 8$ 27. $38 \div 9$ 28. $39 \div 6$ 29. $29 \div 4$ 30. $44 \div 5$

USE WITH PAGES 380–381.

Write the quotient and any remainder. Check your answer.

1. $4\overline{)57}$ 2. $5\overline{)86}$ 3. $7\overline{)95}$ 4. $6\overline{)24}$ 5. $8\overline{)74}$

6. $2\overline{)77}$ 7. $3\overline{)63}$ 8. $5\overline{)87}$ 9. $6\overline{)36}$ 10. $7\overline{)92}$

11. $5\overline{)76}$ 12. $2\overline{)67}$ 13. $8\overline{)38}$ 14. $2\overline{)77}$ 15. $5\overline{)77}$

16. $83 \div 2$ 17. $44 \div 8$ 18. $66 \div 2$ 19. $57 \div 6$

20. $70 \div 6$ 21. $45 \div 9$ 22. $48 \div 5$ 23. $90 \div 7$

24. $81 \div 6$ 25. $60 \div 7$ 26. $66 \div 5$ 27. $50 \div 2$

USE WITH PAGES 382–383.

Divide. Check your answer.

1. $2\overline{)108}$ 2. $8\overline{)183}$ 3. $9\overline{)862}$ 4. $2\overline{)165}$ 5. $4\overline{)365}$

6. $7\overline{)559}$ 7. $6\overline{)525}$ 8. $4\overline{)118}$ 9. $9\overline{)436}$ 10. $9\overline{)853}$

11. $2\overline{)149}$ 12. $2\overline{)155}$ 13. $5\overline{)333}$ 14. $7\overline{)292}$ 15. $6\overline{)381}$

16. $594 \div 6$ 17. $668 \div 9$ 18. $375 \div 5$

19. $330 \div 4$ 20. $663 \div 7$ 21. $258 \div 6$

22. $134 \div 8$ 23. $441 \div 9$ 24. $485 \div 9$

Giant
TREES

Tree	Height (Feet)	State
Balsam poplar	138	Michigan
Douglas fir	158	Oregon
Giant sequoia	275	California
Grand fir	251	Washington
Longbeak eucalyptus	171	California
Pecan	143	Tennessee
Scarlet oak	150	Alabama

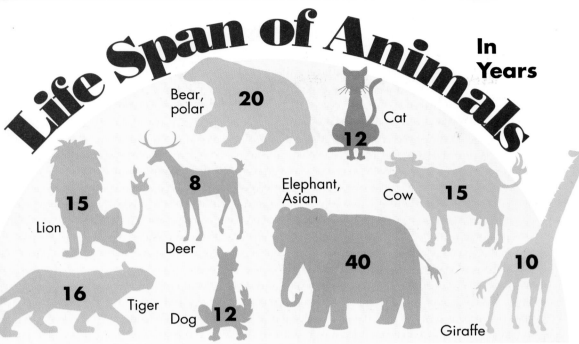

Life Span of Animals

In Years

Bear, polar **20**

Cat **12**

Lion **15**

Deer **8**

Elephant, Asian **40**

Cow **15**

Giraffe **10**

Tiger **16**

Dog **12**

Student Projects on Dinosaurs		
Project	Tally	Number
Book Report	卌 卌	10
Oral Report	卌 I	6
Papier-mâché	IIII	4
Poster	卌 IIII	9

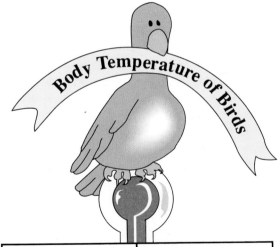

Body Temperature of Birds

Bird	Temperature
House sparrow	105.8° F
Hummingbird	104.2° F
Ostrich	102.6° F
Owl	104.4° F
Wandering albatross	105.3° F

The Great Lakes

Lake Erie
212 ft

Lake Huron
752 ft

Lake Ontario
804 ft

Lake Michigan
925 ft

Lake Superior
1333 ft

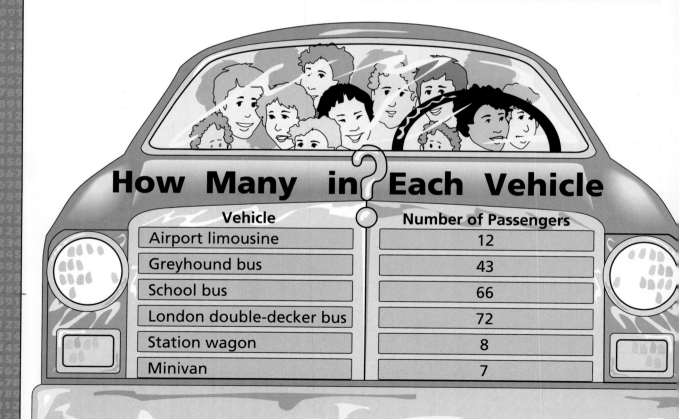

How Many in Each Vehicle

Vehicle	Number of Passengers
Airport limousine	12
Greyhound bus	43
School bus	66
London double-decker bus	72
Station wagon	8
Minivan	7

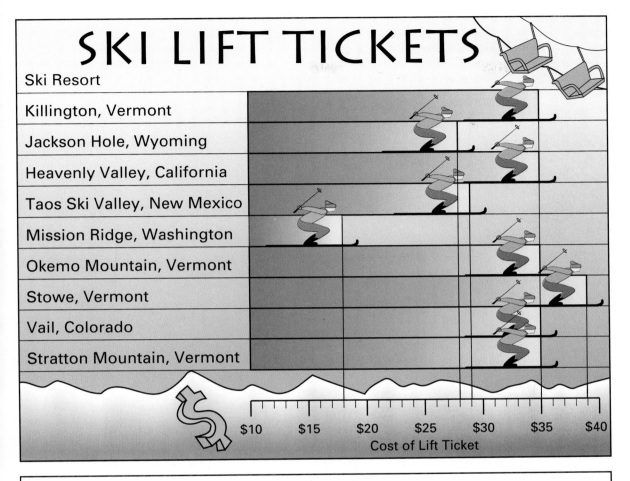

SKI LIFT TICKETS

Ski Resort	
Killington, Vermont	
Jackson Hole, Wyoming	
Heavenly Valley, California	
Taos Ski Valley, New Mexico	
Mission Ridge, Washington	
Okemo Mountain, Vermont	
Stowe, Vermont	
Vail, Colorado	
Stratton Mountain, Vermont	

$10 $15 $20 $25 $30 $35 $40

Cost of Lift Ticket

1988 OLYMPIC HOCKEY STANDINGS

PLACE	TEAM	WON	LOST	TIED
1	Soviet Union	4	1	0
2	Finland	3	1	1
3	Sweden	2	1	2
4	Canada	2	2	1
5	West Germany	1	4	0
6	Czechoslovakia	1	4	0

MINNESOTA

Minneapolis

WISCONSIN

MICHIGAN

Milwaukee

IOWA

Des Moines

Chicago

Detroit

Cleveland

INDIANA

Indianapolis

OHIO

ILLINOIS

Louisville

KENTUCKY

MILEAGE TABLE

0 4 9 7 8

How Many Miles from City to City?

FROM:

TO:	Chicago	Cleveland	Des Moines	Detroit	Indianapolis	Louisville	Milwaukee	Minneapolis
Chicago		348	344	275	185	297	87	410
Cleveland	348		657	172	318	354	435	758
Des Moines	344	657		587	479	588	366	245
Detroit	275	172	587		284	382	360	685
Indianapolis	185	318	479	284		114	270	593
Louisville	297	354	588	382	114		382	705
Milwaukee	87	435	366	360	270	382		337
Minneapolis	410	758	245	685	593	705	337	

STATE FACTS

STATE	AREA (Square Miles)	HIGHEST PLACE (Feet)	YEAR ENTERED UNION
Illinois	56,345	1235	1818
Indiana	36,185	1257	1816
Iowa	56,275	1670	1846
Kentucky	40,410	4145	1792
Michigan	58,527	1980	1837
Minnesota	84,402	2301	1858
Ohio	41,330	1550	1803
Wisconsin	56,135	1951	1848

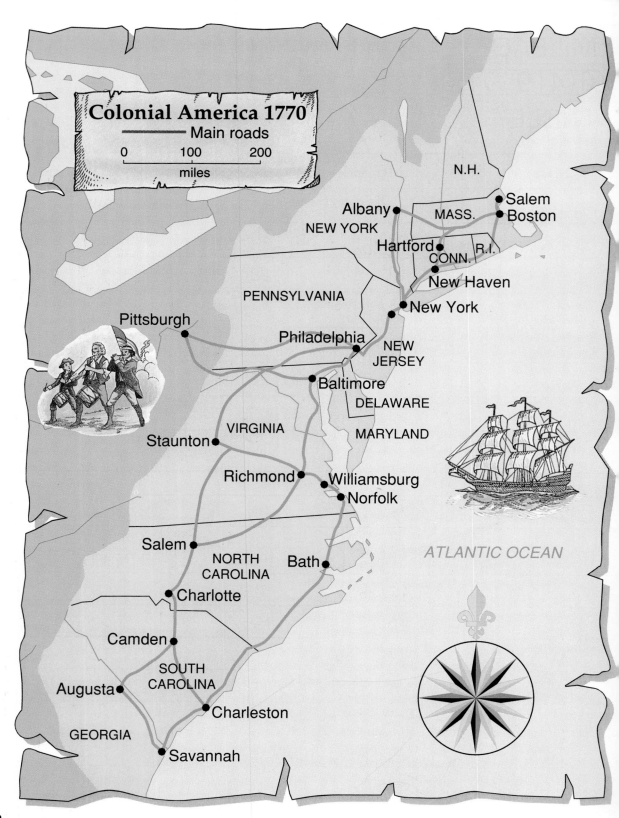

Colonial America 1770

— Main roads

0   100   200
miles

N.H.

Albany

Salem
Boston

MASS.

NEW YORK

Hartford

CONN.   R.I.

New Haven

PENNSYLVANIA

New York

Pittsburgh

Philadelphia

NEW
JERSEY

Baltimore

DELAWARE

MARYLAND

VIRGINIA

Staunton

Richmond

Williamsburg

Norfolk

ATLANTIC OCEAN

Salem

NORTH
CAROLINA

Bath

Charlotte

Camden

SOUTH
CAROLINA

Augusta

Charleston

GEORGIA

Savannah

Meatball Casserole

1 pound ground beef
1 cup condensed tomato soup
1 tablespoon flour
2 tablespoons margarine

1 large onion, chopped
2 cups diced celery
4 medium potatoes, peeled and diced

Put ground beef, soup, and flour into a medium bowl and mix. Shape the mixture into meatballs about the size of walnuts. Melt the margarine in a skillet and brown the meatballs. Then arrange the onion, celery, and potatoes and put on top of the meatballs. Cover and bake at 350°F for 50 minutes.

Serves 4 people

Trail Mix Snack

$2\frac{1}{3}$ cups raisins
1 cup carob chips
1 cup sunflower seeds

$\frac{1}{2}$ cup coconut
$1\frac{1}{2}$ cups peanuts

Mix all the ingredients together in a bowl. Pour mixture into 4 small bags.

Serves 4 people

DATA BOOK

Number of Days in Each Month

Month	Days
January	31
February	28
	29
	(in leap year)
March	31
April	30
May	31
June	30
July	31
August	31
September	30
October	31
November	30
December	31

There are two ways to remember the number of days in each month.

LEARN THIS POEM

Thirty days hath September,
April, June, and November.
All the rest have 31,
except February
which has 28,
or in leap year, 29.

Use four of your knuckles. Every knuckle stands for 31 days. Every dip stands for 30 days or less.

April
March
February
January

TABLE F MEASURES

Customary Measures

Length	1 foot (ft)	=	12 inches (in.)
	1 yard (yd)	=	3 feet, or 36 inches
	1 mile (mi)	=	5280 feet
Liquid	1 pint (pt)	=	2 cups (c)
	1 quart (qt)	=	2 pints
	1 gallon (gal)	=	4 quarts
Weight	1 pound (lb)	=	16 ounces (oz)

Metric Measures

Length	1 decimeter	=	10 centimeters
	1 meter (m)	=	100 centimeters
	1 kilometer (km)	=	1000 meters
Liquid	1 liter (L)	=	1000 milliliters (mL)
Mass	1 kilogram (kg)	=	1000 grams (g)

Time

1 minute (min)	=	60 seconds (s)
1 hour (h)	=	60 minutes
1 day	=	24 hours
1 week	=	7 days
1 year	=	12 months

TIPS FOR PROBLEM SOLVING

INDEPENDENT STUDY

1. If you are stuck on a problem, that is okay. Problems are not supposed to be easy. Otherwise, they would not be problems.

2. There are no magic rules. These tips can only help you think about problem solving. They cannot solve the problem for you.

3. Remember the Problem Solver's Guide.

    - **Understand** Make sure you know what is going on in the problem. What is the problem asking?

    - **Try** Don't give up! Keep trying different things. If one idea does not work, try another.

    - **Look back** Check over what you have done. Does it make sense?

4. If you do *not* understand the problem, try these ideas:

    - Read the problem again slowly.

    - Picture in your mind what is going on in the problem.

    - Make notes or draw pictures.

    - Look up or ask about words you do not know.

    - Cooperate with a friend or a group of friends.

UNDERSTAND TRY
THINK
LOOK BACK

5. Maybe you understand the problem, but you do not know how to start. Try one or more of these strategies:

Use Models	See page 44.
Use Guess and Check	See page 146.
Make a Plan	See page 178.
Make a Diagram	See page 210.
Make a List	See page 318.
Make a Table	See page 344.

6. Try anything that makes sense to you. Take chances! Do not be afraid to explore. Have lots of scrap paper handy.

7. When you look back, ask yourself these questions:

   • Does my answer make sense?

   • Does it fit what the problem is asking for?

   • Are my computations correct?

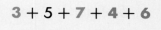
TIPS FOR DOING MENTAL MATH

Mental math is often faster and easier than using a calculator or paper and pencil. When doing mental math, remember these tips:

- Using paper and pencil methods in your head does not work well. There are special mental math strategies that work better.

- There are usually several good ways to do each problem.

The mental math strategies shown on these pages will give you some ideas. Do not be afraid to invent methods of your own!

STRATEGIES FOR BASIC FACTS

Sometimes you forget a basic fact. These strategies can help you figure out the answer.

Doubles

A double is a number plus itself. There are many doubles in real life.

$5 + 5$

$3 + 3$

You can use doubles to add.

$$5 + 6 = \blacksquare$$

Use the double $5 + 5 = 10$.
Add 1 to the double.

$$\text{So, } 5 + 6 = 11.$$

or

Use the double $6 + 6 = 12$.
Subtract 1 from the double.

Counting Up or Back

$$12 - 9 = \blacksquare$$

Count up from 9 until you reach 12. You counted 3 numbers.

$$\text{So, } 12 - 9 = 3.$$

$$11 - 3 = \blacksquare$$

Count back 3 numbers from 11. You stopped at 8.

$$\text{So, } 11 - 3 = 8.$$

INDEPENDENT STUDY

Look for Tens

$8 + 3 = \blacksquare$

Break 3 into $2 + 1$.
$8 + 3 = 8 + 2 + 1$
$\qquad 10 \ + 1 = 11$

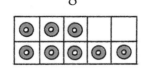

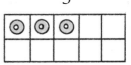

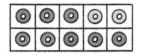

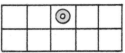

Adding and Subtracting with Nines

$7 + 9 = \blacksquare$

Notice that 9 is 1 less than 10.
First add 10.
$7 + 10 = 17$
This is 1 too much. Subtract 1
from the sum.
$17 - 1 = 16$
So, $7 + 9 = 16$.

Using a Known Fact

$6 \times 8 = \blacksquare$

Suppose you do know that
$5 \times 8 = 40$. You can use this fact.
6×8 means 6 groups of 8.
If 5 groups of 8 is 40, then add 1
more group of 8.
$40 + 8 = 48$
So, 6 groups of 8 is 48.
$6 \times 8 = 48$.

OPERATING WITH MULTIPLES OF 10, 100, AND 1000

Use basic facts to help you add, subtract, multiply,
and divide multiples of 10, 100, and 1000.

$$
\begin{array}{r} 8 \\ +4 \\ \hline 12 \end{array}
\qquad
\begin{array}{r} 80 \\ +40 \\ \hline 120 \end{array}
\qquad
\begin{array}{r} 800 \\ +400 \\ \hline 1200 \end{array}
\qquad
\begin{array}{r} 8000 \\ +4000 \\ \hline 12{,}000 \end{array}
$$

$3 \times 5 \ \ = 15$
$3 \times 50 \ = 150$
$3 \times 500 = 1500$

$$
\begin{array}{r} 15 \\ -\ 7 \\ \hline 8 \end{array}
\qquad
\begin{array}{r} 150 \\ -\ 70 \\ \hline 80 \end{array}
\qquad
\begin{array}{r} 1500 \\ -\ 700 \\ \hline 800 \end{array}
\qquad
\begin{array}{r} 15{,}000 \\ -\ 7{,}000 \\ \hline 8{,}000 \end{array}
$$

$8 \div 2 \ \ = 4$
$80 \div 2 \ = 40$
$800 \div 2 = 400$

Tips for Estimating

About how many people are shown in the picture at the right?

You could count each person, but that would take a very long time.

You could also take a wild guess, but that would not tell you much.

Instead, you can make a close estimate. Here is one good way.

First count the number of people in a small section. There are about 30 people in the white box.

Skip-count to estimate the size of the crowd.

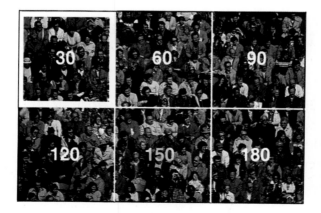

There are about 180 people.

Rounding

Susan and her family drove 387 miles to the Grand Canyon. When someone asked Susan how far they drove, she said, "about 400 miles."
Susan estimated the number of miles by rounding 387 to 400.

Front-end Estimation

Add the front digits.

$$\begin{array}{r} 253 \\ 359 \\ +287 \\ \hline \end{array}$$

rough estimate: **700**

Subtract the front digits.

$$\begin{array}{r} 845 \\ -357 \\ \hline \end{array}$$

rough estimate: **500**

Adjust by looking for groups of about 100.

$$\begin{array}{r} 253 \longleftarrow \text{about 100} \\ 359 \\ +287 \longleftarrow \text{about 100} \\ \hline \end{array}$$

adjusted estimate:
$700 + 100 + 100 = 900$

About how much will 3 paint sets cost?

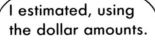 $5.69

I estimated, using the dollar amounts.

$3 \times \$5 = \$15$

Since each paint set costs more than $5, I know the total will be more than $15.

I rounded $5.69 to $6.

$3 \times \$6 = \$18$

Since each paint set costs less than $6, I know the total is less than $18.

Three paint sets cost between $15 and $18.

You remember better if you review what you learn each day. At the end of each math class, answer these questions. Write the answers on a piece of paper because it may help you think more clearly.

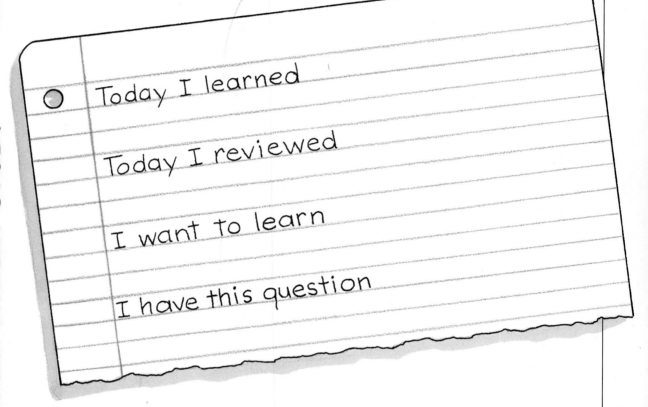

○ Today I learned

Today I reviewed

I want to learn

I have this question

Share your answers with other students in your class.

Answer these questions each day for the next two weeks. This short review may help you remember the new ideas that you are learning in math.

FINDING INFORMATION

Do you know what the word **product** means? If so, write the meaning in your own words.

If you are not sure of the meaning, there are ways to find the meaning. Your math book has a glossary and an index. Find **product** in the glossary at the back of your book. Copy the meaning on a piece of paper.

Find **product** in the index. Turn to the page that is listed and copy that meaning onto your paper.

A dictionary can also give you information. Find the meaning of **product** there and copy it on your paper. You do not have to copy all of the meanings from the dictionary, just the ones that have to do with mathematics.

Which meaning do you like best?

Now, write the meaning of **product** in your own words. Give an example and label it.

Write the meanings of the following words: **quotient, meter**.

Give an example of the meaning of each word.

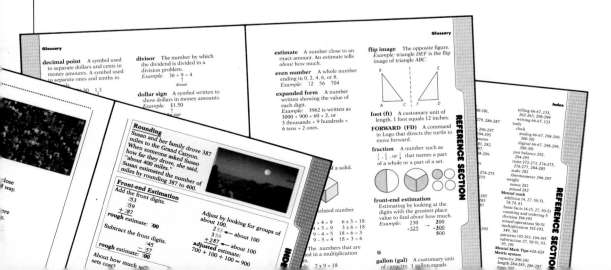

USING YOUR TEXTBOOK

Math can be a lot of fun, and your new book will help make it that way. This book will ask you to think in new and different ways about things you already know.

Some lessons use calculators or computers. You will work with partners to make discoveries and to do projects. You will be exploring many new ideas about math this year!

Knowing about your new book and how to use it can help you. To get started, read about some features you will find.

The **Connections** pages of every chapter tell stories about mathematics. The stories show how mathematics is a part of science, history, art, language, and other subjects. They will help you understand how mathematics connects to the world and why the lessons in the chapters are important for you to learn. (See pages 36 and 37.)

In the lessons, you will learn about new topics by doing activities and thinking, writing, and talking about math.

"Think" questions are a part of many lessons. These are questions you will talk about in class with the help of your teacher. "Think" questions help you make sure you understand the lesson. (See page 4.) For the **Math Log**, you use your own words or a picture to describe what you have learned. (See page 53.)

CHAPTER

1

Connection

Think

INDEPENDENT STUDY

434

In many lessons in your book, you will be able to teach yourself something new about math. You and your classmates will make discoveries about mathematics by drawing diagrams, studying patterns, cutting out shapes, and measuring objects. A lesson of this type is on pages 224 and 225.

CHALLENGE

Math is an important part of your life. You are often "doing" math and you may not even know it! You will learn how to use math in your life, now and in the future. You can find a lesson like this on pages 122 and 123.

Many lessons contain activities for you. Two of these activities are **Projects** and **Challenges.** Projects are a good way to practice and have some fun with the lesson. You will play math games, draw patterns, and build models. (See page 115.) Challenges make you think! You may want to work with a partner to do a challenge activity. (See page 213.)

This Handbook section contains many helpful pages. Look at the **Tips for Problem Solving** guide (page 426) whenever you get stuck on a problem.

The Data Book contains information on many topics, including sports, weather, maps, and population. You will use the Data Book to answer questions and draw graphs. (See page 416.)

You will also find extra practice problems (called **More Practice**) on page 390. There are sections on important **Estimation** and **Mental Math** skills (pages 428 and 430). When you do not know or remember the meaning of a word, you can look it up in the **Glossary** (page 440).

TIPS FOR WORKING TOGETHER

Cooperative learning means "working together." Cooperative learning helps you and your group develop important skills. Here are some skills to work on:

COOPERATING By working together, everyone in the group takes part in the project. No one is left out.

BEING RESPONSIBLE Everyone is responsible for their part of the project. Everyone is responsible for seeing that the whole group finishes the project.

LISTENING Let others talk about their ideas or explain how they got an answer. Let others tell what they do or do not understand.

USING WORDS Help your classmates. Praise a job well done or a good idea. Ask questions when you are having trouble. Talk about your ideas.

MAKING CHOICES Decide who, when, what, where, and how to do the project.

THINKING Be creative. Use what you already know to learn new ideas. Look for patterns, rules, and strategies. Explore and make sense of new ideas.

BEING INDEPENDENT Take charge of your learning. Use your teacher as a helper!

437

LEARNING TO USE A CALCULATOR

A calculator can be a very useful tool when you are doing mathematics. You will not need to know all the keys to get started.

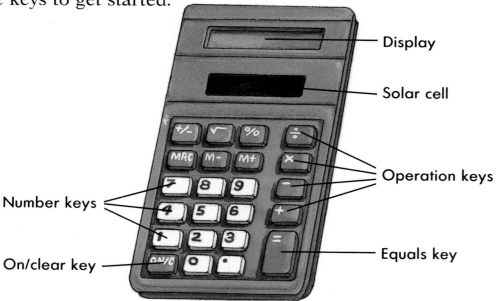

Display

Solar cell

Operation keys

Number keys

Equals key

On/clear key

Entering Numbers

Try putting your telephone number into the calculator. To enter each digit, press a number key. The number should appear in the display.

How many digits does the display hold? Press the numbers in order, starting with 1. What do you see?

Clearing Numbers

If you make a mistake, press the clear key, ON/C . The calculator display will show 0, and you can start again.

Practice entering and clearing. Enter each number below. Press ON/C after each.

203   66008   49135   10278

Using the Operation Keys

The ⊞, ⊟, ⊠, and ÷ signs are used just as they are used with paper and pencil.

Press: 6 2 ⊞ 5 1

You will not see ⊞ in the display, but the calculator will add the numbers.

Using the Equals Key

What do you think the sum is? Check by pressing =. The answer will show in the display.

What happens if you press = again? You should see *164* in the display. Why?

When you press = again, the calculator adds 51 to 113. Each time you press =, the calculator will add 51 to the last sum. This is the way to make the calculator skip-count by 51's.

To make the calculator skip-count by 5's, press 5 ⊞ = = = = = =. Try it!

What did you see? You should see *5 10 15 20 25 30*

Can you make the calculator skip-count backward by 5's starting from 50? Press 5 0 ⊟ 5 = = = = =. Keep pressing = until you get to 0. What did you see?

Your calculator may not be like the one shown. Draw a picture of your calculator and label the keys. Try the activities. Make notes of what your calculator can do and what it cannot do.

Glossary

REFERENCE SECTION

A

addend   A number that is added to another number.
Example: $5 + 9 = 14$
↑   ↑
addends

addition properties
• **grouping property**   No matter how addends are grouped, the sum is always the same.
Example: Add the blue numbers first.
$5 + 1 + 3 = 9$
$5 + 1 + 3 = 9$
$5 + 1 + 3 = 9$
• **order property**   Changing the order of addends does not change the sum.
Example: $5 + 3 = 8$
$3 + 5 = 8$
• **zero property**   If 0 is added to a number, the sum equals that number.
Example: $4 + 0 = 4$ $0 + 26 = 26$

A.M.   The hours from 12:00 midnight to 12:00 noon.

angle   A figure that can be used to show a turn.

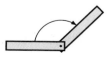

area   The number of square units needed to cover a figure.

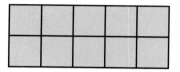

array   Data arranged in rows and columns.

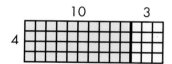

B

BACK (BK)   A command in Logo that directs the turtle to move backwards.

bar graph   A graph that uses bars to show data.

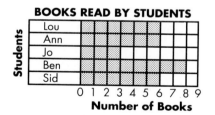

bug   An error in a computer procedure.

C

capacity   The amount a container holds.

center   The middle of a circle.

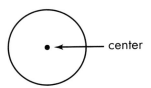

centimeter (cm)   A metric unit of length. 100 centimeters equal 1 meter.

centimeter ruler   A ruler marked in centimeters.

command   In Logo, a direction to do something.

computer program   A set of commands that tells a computer what to do.

cone   A solid that has a circular base and that comes to a point.

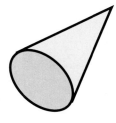

congruent figures   Figures that have the same size and shape.

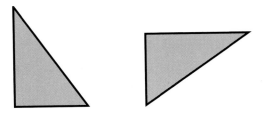

cube   A solid having six square faces the same size.

cup (c)   A customary unit of capacity. 2 cups equal 1 pint.

customary system   The measurement system that uses units such as foot, quart, pound, and degree Fahrenheit.

cylinder   A solid having circles of equal size at each end.

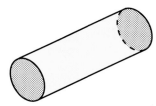

D

data   Information, facts.

day (d)   A unit of time. 1 day equals 24 hours.
Example: Tuesday is the third day of the week.

debug   The act of fixing an error, or bug, in a computer procedure.

decimal   A number with one or more digits to the right of a decimal point.
Example: 0.9, 1.08, 0.621 are decimals

REFERENCE SECTION

441

REFERENCE SECTION

decimal point   A symbol used to separate dollars and cents in money amounts. A symbol used to separate ones and tenths in decimals.
Example: $1.50   1.3
decimal point

decimeter (dm)   A metric unit of length. 1 decimeter equals 10 centimeters.

degree   A unit for measuring temperature.

degree Celsius (°C)   The metric unit for measuring temperature.

degree Fahrenheit (°F)   The customary unit for measuring temperature.

denominator   The number written below the bar in a fraction.
Example: $\frac{1}{4}$ ← denominator

difference   The answer in a subtraction problem.
Example: 7 − 3 = 4
difference

digit   Any one of the symbols 0, 1, 2, 3, 4, 5, 6, 7, 8, or 9 used to write numbers.

dividend   the number that is divided in a division problem.
Example: 12 ÷ 4 = 3
dividend

divisor   The number by which the dividend is divided in a division problem.
Example: 36 ÷ 9 = 4
divisor

dollar sign   A symbol written to show dollars in money amounts.
Example: $1.50
dollar sign

E

edge   Where two faces of a solid meet.

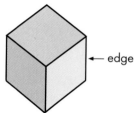
← edge

END   A command in Logo that completes a procedure.

end point   The point at the end of a line segment.
Example:
end points

equivalent fractions   Fractions that show the same amount.
Example:

$\frac{6}{8}$

$\frac{3}{4}$

estimate A number close to an exact amount. An estimate tells *about* how much.

even number A whole number ending in 0, 2, 4, 6, or 8.
Example: 12   56   704

expanded form A number written showing the value of each digit.
Example: 3962 is written as 3000 + 900 + 60 + 2, or
3 thousands + 9 hundreds + 6 tens + 2 ones.

F

face A flat surface of a solid.

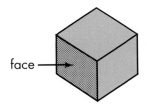

fact family Related number sentences.
Example:
5 + 4 = 9	6 x 3 = 18
4 + 5 = 9	3 x 6 = 18
9 − 4 = 5	18 ÷ 6 = 3
9 − 5 = 4	18 ÷ 3 = 6

factors The numbers that are multiplied in a multiplication problem.
Example: 2 x 9 = 18
           ↑   ↑
          factors

flip A move that makes a figure face in the opposite direction.

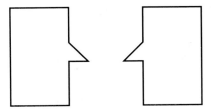

The second figure is a flip image of the first.

foot (ft) A customary unit of length. 1 foot equals 12 inches.

FORWARD (FD) A command in Logo that directs the turtle to move forward.

fraction A number that names a part of a whole or a part of a set.

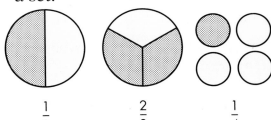

$\frac{1}{2}$ $\frac{2}{3}$ $\frac{1}{4}$

front-end estimation Estimating by looking at the digits with the greatest place value to find *about* how much.
Example:
230 → 200
+325   +300
         500

G

gallon (gal) A customary unit of capacity. 1 gallon equals 4 quarts.

443

gram (g) A metric unit of mass. 1 gram equals 1000 milligrams.

graph A picture that shows information by using bars, lines, or symbols.

H

half turn A turn that causes a figure to point in a different direction.

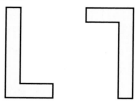

The second figure is a half turn image of the first.

hexagon A figure with six sides. In a regular hexagon, all six sides are equal.

hour (h) A unit of time. 1 hour equals 60 minutes.

I

inch (in.) A customary unit of length. 12 inches equal 1 foot.

inch ruler A ruler marked in inches.

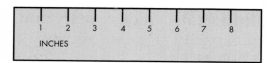

K

key Tells what each picture stands for in a pictograph. *Example:*

kilogram (kg) A metric unit of mass. 1 kilogram equals 100 grams.

kilometer (km) A metric unit of length. 1 kilometer equals 1000 meters.

L

LEFT (LT) A command in Logo that directs the turtle to move left.

line A straight path that goes on forever.

line graph A graph that uses line segments to show changes over time.

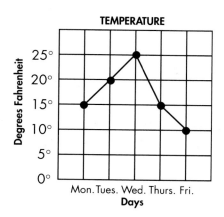

REFERENCE SECTION

line of symmetry   A line along which you could fold a figure so that both halves match.

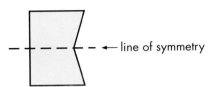
← line of symmetry

line segment   Part of a line having two end points.

liter (L)   A metric unit of capacity. 1 liter equals 1000 milliliters.

Logo   A computer language that uses a turtle to draw pictures.

M

mass   The measure of the amount of matter in an object.

meter (m)   A metric unit of length. 1 meter equals 100 centimeters.

metric system   The measurement system that uses units such as meter, liter, gram, and degree Celsius.

mile (mi)   A customary unit of length. 1 mile equals 5280 feet.

milliliter (mL)   A metric unit of capacity. 1000 milliliters equal 1 liter.

minute (min)   A unit of time. 1 minute equals 60 seconds.

missing factor   A factor that is missing in a multiplication sentence.
Example: 5 x ■ = 45
↑
missing factor

mixed numbers   Numbers that have a whole number part and a fraction part.
Example: $3\frac{1}{2}$

multiplication properties
• **order property**   Changing the order of factors does not change the product.
Example: 6 x 4 = 24
4 x 6 = 24

• **property of one**   If 1 is a factor, the product always equals the other factor.
Example: 6 x 1 = 6
1 x 51 = 51

• **zero property**   If 0 is a factor, the product is always 0.
Example: 8 x 0 = 0
0 x 17 = 0

N

net   A flat pattern that folds into a solid.
Example:

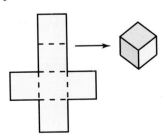

number line   A line showing numbers equally spaced and in order.

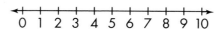

numerator   The number written above the bar in a fraction.
Example: $\frac{1}{4}$ ← numerator

o

odd number   A whole number ending in 1, 3, 5, 7, or 9.
Example: 13   67   429

ounce (oz)   A customary measure of weight. 16 ounces equal 1 pound.

ordered pair   A letter and a number that tell where a square is on a grid.

P

palindrome   A number whose digits are the same from left to right and from right to left.
Example: 22   636   1551

parallel lines   Lines that are always the same distance apart.

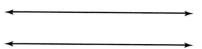

pentagon   A figure with five sides. In a regular pentagon, all five sides are equal.

perimeter   The distance around a figure. The perimeter of the rectangle below is 12 centimeters.

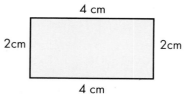

pictograph   A graph showing data with pictures or symbols.

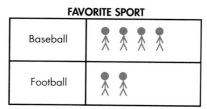

pint (pt)   A customary unit of capacity. 2 pints equal 1 quart.

place value   The value of a position in a number.
Example: In 7943, the digit 7 is in the thousands place.

Thousands	Hundreds	Tens	Ones
7	9	4	3

REFERENCE SECTION

P.M. The hours from 12:00 noon to 12:00 midnight.

point An exact place or position, marked by a dot.

polygon A figure made up of line segments with three or more sides.

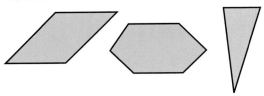

pound (lb) A customary unit of weight. 1 pound equals 16 ounces.

prediction What someone thinks may happen.

prism A solid with two bases that are parallel and are the same size and shape.

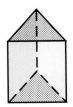

probability The chance that an event will happen.

procedure In Logo, a list of commands that tells the turtle how to move.

product The answer in a multiplication problem.
Example: 5 x 3 = 15
↑
product

pyramid A solid with a polygon base and triangular faces meeting in a point.

Q

quart (qt) A customary unit of capacity. 4 quarts equal 1 gallon.

quarter Another name for a fourth, 25¢, or $\frac{1}{4}$.

quotient The answer in a division problem.
Example: 54 ÷ 9 = 6
↑
quotient

R

rectangle A figure having 4 sides and 4 square corners. A square is a kind of rectangle.

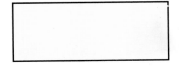

rectangular prism A solid having 6 faces. Each face is a rectangle.

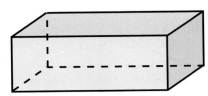

REFERENCE SECTION

447

remainder   The number left over when one number does not exactly divide another.
Example:

$$\overset{4\ R2}{9\overline{)38}} \leftarrow 2 \text{ is the remainder}$$

REPEAT   A command in Logo that directs the turtle to perform a command more than once.

rhombus   A four-sided figure with four equal sides.

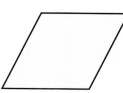

RIGHT (RT)   A command in Logo that directs the turtle to move right.

s

second (s)   A unit of time. 60 seconds equal 1 minute.

side   A line forming part of a figure.

← side

slide   A move in the direction shown by a slide arrow. The slide arrow also tells how far to move the figure.

The second figure is a slide image of the first.

sphere   A solid having the shape of a ball.

square   A figure with 4 square corners and 4 equal sides.

square corner   A right angle.

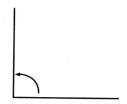

square number   The product shown by a square array. The factors of the product are the same.
Example: $3 \times 3 = 9$
square number

standard form   The usual way of writing a number, using digits.
Example: The standard form of twenty-seven is 27.

sum   The answer in an addition problem.
Example: $5 + 4 = 9$
sum

survey   A way to collect data by asking people questions.

REFERENCE SECTION

T

table A chart showing data.

FAVORITE WAYS TO TRAVEL

Grade	Planes	Trains
3	12	15
4	8	20

tally A count made using tally marks.
Example:

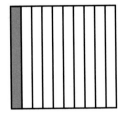

The tally is 12.

temperature The measurement of how warm something is.

tenths One of ten equal parts of a unit.

thermometer An instrument that measures temperature.

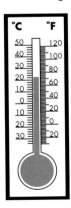

ton (t) A customary unit of weight. 1 ton equals 2000 pounds.

triangle A figure with three sides and three corners.

V

value The worth of a digit, depending on its placement in a number.
Example: In 324, the 2 is in the tens place. Its value is 20.

Y

yard (yd) A customary unit of length. 1 yard equals 3 feet.

yardstick A ruler, marked in inches and feet, that is one yard long.

REFERENCE SECTION

Index

REFERENCE SECTION

Index

M

REFERENCE SECTION

Index

REFERENCE SECTION

Index

REFERENCE SECTION

456